FEB 2017

Understanding the Department of the Interior

The Cabinet Series

Understanding the Department of the Interior

DON PHILPOTT

The Cabinet Series

Lanham • Boulder • New York • London

Published by Bernan Press
An imprint of The Rowman & Littlefield Publishing Group, Inc.
4501 Forbes Boulevard, Suite 200, Lanham, Maryland 20706
www.rowman.com
800-865-3457; info@bernan.com

Unit A, Whitacre Mews, 26-34 Stannary Street, London SE11 4AB

Library of Congress Control Number: 2016942637

ISBN: 978-1-59888-781-5
E-ISBN: 978-1-59888-782-2

⊖™ The paper used in this publication meets the minimum requirements of
American National Standard for Information Sciences—Permanence of Paper
for Printed Library Materials, ANSI/NISO Z39.48-1992.

Printed in the United States of America

Contents

Introduction

In one way or another the Department of the Interior has an impact on almost everybody that lives in the United States. It is a Cabinet-level agency that manages America's vast natural and cultural resources.

It manages millions of acres of public land and shoreline where we picnic, hike, camp and explore. It manages millions of acres that more that provide millions of people with water and almost a quarter of the nation's energy.

The Department manages and provides access to more than 500 million acres of public lands, 700 million acres of subsurface minerals, and 1.7 billion acres of the Outer Continental Shelf. It is the steward of 20 percent of the nation's lands, including national parks, national wildlife refuges, and public lands.

It protects and manages the nation's natural resources that supply 23 percent of the nation's energy; supplies and manages water in the 17 Western States and supplies 17 percent of the nation's hydropower energy. It also upholds Federal trust responsibilities to 566 federally recognized Indian tribes and Alaska Natives.

The DOI is also responsible for migratory bird and wildlife conservation; historic preservation; endangered species conservation; surface-mined lands protection and restoration; mapping, geological, hydrological, and biological science for the Nation; and financial and technical assistance for the insular areas.

In 1849 President Polk signed the bill creating the Home Department under which the Department of the Interior was charged with managing a wide variety of programs, which included overseeing Indian Affairs, exploring the western wilderness, directing the District of Columbia jail, constructing the National Capital's water system, managing hospitals and universities, improving historic western emigrant routes, marking boundaries, issuing patents, conducting the census, and researching the geological resources of the United States.

As the Country matured during the last half of the 19th Century, so did the Department and its mission began to evolve as some of these functions moved to other agencies.

Following Theodore Roosevelt's conservation summit and the conservation movement at the beginning of the 20th Century, there was an increasing urgency and expanding congressional mandate to protect and more effectively manage the country's natural resources. Accordingly, DOI's mission shifted to focus on the preservation, management, understanding, and use of public lands, natural and cultural resources, responsible management of energy and water resources, and responsibilities related to Indian nations and scientific discovery.

The Department of the Interior has a $12 billion total annual budget and in addition, raises billions in revenue annually from energy, mineral, grazing, and timber leases, as well as recreational permits and land sales. It has 70,000 staff, including expert scientists and resource-management professionals, in nine technical bureaus, and is supported by more than 280,000 volunteers who help carry out the Department's mission in more than 2,400 operating locations.

This mission is achieved through the following Bureaus and Offices which are described in greater detail later in this book.

At a glance

Bureau of Land Management (BLM)

It manages and conserves resources for multiple use and sustained yield on approximately 248 million acres of public land, and an additional 700 million acres of subsurface federal mineral estate, including the following:

- Renewable and conventional energy and mineral development
- Forest management, timber and biomass production

- Wild Horse and Burro management
- Management of diverse landscapes for the benefit of wildlife, domestic grazing, and recreational uses
- Resource management at sites of natural, scenic, scientific, and historical value including the National Landscape Conservation System

Bureau of Ocean Energy Management (BOEM)

It manages access to renewable and conventional energy resources of the Outer Continental Shelf (OCS) and administers over 6,400 active fluid mineral leases on approximately 35 million OCS acres. It Issues leases that provide 24 percent of domestic crude oil and eight percent of domestic natural gas supply and oversees lease and grant issuance for off-shore renewable energy .

Bureau of Safety and Environmental Enforcement (BSEE)

The Bureau promotes safety, protects the environment, and conserves resources offshore through regulatory enforcement of offshore oil and gas facilities on the 1.7 billion acre US Outer Continental Shelf (OCS). It oversees oil spills for US facilities in state and federal waters and operates the Ohmsett National Oil Spill Response Research test facility. It also supports research to promote the use of best available safest technology for oil spill response

Office of Surface Mining Reclamation and Enforcement (OSMRE)

It protects the environment during coal mining operations through Federal programs. It provides grants and oversight activities and ensures the land is reclaimed afterwards. It is also responsible for overseeing mitigation efforts from past mining by pursuing reclamation of abandoned coal mine lands

US Geological Survey (USGS)

The Survey conducts scientific research in ecosystems, climate and land use change, mineral assessments, environmental health, and water resources to inform effective decision making and planning. It produces information to increase the understanding of natural hazards such as earthquakes, volcanoes, and landslides, and conducts research on oil, gas, and alternative energy potential, production, consumption, and environmental effects. It also leads the effort on climate change science research for the Department and provides access to natural science information to support decisions about how to respond to natural risks and manage natural resources.

Bureau of Reclamation (BOR)

The Bureau manages, develops, and protects water and related resources in an environmentally and economically sound manner in the interest of the American public. It is the largest wholesale supplier of water in the nation and manages 476 dams and 337 reservoirs. It delivers water to 1 in every 5 western farmers and more than 31 million people. It is also America's second largest producer of hydroelectric power.

Fish and Wildlife Service (FWS)

Manages the 150 million-acre National Wildlife Refuge System primarily for the benefit of fish and wildlife. It also manages 70 fish hatcheries and other related facilities for endangered species recovery and to restore native fisheries populations, and it protects and conserves migratory birds, threatened and endangered species and certain marine mammals. Each year it hosts approximately 47 million visitors at 561 refuges located in all 50 states and 38 wetland management districts.

National Park Service (NPS)

NPS maintains and manages a network of 401 natural, cultural, and recreational sites for the benefit and enjoyment of the American people. It manages and protects over 26,000 historic structures, over 44 million acres of designated wilderness, and a wide range of museum collections and cultural and natural landscapes. In addition, it provides outdoor recreation to over 286 million annual park visitors and provides technical assistance and support to state and local natural and cultural resource sites and programs as well as fulfilling its responsibilities under the National Historic Preservation Act.

Indian Affairs (IA)

IA fulfills its Indian trust responsibilities and promotes self-determination on behalf of 566 federally recognized Indian tribes. It funds compacts and contracts to support natural resource education, law enforcement, and social service programs that are delivered by tribes and operates 182 elementary and secondary schools and dormitories, providing educational services to 42,000 students in 23 states. It also supports 29 tribally controlled community colleges, universities, and post-secondary schools.

1

The Department of the Interior

A little history

In 1789 Congress created three Executive Departments: Foreign Affairs (later in the same year renamed State), Treasury, and War. It also provided for an Attorney General and a Postmaster General. Domestic matters were apportioned by Congress among these departments.

The idea of setting up a separate department to handle domestic matters was put forward on numerous occasions. It wasn't until March 3, 1849, the last day of the 30th Congress that a bill was passed to create the Department of the Interior to take charge of the Nation's internal affairs:

The Interior Department had a wide range of responsibilities entrusted to it: the construction of the national capital's water system, the colonization of freed slaves in Haiti, exploration of western wilderness, oversight of the District of Columbia jail, regulation of territorial governments, management of hospitals and universities, management of public parks, and the basic responsibilities for Indians, public lands, patents, and pensions. In one way or another all of these had to do with the internal development of the Nation or the welfare of its people.

Some significant dates:

1849 Creation of the Home Department consolidating the General Land Office (Department of the Treasury), the Patent Office (Department of State), the Indian Affairs Office (War Department) and the military pension offices (War and Navy Departments). Subsequently, Interior functions expand to include the census, regulation of territorial governments, exploration of the western wilderness, and management of the D.C. jail and water system.

1850-1857 Interior's Mexican Boundary Commission establishes the international boundary with Mexico.

1856-1873 Interior's Pacific Wagon Road Office improved the historic western emigrant routes.

1869 Interior began its geological survey of the western Territories with the Hayden expedition. The Bureau of Education is placed under Interior (later transferred to the Department of Health, Education and Welfare).

1872 Congress establishes Yellowstone as the first National Park.

1873 Congress transferred territorial oversight from the Secretary of State to the Secretary of the Interior.

1879 Creation of the US Geological Survey.

1884 Interior's Bureau of Labor is established (becomes the Department of Labor in 1888).

1887-1889 The Interstate Commerce Commission is established in Interior. The Dawes Act authorizes allotments to Indians.

1902 The Bureau of Reclamation is established to construct dams and aqueducts in the west.

1903 President Theodore Roosevelt establishes the first National Wildlife Refuge at Pelican Island, Florida. The Census Bureau is transferred to the Department of Commerce.

1910 The Bureau of Mines is created to promote mine safety and minerals technology.

1916 President Wilson signed legislation creating The National Park Service.

1920 The Mineral Leasing Act establishes the government's right to rental payments and royalties on oil, gas, and minerals production.

1925 The Patent Office is transferred to the Department of Commerce.

1930 The Bureau of Pensions is transferred to the Veterans Administration.

1934 The Taylor Grazing Act is enacted to regulate economic uses of public lands. The first Migratory Bird Hunting Stamp is issued. The Indian Reorganization Act abolishes the allotment system established in 1887, forms tribal governments, and affirms the Secretary's trust responsibilities. Oversight of Alaska, Hawaii, the Virgin Islands, and Puerto Rico is transferred to Interior.

1935 The Bureau of Reclamation completes construction of Hoover Dam.

1940 The US Fish and Wildlife Service is created from the Bureau of Fisheries and the Bureau of Biological Survey.

1946 Interior's General Land Office and Grazing Service are merged into the Bureau of Land Management.

1950-1951 Interior assumes jurisdiction over Guam, American Samoa, and the Trust Territory of the Pacific Islands.

1977 The Office of Surface Mining Reclamation and Enforcement is established to oversee state regulation of strip coal mining and repair of environmental damage.

1980 The Alaska National Interest Lands Conservation Act is enacted adding 47 million acres to the National Park System and 54 acres to the National Wildlife Refuge System.

1982 The Minerals Management Service (now known as the Bureau of Ocean Energy Management, Regulation, and Enforcement) is established to facilitate mineral revenue collection and manage the Outer Continental Shelf offshore lands.

1993 The President convened the Northwest Forest Plan Summit and released the "Forest Plan for a Sustainable Economy and Sustainable Environment."

1996 Interior science and technology functions are consolidated in the US Geological Survey.

2001 Gale A. Norton is nominated the first woman to serve as Secretary of the Interior.

2010 Secretary Ken Salazar signs order 3302, renaming the Minerals Management Service as the Bureau of Ocean Energy Management, Regulation, and Enforcement.

Key Principles

The DOI operates based on a set of key principles and tenets that guide the efforts of 70,000 employees, volunteers, and other stakeholders that deliver a broad spectrum of services and programs. These principles serve as the standard of operations throughout DOI and ensure achievement of the highest of ideals while performing the mission.

Stewards of the Nation's Natural, Cultural, and Heritage Assets

The DOI is committed to being an outstanding steward of approximately 500 million acres of public lands and 700 million subsurface acres including magnificent vistas, unique ecosystems, and treasured natural, cultural, and heritage assets. The management and oversight of these resources require a dedicated cadre of employees, the contributions of volunteers, and the input of stakeholders to inform decision making. The challenges of managing for a diverse constituency while meeting national goals for energy development and sustaining high levels of recreation and access require technical expertise, the best available science, and a landscape-level understanding of the balance of development and conservation.

Effective and Efficient Operations

The DOI is committed to achieving effective and efficient management. Executives and managers rely extensively on collaboration and partnerships that leverage resources. The DOI utilizes an extensive framework of internal controls to protect against fraud and waste and implements recommendations from the Government Accountability Office and the Office of Inspector General. On an annual basis, DOI reviews program activities for opportunities to eliminate lower priority programs, re-engineer underachieving programs, and investigate new ideas to increase the effectiveness and efficiency of program delivery. Through the President's SAVE awards program and other efforts that incentivize creative cost cutting, DOI is focused on specific management initiatives, which are described in greater detail in the Appendix.

Financial Integrity and Transparency

The DOI is committed to effective financial operations and accountability including high quality and timely reporting, robust internal controls, clean audits, and effective follow-up on audit and internal control findings. The DOI utilizes the Financial and Business Management System for the integration of business functions including budget execution, finance, acquisition, and others with single sign on, improved internal controls, a secure information technology environment, and a community of business innovation, efficiency, and transparency.

Ensuring High Ethical Standards

Key to maintaining public trust and confidence in the integrity of government is the adherence of high ethical standards and ensuring that government business is conducted with impartiality and integrity. The DOI embodies this principle, follows the law and holds people accountable. Accountability is a key theme – DOI expects to be held accountable. The DOI does not tolerate lapses that detract and distract from good, honest service to the American people. Decisions are based on sound science and the best interest of the public. The Department promotes and supports transparency, accountability, and efficiency.

Making DOI the Best and Most Inclusive Place to Work in America

The DOI is committed to making the Department the best and most inclusive place to work. Changing demographics of the population, generational shifts, increased urbanization, and increased use of technology makes the management of a changing cadre of employees challenging. The DOI will foster an environment that is open and accepting of individual differences and encourages employees to maximize their potential and to provide quality public service. The DOI will ensure that policies, practices, and systems do not benefit any one group over another and that the differences that each employee brings to the Department are respected and can enhance the organization's capacity, service, and adaptability.

Safety, Security, Preparedness, Response, and Recovery

One of DOI's top priorities is to focus on safety, security, and preparedness activities. The DOI will uphold its responsibilities for protecting lives, resources, property, and the environment through a wide variety of program areas, including law enforcement, health and safety, security, aviation, environmental compliance and emergency management. The DOI will provide technical expertise and capability for interagency preparedness, response and recovery activities as defined in Presidential Policy Directive 8 and the five National Frameworks (Protection, Prevention, Response, Recovery, and Mitigation), and as required by other interagency plans such as the National Oil and Hazardous Substance Pollution Contingency Plan. The DOI resources are frequently called upon for wildland fire and oil spill response, public works and engineering activities, search and rescue operations, protection of natural and cultural resources and historic properties expertise, rebuilding after storm and hazard events, and law enforcement missions.

Interior has the third largest contingent of Federal law enforcement officers in the Executive Branch with 3,500 officers that patrol vast acres of federal lands, national parks, wildlife refuges, and Indian communities. To ensure DOI is prepared to meet its preparedness, response, and recovery obligations, the Department and Bureaus maintain plans for all-hazards to safeguard the environment.

Respecting Tribal Self-Governance

The DOI recognizes the importance of the nation-to-nation relationship with tribes and will continue to encourage tribal management of resources and self-determination; consultation and support for effective management of the tribal trust; and the need to uphold commitments to tribes and Indian communities. Building coalitions will be an important aspect of these principles, including respect for the viewpoints of the 566 Indian tribes and the importance of maintaining strong tribal communities. Consultation is a key component of respecting Tribal self-governance and supporting the nation-to-nation relationship. The DOI upholds the principles set forth in the President's Executive Order 13175 Consultation and Coordination with Indian Tribal Governments. All of DOI's bureaus and offices operate under a policy consistent with the Executive Order that considers the impacts of policies, processes, rulemaking, and legislation regarding tribes and tribal communities.

International Engagement and Leadership

The DOI participates in the United States' efforts to address climate change; protect biodiversity; sustainably manage energy, water, and natural resources; empower indigenous communities; protect cultural heritage; and ensure sound science as the basis for decision-making. The resources for which DOI is responsible cross jurisdictional boundaries and DOI is a key player in the international community confronting the exploitation of natural resources, trade in wildlife, spread of invasive species, the arctic, and a multiplicity of scientific issues. The DOI is committed to maintaining its relevance and will engage in international efforts as a core mission responsibility, consistent with its unique expertise and mandate.

The DOI's responsibilities for management of lands, waters, and wildlife provide first-hand experience of the impacts of a rapidly changing climate. Impacts observed by Federal resource managers include drought, severe flooding, interrupted pollination of crops, changes in wildlife and prey behavior, warmer rivers and streams, and sea level rise. The DOI will bring the best science to bear to understand these consequences and will undertake mitigation, adaptation, and enhancements to support natural resilience and will take steps to reduce carbon pollution, including through the responsible development of clean energy. The DOI will be a national leader in integrating preparedness and resilience efforts into its mission areas, goals, strategies, and programs; identifying vulnerabilities and systematically addressing these vulnerabilities; and incorporating climate change strategies into management plans, policies, programs, and operations.

Strategic Plan 2014-2018

To ensure the Department meets its goals and objectives it has developed a strategic plan that will guide its actions until 2018. The Plan will facilitate the integration of all programs, the allocation and alignment of resources, and collaboration and coordination with stakeholders to achieve key goals.

A set of 6 mission areas, 24 goals, 38 strategies, and 117 performance measures will guide the DOI's activities over the lifetime of the plan. These mission areas reflect the Secretary of the Interior's priorities, while the goals and strategies describe the means by which those priorities will be achieved. The mission areas, goals, and strategies that compose the Strategic Plan are displayed in the Strategic Plan Framework, followed by a description of the mission areas, goals, and strategic objectives, and performance measures.

An FY 2018 goal is provided for each performance measure that reflects a desirable annual level of achievement that DOI aspires to by FY 2018 assuming the availability of a reasonable level of resources. The anticipated level of performance for these measures on an annual basis began in FY 2014. The Strategic Plan was developed based on collaboration among personnel of the DOI, in collaboration with tribes and other stakeholders. There is a high degree of continuity of performance measures from the FY2011-2016 Strategic Plan, in order to ensure an ongoing ability to gage trends in performance and assist decision makers to assess the likely impact of program changes. Trends in performance related to funding and programmatic plans are available in the DOI's FY 2014 Annual Performance Plan and Report available at www.doi.gov/bpp.

MISSION AREA I. CELEBRATING AND ENHANCING AMERICA'S GREAT OUTDOORS

GOAL #1 Protect America's Landscapes.

We will ensure that America's natural endowment – America's Great Outdoors – is protected for the benefit and enjoyment of current and future generations. Through collaborative, community-driven efforts, and outcome-focused investment, we will work to preserve and enhance rural landscapes, urban parks and rivers, important ecosystems, and essential wildlife habitat.

STRATEGY #1. Improve land and water health by managing the wetlands, uplands, and riparian areas that comprise our national parks, wildlife refuges, and BLM lands.

The Bureau of Land Management, the Fish and Wildlife Service, the National Park Service, and the Bureau of Reclamation are stewards of the lands and waters managed by the Department. These Bureaus maintain and restore uplands, wetlands, and streams through efforts that include controlling invasive plants and animals, restoring land to a condition that is self-sustaining, and ensuring that habitats support healthy fish and wildlife populations. The DOI's Natural Resource Damage Assessment and Restoration program works with the bureaus to assess the impacts of oil spills and hazardous waste sites and coordinates restoration efforts.

Annually, Bureaus administer resource protection programs on more than 400 million acres of upland, wetland, and aquatic lands within their jurisdiction. Many of these lands have special status as national parks, seashores, monuments, wildlife refuges, wilderness areas, or wild and scenic rivers. They are protected because of their important and often unique ecological characteristics, physical geography, or historical features. The DOI manages these lands on a landscape-scale basis because of increasing stressors such as climate change, habitat fragmentation, exotic invasive species, and other broadly influencing factors. The DOI also works in partnership with others by providing and leveraging resources for conservation activities on non-Federal lands.

STRATEGY #2. Sustain fish, wildlife, and plant species by protecting and recovering the Nation's fish and wildlife populations in cooperation with partners, including states.

The Fish and Wildlife Service is tasked with the conservation and protection of populations of fish, wildlife, plants, and their habitats. The FWS conducts these activities in partnership with others including NPS, BLM, Reclamation, and state and local agencies. The strategy to sustain species focuses on identifying and implementing corrective actions that will lead to species recovery. The DOI's responsibility to protect fish, wildlife, and native plants transcends jurisdictional boundaries, and includes efforts that affect almost 1,500 species with special status under the Endangered Species Act and more than 1,000 migratory birds that receive Federal protection under the Migratory Bird Treaty Act. The DOI is instrumental in combating domestic and international wildlife trafficking by improving enforcement of domestic laws, strengthening international cooperation and global enforcement, and helping to reduce demand for illegal wildlife products.

STRATEGY #3. Manage wildland fire for landscape resiliency, strengthen the ability of communities to protect against fire, and provide for public and firefighter safety in wildfire response.

The Department's Office of Wildland Fire coordinates fire programs across four Bureaus (BLM, FWS, NPS, and BIA) that manage and operate wildland fire programs along with the Department of Agriculture's Forest Service. The DOI Bureaus deploy strategies to mitigate the effects of wildland fire and restore burned acres, support communities that are at highest risk from fire by assisting in the development of fire action plans, and respond quickly when fire strikes. The DOI strives to achieve a technically effective fire management program that meets resource and safety objectives, while minimizing the cost of suppression and damage to resources. Ensuring resilient landscapes and fire-adapted communities depends on implementation of a broad-based, intergovernmental, collaborative, and national cohesive strategy to better address the mounting challenges of escalating fire behavior, increased risk to responders, greater home and property losses, and increased threats to communities. The DOI is a lead agency in this collaborative approach with the Forest Service and other Federal, state, tribal, and local governments and stakeholders. Three supporting performance measures were developed to demonstrate and evaluate progress in achieving the national goals to restore and maintain resilient landscapes, promote fire-adapted communities, and respond to wildfires.

GOAL #2. Protect America's Cultural and Heritage Resources.

We will ensure that our Nation's rich cultural heritage and abundant historic and prehistoric resources are preserved for the enjoyment and enlightenment of current and future generations.

STRATEGY #1. Protect and maintain the Nation's most important historic areas and structures, archaeological sites, and museum collections.

A cornerstone of DOI's mission is the protection of America's cultural heritage and resources for future generations and the obligation to honor and protect cultural resources of tribal communities. The Department maintains over 29,000 historic structures among 5 Bureaus – NPS, BLM, BOR, FWS, and BIA. The largest portion of historic structures on DOI lands is found in the National Park System. The Department also protects many of the Nation's most important cultural heritage sites. They range in size from pioneering homesteads to the massive granite carvings of Mount Rushmore. The DOI is the steward of millions of cultural and natural artifacts, including those from the earliest days of North American occupation over 15,000 years ago through colonial and westward expansion settlements to those from monuments commemorating recent heroic events, such as the Flight 93 National Memorial in Pennsylvania. These valued collections tell the history of the Nation. These Bureaus work closely with Native American tribes, Alaska Native corporations, and Native Hawaiian communities to help ensure respect for and preservation of the sacred cultural sites of our native peoples, as well as repatriation of Native American cultural items.

The Department, universities, historians, and others use America's cultural and heritage resources to expand understanding of our culture. They remind us of who we are and where we came from.

GOAL #3. Enhance Recreation and Visitor Experience.

We will encourage the appreciation and use of our lands by facilitating visitor use and recreational experiences. We will support tourism and outdoor recreation—powerful economic engines that bolster communities across the Nation. We will strive to provide visitors with beneficial physical, mental, and social opportunities, including those that result from outdoor recreational experiences.

STRATEGY #1. Enhance the enjoyment and appreciation of our natural and cultural heritage by creating opportunities for play, enlightenment, and inspiration.

About 417 million Americans and foreign visitors traverse public lands each year. The Bureaus that provide recreational opportunities – BLM, FWS, and NPS – are particularly dedicated to ensuring that visitors have the best possible experiences through interpretive guides, displays, videos, and other materials, in addition to the spectacular land, water, wildlife, and cultural features themselves. In a national dialogue about America's Great Outdoors, citizens reiterated the importance of open spaces and recreation to their quality of life, health, and commitment to conservation. National parks, FWS refuges, and BLM public lands provide recreation experiences that include many forms: camping or hiking; catch and release trout fishing; canoeing; bird watching; biking, swimming, and many other activities. Many water-related recreational activities are also available as a result of Bureau of Reclamation projects. These Bureaus make special accommodations to address the need for accessibility to public lands and to better engage underserved communities, especially in response to the increasing urbanization and shifting demographics of America's population. This requires focused research and close coordination with existing partners, as well as cultivating new partnerships with organizations representing diverse constituents.

By focusing on visitor services, increasing volunteer opportunities, and ensuring access for recreation, education, and contemplation, the Department ensures that the public is offered valuable, high-quality experiences at our sites.

MISSION AREA 2. STRENGTHENING TRIBAL NATIONS AND INSULAR COMMUNITIES.

GOAL #1. Meet Our Trust, Treaty, and Other Responsibilities to American Indians and Alaska Natives.

We will restore the integrity of nation-to-nation relationships with tribes and work diligently to fulfill the United States' trust responsibilities. We will work in partnership with tribes to build stronger economies and safer Indian communities.

STRATEGY #1. Protect reserved Indian treaty and subsistence rights.

The DOI will assist American Indian tribes and Alaska Natives in developing the most effective practices for responsible and successful use of subsistence resources and treaty reserved rights to natural resources. For the purposes of this measure, subsistence means the gathering and harvest, processing, consumption, and use of all wild resources – birds, mammals, fish, and plants – from all the varied environments found throughout tribal communities. For American Indians and Alaska Natives, subsistence use embodies a culturally significant lifestyle and is an important component of their communities. Subsistence resources are important to these economies and for the continuation of traditions and practices that are a part of these diverse cultures. The term "customary and traditional" is included in the Code of Federal Regulations to describe the historic and current use of wildlife and fisheries resources for subsistence by residents of rural communities.

STRATEGY #2. Fulfill Fiduciary Trust.

The DOI has ongoing responsibilities for timely reporting of Indian trust ownership information to its beneficiaries. We will ensure that trust and restricted Federal Indian-owned lands are managed effectively and accurately account for revenues in a timely and efficient manner. The Office of the Special Trustee for American Indians and Bureau of Indian Affairs oversee fiduciary trust activities.

GOAL #2. Improve the Quality of Life in Tribal and Native Communities.

With self-governance and self-determination as our North Star, the Department will work to restore tribal homelands, settle Indian water rights claims, increase opportunities for renewable and conventional energy on Indian lands, expand educational opportunities for Native American youth, and protect natural and cultural resources in the face of climate change.

STRATEGY #1. Support self-governance and self-determination.

The DOI is strengthening the nation-to-nation relationship between the Federal Government and tribal nations because self-determination, sovereignty, self-government, and self-reliance are the tools that will enable tribal nations to shape their collective destiny. Tribes have also assumed an expanded role in the operation of Indian programs through Public Law 93-638 contracting. Tribes contract with the Federal Government to operate programs serving their tribal members and other eligible persons.

STRATEGY #2. Create economic opportunity.

The DOI assists Indian Nations in developing capacity and infrastructure needed to attain economic self-sufficiency on reservations to enhance their quality of life. One critical path is economic development and job creation. The BIA coordinates development of comprehensive tribal programs with the Departments of Labor and Health and Human Services. The DOI offers programs and financial services that encourage start-ups and help position Indian businesses and individuals to compete in today's economy. The Department supports tribal communities in increasing opportunities to develop conventional and renewable energy resources (e.g. solar and wind) and non-energy mineral resources on trust land.

An integral part of building stronger economies within American Indian and Alaska Native communities is developing conservation and resource management plans that ensure sustainable use of trust land. Income is derived from leasing the land for timber and forest biomass harvests, grazing, and farming. These plans are reviewed by BIA to help safeguard the income-generating assets that sustain the economy of communities.

STRATEGY #3. Strengthen Indian education.

The DOI is allocating funds to improve its Bureau of Indian Education (BIE) funded schools, and improve the learning environment of BIE students. Improving performance in BIE schools is a challenge the DOI is addressing through initiatives aimed at increasing student achievement with a focus on reading and math. Schools are assessed for their Adequate Yearly Progress (AYP) which is defined by each state based on judging reading and mathematics proficiency along with attendance for elementary and middle schools, and graduation rates for high schools.

STRATEGY #4. Make communities safer.

The DOI will strengthen law enforcement in Indian Country by putting more officers on the streets, bolstering tribal courts, and helping fight violent crime and drug abuse. Crime control, however, is only one component of a safe community. New construction, renovation, and maintenance of facilities, including detention facilities and roads and bridges, also contribute to the safety and well-being of the tribal populace.

Tribal justice systems are an essential part of tribal governments, which interface with BIA and tribal law enforcement activities. Congress and the Federal courts have repeatedly recognized tribal justice systems as the appropriate forums for adjudicating disputes and minor criminal activity within Indian Country. It is important that the BIA and tribal law enforcement activities complement the operations of the tribal courts to ensure that justice in the tribal forums is administered effectively.

GOAL #3. Empower Insular Communities.

The Department empowers insular communities by improving the quality of life, creating economic opportunity, and promoting efficient and effective governance. The US-affiliated insular areas include: the territories of American Samoa, Guam, the US Virgin Islands, and the Commonwealth of the Northern Mariana Islands. The DOI also administers and oversees Federal assistance provided to the three Freely Associated States: the Federated States of Micronesia, the Republic of the Marshall Islands, and the Republic of Palau. The Assistant Secretary for Insular Affairs and the Office of Insular Affairs carry out these responsibilities on behalf of the Secretary.

STRATEGY #1. Improve quality of life.
The DOI will assist the insular areas to improve the quality of life by pairing access to financial resources for capital improvements and public services with robust oversight, and by improving interagency coordination on insular issues. We will also pursue sustainable, indigenous energy strategies to lessen dependence on oil imports and provide more reliable and affordable energy. In addition, we are working with other partners, such as the Department of Health and Human Services, to improve the quality of healthcare across the insular areas.

STRATEGY #2. Create economic opportunity.
The DOI will help create economic opportunity by forging partnerships that bolster tourism and attract industry by promoting the unique island cultures, natural resources, and by preparing the next generation of business leaders. We will pursue economic development initiatives that encourage private sector investment in the insular areas.

STRATEGY #3. Promote efficient and effective governance.
The DOI will work with the insular areas to ensure that local and Federal funding is being used efficiently and effectively by improving insular government financial policies and procedures, financial management systems, and technical planning abilities. We will also strive to equip insular area leadership with the statistical tools necessary for informed decision making.

MISSION AREA 3. POWERING OUR FUTURE AND RESPONSIBLE USE OF THE NATION'S RESOURCES

GOAL #1. Secure America's Energy Resources.

As manager of one-fifth of the Nation's landmass and energy resources on 1.7 billion acres of the Outer Continental Shelf (OCS), the Department plays a central and essential role in powering America's future through the responsible development of our Nation's abundant domestic energy resources. Through early planning, thoughtful mitigation, and the application of sound science, DOI can ensure that the Administration's "all-of-the-above" energy strategy includes not only traditional sources, but also the further development of new, cleaner resources to help mitigate the causes of climate change. Included in this development is a reliable, resilient, and well-planned energy transmission system that forms the backbone of the Nation's energy economy and is crucial to bringing both conventional and renewable energy to households across America. By modernizing practices, leveraging technology, and looking across the government and industry for best practices, DOI is improving the transparency and timeliness of the resource development permitting process while providing greater certainty to industry and strengthening inspection and regulatory enforcement programs.

STRATEGY #1. Ensure environmental compliance and the safety of energy development.

One of the keys to further expanding safe and responsible energy development is maintaining the public's confidence that this activity can be conducted in an environmentally responsible manner and is subject to strong oversight. The DOI is pressing forward with a reform agenda, both onshore and offshore, and is bolstering oversight and inspections. The DOI is focused on risk and is appropriately devoting limited oversight resources based on robust assessments of risk.

STRATEGY #2. Develop renewable energy potential.

The DOI is working to move America to a clean and sustainable energy future and, as called for in President Obama's Climate Action Plan, will re-double efforts on renewable energy as we transition to a landscape-level approach to wind, solar, geothermal, and hydropower energy development. Standing up new sources of clean energy generation and facilitating the construction of new or upgraded transmission networks are helping to create new industries and supply chains, driving economic growth and job creation. Connecting renewable energy projects to the grid and key markets is central to making renewable energy generation projects viable. Through partnerships and close coordination, the DOI works to site renewable energy projects in the right places where potential environmental and social conflicts can be minimized and potential effects mitigated, consistent with landscape-level planning.

Hydropower is the Nation's largest renewable energy resource, and the Bureau of Reclamation is the second largest hydropower producer in the United States. Our 53 power plants generate more than 40 billion kilowatt hours annually, enough electricity to serve 3.5 million homes. Over the next 12 years, Reclamation is initiating major rehabilitation and upgrades to many of its large hydropower assets which will yield over 250 Megawatts of additional capacity via increased efficiencies. These actions may affect peak availability of units in a given year during this period.

STRATEGY #3. Manage conventional energy development.

The DOI oversees vast resources that, when developed the right way and in the right places, support "all of the above" energy strategy that expands the production of energy at home, promotes energy security, and helps drive the economy and job growth.

STRATEGY #4. Account for energy revenue.

The DOI is committed to providing reasonable assurance that it is collecting every dollar due from Federal and Indian lands leased for energy development. The Department will fulfill its role by accurately and efficiently collecting, accounting for, analyzing, auditing, and disbursing revenues associated with offshore and onshore energy production. Revenues generated from these activities are distributed to states and tribes, fund land protection and historic preservation, and are deposited in the US Treasury. The DOI also is committed to working with industry, as well as public and nongovernmental entities, as part of the international Extractive Industries Transparency Initiative (EITI), which offers a voluntary framework for governments to disclose revenues received from oil, gas, and mining assets, with parallel disclosure by companies of what they have paid governments in royalties, rents, bonuses, taxes and other payments. The Department is working diligently towards obtaining compliance with the international EITI standards and in December 2013 submitted the US Candidacy Application to the International EITI Board.

GOAL #2. Sustainably Manage Timber, Forage, and Non-energy Minerals.
STRATEGY #1 Manage timber and forest product resources.
The DOI's forests or woodlands are managed by BLM for the benefit of the American public. The BLM maintains a permanent source of timber supply, which supports the production of commodities such as lumber, plywood, and paper, while also protecting watersheds, regulating stream flow, contributing to the economic stability of local communities and industries, and providing recreational opportunities.

STRATEGY #2. Provide for sustainable forage and grazing.
The BLM manages livestock grazing on over half of its public lands. The BLM's overall objective is to ensure the long-term health and productivity of these lands. The BLM uses a variety of methods to accomplish this objective – periodic rest or deferment of grazing in pastures in specific allotments during critical growth periods; vegetation treatments; and projects such as water development and fences. The terms and conditions for grazing on BLM managed lands, such as stipulations on forage use and season of use, are set forth in the permits and leases issued by the Bureau to public land ranchers.

STRATEGY #3. Manage non-energy mineral development.
Non-energy minerals development on DOI lands and waters, such as gold, zinc, lead, copper, iron, salt, sand, potassium, phosphate, stone, gravel, and clay, support a broad array of uses, including medical applications, computer production, coastal restoration, automobile production, and highway construction and maintenance. The DOI is committed to sustaining mineral development in an environmentally responsible way by ensuring the

reclamation of areas that have been mined and minimizing environmental impacts during the mining process.

MISSION AREA 4. ENGAGING THE NEXT GENERATION

"For the health of our economy and our public lands, it's critical that we work now to establish meaningful and deep connections between young people – from every background and every community – and the great outdoors." Secretary Sally Jewell October 31, 2013.

The future of our public lands depends upon young people serving as active stewards of the environment throughout their lives. However, there is a growing disconnect between young people and the great outdoors – and it's a gap that DOI has the power to help bridge. The Department has a unique opportunity to harness the strong spirit of community service and volunteerism that is alive within our Nation's youth, and encourage them to use their time, energy, and talent to better our natural and cultural treasures. Through public-private partnerships and in conjunction with all levels of government, DOI will expand its efforts to inspire millions of young people to play, learn, serve, and work outdoors.

GOAL #1. Play.

Develop or enhance outdoor recreation partnerships in a total of 50 cities over the next 4 years to create new, systemic opportunities for outdoor play for over 10 million young people.

By participating in recreation opportunities on public lands, our youth strengthen their ties to America's backyard. However, nearly 80 percent of the United States' population lives in cities. The DOI can leverage our experience and expertise to help communities engage more young people on all public lands. To increase the number of youth who play outside, we must overcome the major obstacles including a lack of access in communities, a lack of interest from children, and a lack of time for young adults. To address these problems, DOI will develop or enhance outdoor recreation partnerships in 50 cities with the goal of creating new systemic opportunities for outdoor play for over 10 million young people.

This goal will build upon the National Park Service's plan for the Centennial. As part of the NPS Call to Action for the Centennial, the NPS has committed to developing proactive Rivers, Trails and Conservation Assistance Programs and collaborative park-based programs in the 50 largest urban areas and those with the least access to parks. The NPS is also establishing 50 formal partnerships with health and medical providers across the Country.

GOAL #2. Learn.

In 4 years, provide educational opportunities to at least 10 million of the Nation's K-12 student population annually.

Our public lands and waters are our outdoor laboratories, and by getting students–from grammar school to graduate school–to learn about our public lands and waters, we can develop their interest in nature and the science, technology, engineering, and mathematics (STEM) education fields that are essential to our future. There are approximately 50–55 million K-12 students in the US. The DOI currently reaches at least 3 million students a year through its education programs. With new online education resources, we have the ability to reach more teachers and students than those that can come for an in-person visit.

Leveraging the NPS' newly launched teacher portal, DOI will provide educational opportunities to at least 10 million of the Nation's K-12 student population annually.

GOAL #3. Serve.

In 4 years, attain 1,000,000 volunteers annually on public lands.

Currently 332,000 volunteers provide 9.6 million hours of service annually valued at $209 million per year. We know that many more people are interested in volunteering but there is insufficient volunteer coordination and management capacity. By prioritizing volunteer management and coordination positions as part of our efforts to expand youth work opportunities and leveraging the expertise of partners like the Corporation for National and Community Service, we will expand volunteer opportunities across DOI's public lands.

GOAL #4. Work.

Provide 100,000 work and training opportunities to young people over the next 4 years.

To develop the next generation of lifelong conservation stewards and ensure our own skilled and diverse workforce pipeline, DOI will provide 100,000 work & training opportunities to young people (ages 15 to 25) over 4 years. In order to achieve the goal, we will utilize public-private partnerships to leverage additional resources and provide additional work and training opportunities than those we could do on our own. Our work and training opportunities will support the 21st Century Conservation Service Corps (21CSC) which is a multi-agency effort to provide work and training opportunities in stewardship of our public lands to young people and veterans, helping them develop skills to serve both the Nation's natural and cultural resources, but also their own futures. The other 21 CSC Federal agency partners are Agriculture, Commerce, Labor, Environmental Protection Agency, Army, Council on Environmental Quality, and the Corporation for National and Community Service.

MISSION AREA 5. ENSURING HEALTHY WATERSHEDS AND SUSTAINABLE, SECURE WATER SUPPLIES

Healthy watersheds provide sustainable, secure water that is the foundation for healthy communities and economies, but water supplies are challenged by climate change, record drought conditions, and increasing demands. Recognizing the states' primary role in managing water resources, the Department will work as a partner to increase reliability of water supplies, for the benefit of the people, the economy, and the environment by providing better tools for water management, promoting water conservation and efficiency, and wisely maintaining and improving infrastructure. To achieve this goal it will be critical to inculcate these concepts in the next generation of water managers.

GOAL #1. Manage Water and Watersheds for the 21st Century.

We deliver water in the 17 Western States for agriculture, municipal and industrial use, and providing flood control and recreation for millions of Americans. To achieve these goals, BOR balances water supply demands, promotes water conservation, improves water management, and protects the environment through the safe and effective performance of our facilities. The Department has a role in developing innovative approaches to meet water needs and anticipate future challenges.

STRATEGY #1. Improve reliability of water delivery.

The BOR and its managing partners operate and maintain its water facilities in a safe, efficient, economical, and reliable manner, and assure that systems and safety measures are in place to protect the facilities and the public. The BOR's Facility Reliability Rating (FRR) system was established to score and provide a general indication of BOR's ability to maintain the reliability of its facilities. The BOR uses FRR data, on both reserved and major transferred facilities, to focus on activities that help ensure water storage and delivery for its customers. Approximately 40% of the total facilities subject to FRR are managed by Reclamation's water partners. These partnerships create significant operational efficiencies but will also require close coordination to effectively utilize available Federal and non-Federal resources needed to achieve the stated goal.

STRATEGY #2. Better ensure the future of watersheds against the impacts of climate change.

The BOR is currently conducting assessments of existing and future water supply demand imbalances in watersheds within its 17 Western States through Basin Studies and Impact Assessments. When completed, these studies will analyze the risks and impacts of climate change to water resources and identify actions to adapt to the potential effects of climate change. To address projected imbalances in supply and demand, the studies identify adaptation strategies, including strategies for non-structural and structural changes. A wide range of Federal and non-Federal stakeholders participate in the basin studies, which are selected through a competitive process using established criteria.

GOAL #2. Extend the Supply of Water through Conservation.

STRATEGY #1. Expand Water Conservation Capabilities.

The American West is now the fastest growing region of the Country and faces serious water challenges. Competition for finite water supplies is increasing as a result of population growth, agricultural demands, and water for environmental needs. An increased emphasis on domestic energy development will place additional pressure on limited water supplies, as significant amounts of water may be required for unconventional and renewable energy development.

Impacts of climate change, as evidenced by increases in temperature, decreases in precipitation and snowpack, extended droughts, and depleted aquifers and stream flow in several Reclamation river basins are reducing water supplies. Water is vital for the environment and the economies of rural and urban communities in the west. The DOI will "increase" water supplies through BOR's Priority Goal conservation programs.

GOAL #3. Availability of Water to Tribal Communities.
STRATEGY #1. Protect tribal water rights.

The BIA water program functions are divided into two distinct but overlapping elements. The Water Rights Negotiation/Litigation Program defines and protects Indian water rights and settles claims through negotiations if possible, or alternatively, through litigation. The Water Management Program assists tribes in managing, conserving, and utilizing trust water resources.

STRATEGY #2. Improve infrastructure and operational efficiency of tribal water facilities

The BIA Irrigation, Power and Safety of Dams program operates and manages irrigation, power, and dam infrastructure. The program sets high standards for maintenance, collaboration with stakeholders, and effective water and power distribution. The BIA manages facilities to ensure they do not present an unacceptable risk to downstream lives and property; and are managed in an economically, technically, environmentally, and culturally sound manner.

MISSION AREA 6. BUILDING A LANDSCAPE-LEVEL UNDERSTANDING OF OUR RESOURCES

To effectively carry out its mission, the Department of the Interior must understand and make decisions at the landscape-level. Decisions affecting the siting of energy development, water resource management, recreation, the conservation of habitat for sensitive flora and fauna, the identification of transmission line rights-of-way, mitigation for development activities, and other land uses are increasingly interconnected with one another on an ever changing, climate-impacted landscape.

The Department conducts science to inform these decisions; develops tools to analyze, visualize, translate, and extrapolate science; and is leading efforts to apply it at multiple scales and across multiple landscapes and jurisdictions to inform land and resource planning, policy, mitigation, and management. Additionally, as the managing partner for the Geospatial Platform, DOI can leverage 21st Century Geographic Information System (GIS) tools to transform vast amounts of data regarding our landscapes and resources into useful information to inform decisions about powering our future and ensuring healthy landscapes and sustainable supplies of water.

GOAL #1. Provide Shared Landscape-level Management and Planning.

Tools Harnessing emerging technologies, tools, and methodologies, DOI works with partners to elevate understanding of resources on a landscape-level. The DOI will leverage these partnerships and its role as the managing partner for the National Geospatial Platform to turn vast amounts of data into usable information and advance broader based and more consistent landscape and resource management.

STRATEGY #1. Ensure the use of landscape-level capabilities and mitigation actions.

Landscape-level approaches to management hold the promise of a broader-based and more consistent consideration of both development and conservation, as opposed to a piecemeal approach. Over the last few decades, ecologists and conservationists have increasingly worked at larger geographic scales to improve their ability to characterize and combat complex threats and stressors such as habitat fragmentation and climate change. When conservation is planned for and carried out at these larger scales, it is often easier to detect ecological patterns and population dynamics than with conservation undertaken within smaller units of habitat, improving the ability of conservationists to address limiting factors, adapt to changing circumstances, and achieve long-term benefits to species. The rigorous science underlying our landscape-scale databases, tools, and methodologies provides the foundation for a new generation of citizen scientists, professional experts, and organizations to better understand and care for our landscapes. By improving coordination with partner agencies, a landscape-level understanding of resources will be available for these needs.

Strong science based evidence will allow DOI to make strategic decisions relative to conservation priorities and maximize our conservation investments to achieve the best possible outcomes, while learning from our experience and new evidence on changing conditions. Changes in ecosystems and habitats in the face of changing climatic conditions require that future conservation strategies can be adaptive, including the use of vulnerability assessments, scenario planning, and explicit statements of expected biological outcomes.

This information can be used to identify conservation targets and objectives that best represent our desired outcomes and then to develop landscape conservation designs, long-term strategies, and forward-looking resource management decisions to achieve them. Implementation occurs using a collection of tools and methodologies including the Geospatial Platform,

Landscape Conservation Cooperatives, Climate Science Centers, and other specialized programs and processes. This information is essential to the successful use of the landscape-scale mitigation approaches being implemented throughout the DOI. Mapping and imagery tools facilitate sound planning and management, ensuring the functionality of entire ecosystems, the resiliency of species and the predictability of decisions for industry. The Geospatial Platform offers an Internet-based tool for sharing trusted geospatial data. It provides services and applications for use by the public, government agencies, and partners to meet their mission needs. This resource facilitates landscape-level planning by providing a platform for integrated data from Federal and non-Federal partners (e.g., universities, private organizations, and tribal, state, and local governments). By centralizing such critical inputs as habitat characteristics, risk vulnerabilities, mineral resources, energy potential, conservation priorities, cultural resources, water resources, surface elevation, and property ownership, these tools will provide policy and decision makers from Federal and state governments, local communities, businesses, and non-profit organizations with reliable, transparent, science-based information to effectively manage the resources and enable integrated early analysis in a programmatic way.

The National Map, a collection of geospatial data of the Nation's topography, natural landscape and built environment is also available. Updating high-resolution geospatial databases such as surface water and elevation data and topographic map images on a 3 year cycle supports public purposes such as resource management, climate and environment, infrastructure and human services, energy, disaster response, and public safety.

GOAL #2. Provide Science to Understand, Model, and Predict Ecosystem, Climate, and Land Use Changes at Targeted and Landscape Levels (biota, land cover, and Earth and ocean systems).

We will support scientific research to assess, understand, model, and forecast the impacts of climate change and other environmental drivers on our ecosystems, natural resources, and communities. Our Bureaus will develop and construct strategies for adapting to climate change based on scientific analysis. The DOI will assist Federal, state, local, and tribal entities by monitoring water quality and quantity; analyzing energy and mineral resources potential and environmental effects of their extraction and use; and analyzing and monitoring changes to the land and ocean environments.

STRATEGY #1. Identify and predict ecosystem and land use change.

The DOI will conduct ongoing research to support and inform decisions related to ecological systems for land, water, and fish and wildlife population management. Climate and land use changes are the key drivers of changes in ecosystems, and strategies for protecting climate-sensitive ecosystems will be increasingly important. The USGS uses satellite data such as Landsat to detect, analyze, and monitor changes on the land, study the connections between people and the land, and provide society with relevant science information to inform public decisions. These data are necessary to provide a baseline composite of the characteristics and geographic variability of land cover, such as seen in the National Land Cover Database. Terrestrial and aquatic populations and their habitats are studied to understand their condition and function within ecosystems and provide information to improve management and conservation actions. Managing and protecting the biological and physical components that support ecosystem services and processes is a priority of the DOI, especially as it relates to the impacts of climate change.

STRATEGY #2. Assess and forecast climate change and its effects.

The extent to which US communities and ecosystems may be affected by climate change will depend on the nature of the impacts and the sensitivity of the ecosystem to the changes. Successful adaptation to climate change will depend on access to a variety of options for effective management responses. The DOI will support research and monitoring initiatives of carbon, nitrogen, and water cycles, and their effects on ecosystems. The USGS will provide tools for managers to develop, implement, and test adaptive strategies, reduce risk, and increase the potential for ecological systems to be self-sustaining, resilient, and adaptable to environmental changes. The DOI also considers the application of traditional knowledge when making decisions affecting tribal communities. The Department and the USGS strategies and measures align to achieve the goals of the Climate Action Plan. The USGS will, through its existing scientific assets and the DOI Landscape Conservation Cooperatives and Climate Science Centers, implement partner-driven science to improve understanding of past and present land use change, develop relevant climate and land use forecasts, and identify lands, resources, and communities that are most vulnerable to adverse impacts of change from the local to global scale.

GOAL #3. Provide Scientific Data to Protect, Instruct, and Inform Communities.

We will support scientific research to improve the resilience of communities to natural hazards and wildlife diseases in order to preserve the quality of life and reduce the likelihood of fatalities and economic losses. The USGS will lead the scientific research on the environment and natural hazards and provide information to partners and stakeholders for use in making decisions that will protect lives.

STRATEGY #1. Monitor and assess natural hazards risk and resilience.

The DOI's monitoring and assessments provide information and the scientific understanding that will help protect communities by significantly reducing the vulnerability of millions of people to natural hazards. For example, USGS, working with many partners, collects accurate and timely data from modern earth observation networks and surveys, analyzes those data to assess areas that are at risk due to natural hazards, and conducts focused research to improve hazard predictions.

STRATEGY #2. Provide environmental health science to guide decisionmaking.

Human health is often related to the health of the environment and wildlife. The emergence of diseases from exposure to environmental contaminants and diseases transferred between animals and humans is a growing concern. The DOI is taking a leadership role in providing the natural science information needed by health researchers, policy makers, and the public to safeguard public health by monitoring the quality of the environment and wildlife disease reservoirs, by identifying emerging environmental quality concerns and emerging threats from disease transmitted from animals to humans, and by providing critical knowledge that helps guide actions to manage, mitigate, and prevent adverse impacts on the environment, wildlife, and human health.

GOAL #4. Provide Water and Land Data to Customers.

The Department, through USGS, will lead the effort to provide water and land data to customers for their various uses. The USGS will gather and present data at targeted and landscape-levels to advance and refine our understanding of the earth and its geologic and ecologic systems. Three dimensional models of ground water aquifers and energy and mineral deposits in the subsurface will be generated to help identify prospective areas for exploration and utilization. We will produce vegetation maps and data to support and inform risk management of wildland fires, wildlife, and other natural resources. We will deliver high resolution geospatial databases and topographic map images to support public purposes and enhance resource management.

STRATEGY #1. Monitor and assess water availability and quality.

The Nation faces an increasing set of water resource challenges. The DOI will continue to monitor and conduct research to generate a more precise estimate of water availability and use for meeting current and future human, environmental, and wildlife requirements. These research and monitoring activities will help identify water resources for use by humans and the environment while also developing tools to forecast likely outcomes for landscape-level planning needs including water use and quality, and aquatic ecosystem health affected by changes in land use and land cover, natural and engineered infrastructure, water use, and climate. State and local governments rely heavily on the monitoring data that is provided by USGS monitoring systems that operate across the Country.

STRATEGY #2. Generate geologic maps.

As the DOI's science arm, USGS produces accurate geologic maps and three-dimensional geologic frameworks that provide indispensable data for sustaining and improving the quality of life and economic vitality of the Nation. Geologic maps and research are foundational for exploring, developing, and preserving mineral, energy, and water resources; evaluating and planning for land management and environmental protection; supporting DOI's land management decisions, reducing losses from natural hazards, including earthquakes, volcanoes, landslides, and other ground failures; mitigating effects of coastal and stream erosion; placement of critical infrastructure and facilities; and conducting basic earth science research. The geologic maps and interpretive products produced through the USGS and its state partners are served through the National Geologic Map Database, which is an authoritative and landscape-level data source for the general public, scientists, and decision makers.

STRATEGY #3. Assess national and international energy and mineral resources.

The Nation faces increasing demands for energy and mineral resources, particularly in light of concerns about our dependence on resources imported from other countries. The DOI's energy and mineral resources research, assessments, and information will improve our understanding of resource occurrence, distribution, quality, and supply and foster multidisciplinary analyses of the broad economic, environmental, and societal consequences of resource extraction and use. The outcomes of these activities will inform decision making with respect to such issues as natural resource protection, environmental health, economic vitality, and responsible resource management on DOI and other lands.

2

Bureau of Land Management

The Bureau of Land Management (BLM) manages billions of acres of land on the surface, below the surface and under the oceans within our territorial waters.

These vast tracts of public lands have the potential to make significant contributions to the nation's renewable energy portfolio. This gives the BLM a leading role in fulfilling the Administration's goals for a new energy economy based on a rapid and responsible move to large-scale production of solar, wind, geothermal, and biomass energy. The BLM also manages Federal onshore oil, gas and coal operations that make significant contributions to the domestic energy supply as the Nation transitions to a clean energy future.

Energy

The BLM manages more Federal land than any other agency – about 245 million surface acres as well as 700 million sub-surface acres of mineral estate. As these lands are increasingly tapped to develop clean, renewable energy, the US reduces its dependence on foreign oil and provides opportunities for creating new jobs to support local communities. Public lands also provide sites for new modern transmission facilities needed to deliver clean power to consumers.

Not all lands with energy potential are appropriate for development. The BLM reviews and approves permits and licenses from companies to explore, develop, and produce both renewable and nonrenewable energy on Federal lands.

The BLM ensures that proposed projects meet all applicable environmental laws and regulations. The bureau works with local communities, the states, industry, and other federal agencies in this approval process and has set up four Renewable Energy Coordination Offices and five oil and gas Pilot Offices to facilitate reviews. In addition, The BLM participates in a Cabinet-level working group that is developing a coordinated federal permitting process for siting new transmission projects that would cross public, State and private lands.

Once projects are approved, the BLM is responsible for ensuring that developers and operators comply with use authorization requirements and regulations. Although the Bureau of Indian Affairs issues mineral leases on Indian lands, the BLM approves and supervises mineral operations on these lands.

Companies pay for development of public energy resources. Total royalty, rentals, and bonus payments vary from year to year but Federal and State governments receive billions of dollars for onshore energy leasing and production. For oil and gas, half of this money goes to the States and half goes to the US Treasury. Distribution of revenue from renewable energy varies depending on the authority used.

Renewable Energy

The US Department of the Interior and the BLM are working with local communities, state regulators, industry, and other federal agencies in building a clean energy future by providing sites for environmentally sound development of renewable energy on public lands. Renewable energy projects on BLM-managed lands include wind, solar, geothermal, and biomass projects and the siting of transmission facilities needed to deliver this power to the consumer.

Solar Energy

Solar radiation levels in the Southwest are some of the best in the world, and the BLM manages more than 19 million acres of public lands with excellent solar energy potential in 6 states: California, Nevada, Arizona, New Mexico, Colorado and Utah. State renewable energy portfolios, investment tax credits for solar energy projects, volatile oil prices, and international concern about global warming have all contributed toward public and industry interest in utility-scale solar energy development. Solar energy projects can provide significant amounts of electricity while emitting virtually no greenhouse gases, but they require large areas of relatively flat land, and some technologies use substantial amounts of water—a scarce commodity in the arid climates where the solar resources are the best.

Solar energy development projects on BLM-administered public lands are authorized as rights-of-way under Title V of the Federal Land Policy and Management Act if the proposed project is consistent with BLM land use planning. The applicant is required to pay the BLM's costs in processing the right-of-way application, and all projects require an environmental review under the National Environmental Policy Act. Any entity that receives a solar energy right-of-way authorization must comply with the terms and conditions of the authorization and pay fair market value for use of the public lands.

Since 2010, the BLM has approved 29 utility-scale solar energy projects, including connected-action projects that include electric transmission support authorizations, with a total approved capacity of over 8,500 megawatts of clean, renewable energy — enough energy to power roughly 2.6 million homes. In addition, the BLM currently has some 70 pending solar energy applications.

In October 2012, the Secretary of the Interior signed the Record of Decision finalizing a program to facilitate development of solar energy on public lands in six southwestern states. The Western Solar Plan provides a blueprint for utility-scale solar energy permitting in Arizona, California, Colorado, Nevada, New Mexico and Utah by establishing solar energy zones with access to existing or planned transmission, incentives for development within those zones, and a process through which to consider additional zones and solar projects. The Western Solar Plan established an initial set of 17 Solar Energy Zones, totaling about 285,000 acres of public lands that serve as priority areas for commercial-scale solar development, with the potential for additional zones through ongoing and future regional planning processes. Two additional Solar Energy Zones were designated in 2013 in Arizona and California. If fully built out, projects in the designated areas could produce as much as 27,000 megawatts of solar energy, enough to power approximately 8 million homes. The program also keeps the door open, on a case-by-case basis, for the possibility of carefully sited solar projects outside SEZs on about 19 million acres in "variance" areas.

Wind Energy

The BLM manages 20.6 million acres of public lands with wind potential. The BLM has authorized 39 wind energy development projects, including connected-action projects that include electric transmission support authorizations, with a total approved capacity of 5,557 megawatts, enough to supply the power needs of over 1.5 million homes. In addition, the BLM has authorized over 100 wind energy testing sites.

A Programmatic Environmental Impact Statement (EIS) relating to the development of wind energy on the public lands was completed in June 2005. This EIS provides an analysis of the development of wind energy projects on the public lands in the West. In conjunction with the publication of this EIS, the BLM amended 52 land use plans to allow for the use of applicable lands for wind energy development. BLM offices are able to use this EIS as an aid in analyzing impacts for specific applications for the use of public lands for wind energy use. The BLM issued a wind energy policy in December 2008 to provide guidance on best management practices (BMPs); measures to mitigate potential impacts on birds, wildlife habitat, and other resource values; and guidance on administering wind energy authorizations.

Wind power uses the naturally occurring energy of the wind for practical purposes like generating electricity, charging batteries, or pumping water. Wind turbines capture the kinetic energy in the wind, converting it into electrical energy. Utility-scale turbines are mounted on tall towers, usually 300 feet or more above the earth's surface, where the wind is faster and less turbulent. In utility-scale power applications, multiple turbines are connected to the utility grid, providing electricity when the wind blows.

For more than a decade, wind energy has been the fastest growing energy technology worldwide, achieving an annual growth rate of over 30%. In the United States, the current total installed capacity is over 60,000 megawatts of wind projects.

Laws enacted in most of the Western states require energy companies to provide a portion of their energy from renewable energy sources. As a result, the BLM anticipates a continued interest in the use of public lands for renewable energy development.

The BLM continues to conduct studies necessary to evaluate and process applications for rights-of-way for the siting of wind energy projects and applications for rights-of-way for electric transmission lines from these projects. The BLM has approved wind energy projects in Arizona, California, Idaho, Nevada, Oregon, Utah, and Wyoming. The BLM currently has some 29 pending wind energy development applications on the public lands.

The BLM's wind energy program is part of an "all-of-the-above" strategy to improve the management of energy resources found on Federal lands in a balanced way to ensure the Nation's economic and energy security and quality of life.

Geothermal Energy

The BLM has the delegated authority for leasing 245 million acres of public lands, including 104 million acres managed by the US Forest Service, with geothermal potential in 11 Western States and Alaska. The BLM presently manages 818 geothermal leases, with 59 geothermal leases in producing status, with a total capacity of 1,500 megawatts of geothermal energy on public lands. This amounts to over 40 percent of US geothermal energy capacity and supplies the electrical needs of about 1.5 million homes. The BLM's geothermal leases provide not only electrical power generation but also alternative heat sources for direct-use commercial endeavors.

In May 2007, the Department of the Interior published regulations on geothermal energy development on public lands requiring more competitive leasing, offering simplified royalty calculations, and providing for the administration of geothermal leases. Geothermal leases generate over $12 million in Federal royalties each year, with 50 percent shared with the states and 25 percent shared with local counties.

Competitive lease sales since 2007 have netted over $76 million in bonus bids for geothermal lease parcels in Colorado, Idaho, Oregon, Utah, Nevada, and California. A competitive auction of public lands in Nevada held in August 2008 was the largest geothermal sale ever in terms of dollars bid, bringing in a record $28.2 million for a total of 105,211 acres. The development and production of the geothermal resources on these lands will bring the

Nation closer to meeting its targets for electrical energy production from renewable resources.

A Programmatic Environmental Impact Statement (EIS) relating to the authorization of geothermal leasing was completed in October 2008, and the Record of Decision was signed in December 2008. The Record of Decision amended 114 BLM resource management plans and allocated about 111 million acres of Bureau-managed public lands as open for leasing. An additional 79 million acres of Forest Service lands are also available for leasing.

Since the completion of the Programmatic EIS, the BLM has competitively leased over one million acres of Federal lands, generating over $76 million in bonus bids for geothermal lease parcels. The overall lease sales include 67 parcels in Utah, totaling 241,490 acres; 11 parcels in Oregon, totaling 41,362 acres; 13 parcels in Idaho totaling 17,580 acres; 14 parcels in California, totaling 14,110 acres; 1 parcel in Colorado, totaling 799 acres; and 260 parcels in Nevada, totaling 734,447 acres.

Woody Biomass and Bioenergy

BLM manages approximately 65 million acres of forests and woodlands in Alaska and 14 Western States. An estimated 16 million acres are in need of restoration. Woody biomass is a part of BLM's forest product line and is primarily comprised of restoration residues and smaller diameter material from forestry, fuels and rangeland treatments. Biomass utilization is expected to increase as an increasing number of renewable and bioenergy facilities come on-line.

When trying to reduce hazardous wildland fire fuels and utilize biomass as part of forest health and restoration treatments, the BLM lands are not unique. They share many of the same barriers, and offer the same opportunities as other federal, state and private lands. Most of the 16 million acres needing restoration are in rural areas, a long distance away from many existing woody biomass markets. Transportation costs to these markets can be quite high, and establishing new markets for woody biomass is often difficult. The BLM is actively working with partners in local communities to identify and promote opportunities.

The Interdepartmental Woody Biomass Utilization Working Group (Woody BUG or WBUG) includes the Departments of Agriculture, Energy and Interior.

Additional membership includes the Departments of Commerce, Defense, Environmental Protection Agency and others.

Since the passage of the 2005 Energy Policy Act, the BLM and the Forest Service have developed a joint Action Plan for Title II - Renewable Energy, Section 210, which authorizes transportation and research grants for BLM and FS. Currently the Woody Biomass Utilization Grants are funded through the USDA Forest Service Forest Products Laboratory in Madison, Wisconsin.

Electric Transmission Facilities & Energy Corridors

The US Department of the Interior and the Bureau of Land Management are committed to processing applications in an environmentally responsible manner for electric transmission facilities that expand and modernize the transmission grid. Processing of the applications will be done in accordance with applicable laws and through a coordinated approach that involves local and state governments, tribes, other federal agencies, local communities, and other stakeholders.

"To build America's clean energy economy the US must update its transmission grid for the 21st century, so that it can efficiently move power from the new energy frontier to the places it is consumed." - Secretary of the Interior Ken Salazar

Transmission towers at sunset

"We know the country that harnesses the power of clean, renewable energy will lead the 21st century." - President Obama

These transmission facilities will accommodate additional electric capacity over the next several decades, including new renewable generation as well as improve reliability and reduce congestion in the western grid. They will also transmit the energy that will power our future.

Transmission towers in the Western US
Interagency Rapid Response Team for Transmission (RRTT)

The RRTT aims to improve the overall quality and timeliness of electric transmission infrastructure permitting, review, and consultation by the Federal government on both Federal and non-Federal lands through:

- Coordinating statutory permitting, review, and consultation schedules and processes among involved Federal and state agencies, as appropriate, through Integrated Federal Planning;
- Applying a uniform and consistent approach to consultations with Tribal governments; and,
- Resolving interagency conflicts and ensuring that all involved agencies are fully engaged and meeting timelines.

Participating Agencies include: the Department of Agriculture, the Department of Commerce, the Department of Defense, the Department of Energy, the Department of the Interior, the Environmental Protection Agency, the Federal Electric Regulatory Commission, the Advisory Council on Historic Preservation, and the White House Council on Environmental Quality.

"Transmission is a vital component of our nation's energy portfolio, and these seven lines, when completed, will serve as important links across our country to increase our power grid's capacity and reliability," said then Secretary of the Interior Ken Salazar.

"This is the kind of critical infrastructure we should be working together to advance in order to create jobs and move our nation toward energy independence."

The RRTT will initially focus on seven projects. Four projects that involve BLM-managed public lands are:

Boardman to Hemingway Line to power Oregon and Idaho: The new 500 kilovolt (kV) transmission line proposed by Idaho Power would create an approximately 300 mile long, single-circuit electric transmission line from a proposed substation near Boardman, Oregon to the Hemingway Substation near Melba, Idaho--known as the Boardman to Hemingway Transmission Line Project or B2H Project. According to the developer of this project during peak construction, this project is estimated to create about 500 jobs in Idaho and Oregon.

Gateway West Project to bring new transmission across Wyoming and Idaho

Jointly proposed by Idaho Power and Rocky Mountain Power, this project would add approximately 1,150 miles of new, high-voltage transmission lines between the Windstar Substation near Glenrock, Wyoming and the Hemingway Substation near Melba, Idaho. According to the developer of this project, during peak construction, it is estimated to create between 1,100 and 1,200 jobs.

SunZia Transmission, LLC to bring power to New Mexico and Arizona

SunZia Transmission, LLC plans to construct and operate up to two 500 kV transmission lines originating at a new substation in Lincoln County in the vicinity of Ancho, New Mexico, and terminating at the Pinal Central Substation in Pinal County near Coolidge, Arizona. According to the developer estimated job creation will be about 3,408 direct jobs during the construction period.

TransWest Express to stand-up transmission from Wyoming to Utah and Nevada

TransWest Express LLC plans to construct and operate a more than 700 mile, 600 kV, transmission line which is estimated by the developer to create 1,035-1,550 direct jobs per year at peak construction. This project will facilitate the development of new wind projects in Wyoming.

Interagency Transmission MOU

The Memorandum of Understanding (MOU) was signed by nine Federal Departments and Agencies on October 23, 2009. The goal of the agreement is to speed approval of new transmission lines, reduce expense and uncertainty in the process, generate cost savings, increase accessibility to renewable energy and jumpstart job creation. The agreement will cut approval time off the normal Federal permit process and help break down the barriers to siting new transmission lines by:

- Designating a single Federal point-of-contact for all Federal authorizations;
- Facilitating coordination and unified environmental documentation among project applicants, Federal Agencies, states, and tribes involved in the siting and permitting process;
- Establishing clear timelines for agency review and coordination; and
- Establishing a single consolidated environmental review and administrative record.

Instead of applicants going to multiple agencies, a single lead agency will coordinate all permits and approvals. The new process will keep applications on track by requiring agencies to set and meet clear deadline and improve transparency by creating a single record to be posted on line at the following webpage: www.doe-etrans.us.

West Wide Energy Corridors

Section 368 (a) of the Energy Policy Act of 2005 (the Act), Public Law 109-58 (H.R. 6), enacted August 8, 2005, directs the Secretaries of Agriculture, Commerce, Defense, Energy, and the Interior (the Agencies) to designate under their respective authorities corridors on federal land in 11 Western States (Arizona, California, Colorado, Idaho, Montana, Nevada, New Mexico, Oregon, Utah, Washington, and Wyoming) for oil, gas, and hydrogen pipelines and electricity transmission and distribution facilities (energy corridors). A Programmatic Environmental Impact Statement (PEIS) was prepared that proposed the designation of more than 6,000 miles of Section 368 energy corridors among the various Agency land use plans is a forward-looking response, mandated by statute, to address a national concern.

BLM Approved a Record of Decision for the PEIS on January 14, 2009. The ROD included a listing of Interagency Operating Procedures (IOP) intended to foster long-term, systematic planning for energy transport development in the West, provide industry with a coordinated and consistent interagency permitting process, and provide practicable measures to avoid or minimize environmental harm from future development within the corridors.

On July 7, 2009 multiple organizations (Plaintiffs) filed a Complaint in the Wilderness Society, et al. v. United States Department of the Interior, et al., No. 3:09-cv-03048-JW (N.D. Cal.). The Plaintiffs raised a variety of challenges in response to the BLM's January 2009 Record of Decision.

The BLM, United States Forest Service (USFS), Department of Energy (DOE), and the Department of Justice worked collaboratively with the Plaintiffs to develop a settlement with specific actions to mutually resolve the challenges in the Complaint. The agencies and Plaintiffs agreed to settle these matters without any adjudication or admission of fact or law by any party and to avoid protracted and costly litigation as well as preserve judicial resources. The case was dismissed pursuant to the Settlement Agreement on July 11, 2012.

"This is a win-win outcome that will support the Obama administration's all-of-the-above energy approach by increasing the reliability of our pipeline and power line networks and unlocking American-made energy, while helping to ensure that transmission lines and natural gas pipelines that cross public lands are sited in the right places.

"By requiring periodic review of our nation's energy corridors, with the benefit of thorough public participation, the settlement agreement will help meet our nation's needs for expanded domestic energy infrastructure while protecting land, water and wildlife.

"The interagency agreements outlined in the settlement will provide greater certainty for transmission and pipeline developers, whose proposals are subject to environmental analysis under the National Environmental Policy Act." – Secretary of the Interior Ken Salazar.

In fulfillment of the Settlement Agreement, BLM, USFS, and DOE executed a Memorandum of Understanding (MOU) on July 8, 2013. The MOU includes a Work Plan for the Regional Periodic Reviews as Attachment A. The Agencies also approved a Work Plan for the Corridor Study with the execution of the MOU. As required by the Settlement Agreement the BLM, USFS and DOE identified and prioritized regions where corridors will be reviewed (Maps of Priority Regions).

Included in the Settlement Agreement was the recognition of 36 of the 119 BLM approved corridors as Corridors of Concern (COC). The BLM Washington Office has developed a series of Corridor Maps showing all the approved corridors with COC highlighted in red. As part of the Settlement Agreement the BLM and USFS agreed to issue new policy for use of the West Wide Energy Corridors on Agency administered lands. In fulfillment of that requirement the BLM issued a policy for the administration of West Wide Energy Corridors on BLM administered lands, IM-2014-080, effective April 7, 2014.

Oil and Gas

The BLM Oil and Gas Management program is one of the most important mineral leasing programs in the Federal government. Domestic production from over 63,000 Federal onshore oil and gas wells accounts for 11 percent of the Nation's natural gas supply and five percent of its oil.

A significant portion of funding in the BLM Oil and Gas program is used to fulfill the Federal government's trust responsibilities to American Indian Tribes and individual Indian mineral owners. The BLM supervises operational activities on 3,700 Indian oil and gas leases, and provides advice on leasing and operational matters to the Bureau of Indian Affairs, Indian Tribes, and Indian mineral owners.

The Oil and Gas program also processes applications for the permits required to develop leased resources. The most common of these is the Application for Permit to Drill (APD). Operators or permit agents can use the BLM's electronic permitting system (a form of E-Commerce, or EC), to submit oil and gas permit applications and reports via the Internet.

Under the direction of the Energy Policy Act of 2005, the BLM has also established seven Federal Permit Processing Pilot Offices, where improvements in coordinating permit processing among Federal agencies and inspection & enforcement can be tested. Pilot Offices have been established in these BLM Field Offices, which together receive more than 70 percent of the APDs each year:

- Montana - Miles City
- Wyoming - Buffalo and Rawlins
- Utah - Vernal
- Colorado - Grand Junction/Glenwood Springs
- New Mexico - Farmington and Carlsbad

The Pilot Project is a vehicle for fostering innovation, creating efficient management processes, and testing new and emerging technologies.

Coal

BLM has responsibility for coal leasing on approximately 570 million acres where the coal mineral estate is owned by the Federal Government. The surface estate of these lands could be controlled by BLM, the United States Forest Service, private land owners, state land owners, or other Federal agencies.

BLM receives revenues on coal leasing at three points:

- a bonus paid at the time BLM issues the lease
- an annual rental payment of $3.00 per acre or fraction thereof
- royalties paid on the value of the coal after it has been mined

The Department of the Interior and the state where the coal was mined share the revenues.

The Mineral Leasing Act of 1920, as amended, and the Mineral Leasing Act for Acquired Lands of 1947, as amended, give the BLM responsibility for coal leasing on approximately 570 million acres of the 700 million acres of mineral estate that is owned by the Federal Government, where coal development is permissible. The surface estate of these lands could be controlled by the BLM, United States Forest Service, private landowners, state landowners, or other Federal agencies. The BLM works to ensure that the development of coal resources is done in an environmentally sound manner and is in the best interests of the Nation.

Regulations that govern the BLM's coal leasing program may be found in Title 43, Groups 3000 and 3400 of the Code of Federal Regulations (CFR). This publication is available in law libraries and most large public libraries. The CFR is also available online from the Government Printing Office (www.access.gpo.gov).

Lands Available for Leasing

- Public lands are available for coal leasing only after the lands have been evaluated through the BLM's multiple-use planning process. Leasing federal coal resources is prohibited on public lands such as military reservations, National Parks, or National Wildlife Refuges. In areas where development of coal resources may conflict with the protection and management of other resources or public land uses, the BLM may identify mitigating measures which may appear on leases as either stipulations to uses or restrictions on operations.

Not all public lands are available for coal exploration or leasing. There is a rigorous land use planning process through which all public lands are reviewed for potential coal leasing. Requirements for the land use plan include multiple use, sustained yield, protection of critical environmental areas, application of specific unsuitability criteria, and coordination with other government agencies.

There are four specific land use screening steps that are unique to developing land use planning decisions for federal coal lands. These are:
- Identification of coal with potential for development
- Determination if the lands are unsuitable for coal development
- Consideration of multiple use conflicts
Surface owner consultation

The purpose of the coal screening part of the land use planning process (43 CFR 3420.1-4) is to identify those federal lands that are acceptable for further consideration for coal leasing and development.

You are qualified to hold a Federal coal lease if you are one of the following:
- A citizen of the United States
- An association of citizens organized under the laws of the United States or any state thereof
- A corporation organized under the laws of the United States, or of any state thereof, including a company or corporation operating a common carrier railroad
- A public body, including municipalities

In addition to these general qualifications, you must also comply with several special leasing qualifications including:
- The aggregate acreage in leases and applications in which you can hold an interest, directly or indirectly, cannot exceed 75,000 acres in any one state and no more than 150,000 acres in the United States.
- You may not acquire any other mineral leases under the Mineral Leasing Act of 1920, as amended, if you hold or have held a federal coal lease for 10 or more years that has not produced commercial quantities of coal. Other minerals that can be leased under the Mineral Leasing Act of 1920 include oil, natural gas, sodium, potassium, phosphate, sulfur, and gilsonite.

- As a part of your application for a new coal lease, you must provide a self-certified statement that you are in compliance with all applicable laws and regulations.
- An alien may hold interests in leases only by stock ownership in US corporations holding leases and only if the laws of his/her country do not deny similar privileges to citizens of the United States. However, an alien may not hold a lease interest through units in a publicly traded partnership.

Types of Coal Leases

The Federal Coal Leasing Amendments Act of 1976 (FCLAA), which amended Section 2 of the Mineral Leasing Act of 1920, requires that all public lands available for coal leasing be leased competitively. There are two notable exceptions to this requirement: (1) preference right lease applications where a lease may be issued on a noncompetitive basis to owners of pre-FCLAA prospecting permits and (2) modifications of existing leases where contiguous lands of as much as 960 acres are added noncompetitively to an existing lease.

There are two distinct procedures for competitive coal leasing: (1) regional leasing where the BLM selects tracts within a region for competitive sale and (2) leasing by application where the public nominates a particular tract of coal for competitive sale.

Regional coal leasing requires the BLM to select potential coal leasing tracts based on multiple land use planning, expected coal demand, and potential environmental and economic impacts. This process requires close consultation with local governments and citizens through a Federal/state advisory board known as a Regional Coal Team. However, because demand for new coal leasing in recent years has been associated with the extension of existing mining operation on authorized federal coal leases, all current leasing is done by application.

Leasing by application begins with BLM review of an application to lease a coal tract to ensure that it conforms to existing land use plans and contains sufficient geologic data to determine the "fair market value" of the coal. Upon review of the application and consideration of public comments, the BLM will reject, modify, or continue to process the application.

Once the BLM accepts an application, the agency begins either an Environmental Analysis (EA) or Environmental Impact Statement (EIS). When an EA or a draft version of an EIS has been prepared, the BLM seeks public comment on the proposed lease sale. At the same time, the BLM will also consult with other appropriate Federal, state, and tribal government agencies.

Preparations for the actual lease sale begin with the BLM formulating an estimate of the "fair market value" of the coal. This number is kept confidential and is only used to evaluate the bids received during the sale.

Sealed bids are accepted prior to the date of the sale and are publicly announced during the sale. The winning bid will be the highest bid that meets or exceeds the coal tract's presale estimated fair market value, assuming that all eligibility requirements are met and the appropriate fees and payments are attached (at a minimum, this amounts to the first year's annual rental payment and one-fifth of the amount bid).

The applicant for a new federal coal lease is required to reimburse the BLM for all processing costs that are incurred by the BLM. The BLM provides an estimate of the total processing fee before any work begins. The applicant must make payment toward the total process fee in advance of the BLM initiating any work on the application. Any excess payments are refunded to the applicant. The total actual processing cost incurred by the BLM is disclosed in the lease sale notice. Entities other than the applicant that may desire to competitively bid on the prospective coal lease must provide, in addition to their competitive bid for the coal resource, funds equal to the total BLM processing cost that will be used to reimburse the applicant if the third-party entity is determined to be the successful high bidder.

Lease Terms and Conditions
A federal coal lease grants the right to explore for, extract, remove, and dispose of some or all of the coal deposits that may be found on the leased lands. Coal leases are granted on the condition that the lessee will obtain the appropriate permits and licenses from the BLM, the Office of Surface Mining, and any affected state and local governments.

The BLM receives revenues from coal leasing at three points:

- A bonus that is paid at the time BLM issues a lease.
- Rental Fees. The annual rental rate for coal leases is $3 per acre (or fraction thereof). After the lease is issued, rentals must be received by the Department of the Interior's Office of Natural Resourses Revenue (ONRR) on or before the lease anniversary date to prevent cancellation of the lease.
- Production Royalties. The royalty for federal coal has been established by law at 12.5% of the gross value of the coal produced. The 12.5% royalty rate applies to coal severed by surface mining methods. For coal mined by underground methods, the statute provides that the Secretary may establish a lesser royalty rate. By regulation, the BLM requires an 8% royalty for coal severed by underground mining methods.
-

All receipts from a lease are shared equally with the state in which the lease is located.

Before the BLM issues a coal lease, the lessee must furnish a bond in an amount determined by the agency to ensure compliance with the terms and conditions of the lease. At a minimum, a bond is required that will cover one-fifth of the bonus bid if there is any remaining unpaid balance, as well as one year of advance rental and one-quarter year of estimated royalties if the lease is in production. In addition, the Surface Mining Control and Reclamation Act of 1977 requires sufficient bonding to cover anticipated reclamation costs. This bond is submitted to the Office of Surface Mining Reclamation Enforcement or the state regulatory office. The BLM may require a change in bond amount, either an increase or decrease, at any time the agency believes it is warranted.

Transfer or Sale of a Lease

The BLM must approve the assignment of a lease in whole or in part to another entity. The other entity must be qualified to hold a Federal coal lease. The rights of the entity receiving the lease, however, will not be recognized by the BLM until the assignment is approved. The original lessee remains responsible for all obligations of the lease until the assignment is approved by the BLM. Under certain circumstances, an exchange of coal leases may be allowed for the purposes of compensation, or when the exchange is in the public interest.

Termination of a Lease

A federal coal lease has an initial term of 20 years, but it may be terminated in as few as 10 years if the coal resources are not diligently developed. A federal coal lease can also terminate if a lessee fails to pay any of the deferred bonus bid payments. In addition, if the lessee fails to comply with the provisions of the Mineral Leasing Act of 1920, as amended, or fails to comply with any applicable regulations, lease terms, or stipulations, the BLM may take legal steps to cancel the lease.

A lessee may, at any time, seek to surrender a lease in whole or in part by filing a written request for relinquishment with the jurisdictional BLM office. However, the lessee must be in compliance with all lease terms and conditions and have paid all payments and fees. The lease bond may be used to ensure compliance with the terms and conditions of the lease.

Logical Mining Units (LMU)

A logical mining unit (LMU) allows the lessee or operator to consolidate the diligent development and continued operations requirements for all the federal leases and other coal tracts within the boundaries of a mine. An LMU provides for continuity in management of the coal resource whenever the geologic characteristics of a coal seam cross property boundaries. In addition, LMUs allow development of the coal deposit as a unit in an efficient, economical, and orderly manner with due regard for conservation of the coal and other resources. The acreage of both federal and non-federal lands within an LMU cannot exceed 25,000 acres. Formation of an LMU requires an application and approval by BLM.

Oil Shale and Tar Sands

The United States holds the world's largest known concentration of oil shale. Nearly five times the proven oil reserves of Saudi Arabia underlies a surface area of 16,000 square miles.

The enormous potential of this domestic resource, if it can be economically produced in an environmentally acceptable way, could be a key to the Nation's energy security and economic strength.

More than 70 percent of American oil shale — including the thickest and richest deposits — lies on federal land, primarily in Colorado, Utah, and Wyoming. These federal lands contain an estimated 1.23 trillion barrels of oil — more than 50 times the nation's proven conventional oil reserves. More than 50 tar sands deposits are found in eastern Utah, containing an estimated 12 to 19 billion barrels of oil. As oil prices rise, there is new interest in developing both of these domestic resources.

The BLM is working to ensure that development of federal oil shale and tar sands resources will be economically sustainable and environmentally responsible. In the Energy Policy Act of 2005, Congress directs the BLM to manage oil shale development on public lands on three tracks:
- research development and demonstration (RD&D) leasing
- a programmatic Environmental Impact Statement (PEIS)
- regulations for commercial leasing

The BLM planning process provides extensive opportunities for public involvement and consultation with States, Indian Tribes, and local governments within each track. On February 15, 2011, Secretary of the Interior Ken Salazar and BLM Director Bob Abbey announced a review of commercial rules for the development of oil shale resources on public lands. Secretary Salazar described the need to update oil shale plans and, if necessary update them based on the latest research and technology, the water demands of the West, and ensure they would provide a fair return to taxpayers.

BLM is beginning the process by:
- Updating the Oil Shale Programmatic Environmental Impact Statement (PEIS)
- Development of Research Demonstration and Development (RD&D) Leases

- Development of regulations that reflect current information and fair royalty rates.

In addition, BLM is working with the US Geological Survey to analyze baseline water conditions in areas where oil shale might be developed. The BLM is proposing to begin a new public planning process related to oil shale and tar sands. Specifically, on April 14, 2011, BLM published in the *Federal Register* a Notice of Intent to Prepare a Programmatic Environmental Impact Statement (PEIS) and Possible Land Use Plan Amendments for Allocation of Oil Shale and Tar Sands Resources on Lands Administered by the Bureau of Land Management in Colorado, Utah, and Wyoming.In the current Notice of Intent, the BLM is considering whether it is still appropriate for the land identified in 2008 to remain open for oil shale and tar sands leasing and development, in light of the nascent character of the technology for development of these resources.

Rights-of-way

Each year, thousands of individuals and companies apply to the Bureau of Land Management (BLM) to obtain a right-of-way (ROW) on public land. A ROW grant is an authorization to use a specific piece of public land for a certain project, such as roads, pipelines, transmission lines, and communication sites. A ROW grant authorizes rights and privileges for a specific use of the land for a specific period of time. Generally, a BLM ROW is granted for a term appropriate for the life of the project.

The Bureau of Land Management (BLM) and the Bureau of Ocean Energy Management (BOEM) are committed to ensuring that the public receives a fair return on publicly owned energy resources. The *Comparative Assessment of the Federal Oil and Gas Fiscal System* report provides useful analysis and tools that support both agencies in achieving this goal. The report, prepared under contract by IHS-CERA, examines 29 fiscal systems worldwide, including the current systems relating to Federal offshore oil and gas resources and onshore gas resources in Wyoming.

The BLM and BOEM commissioned this study in response to Government Accountability Office (GAO) recommendations outlined in a report titled, Oil and Gas Royalties: The Federal System for Collecting Oil and Gas Revenues Needs Comprehensive Reassessment (GAO-08-691). The GAO recommended that the Department of the Interior periodically collect data and information and conduct "analyses to determine how the federal government take and the attractiveness for oil and gas investors in each federal oil and gas region compare to those of other resource owners." This study's emphasis on international comparisons is consistent with the primary focus of the GAO's recommendations.

A comprehensive analysis of fair return must consider more than a comparison of "government take" or royalty and tax rates. The IHS-CERA study identifies four fiscal-related factors that it suggests are amenable to relative comparisons:
- government take
- internal rate of return
- profit-investment ratio, and
- progressivity.

The study also considers measures of revenue risk, as well as an index of fiscal system stability. The report constructs a hypothetical, composite index using all of these measures and concludes that the Federal Government's fiscal systems and take are generally in the mainstream internationally and nationally. The report also provides an assessment of how changes in the Federal royalty rate for oil and gas production could potentially affect industry interest in Federal offerings, relative to other jurisdictions, based on assumptions that all oil and gas operators can easily substitute among different drilling opportunities.

In order to ensure that the public receives a fair return on its resources BLM and BOEM balance all economic, employment, environmental, and national-security considerations.

Bureau of Land Management's Directorates

The Fire and Aviation Directorate (FAD)

FAD is a diverse, professional organization dedicated to providing national direction, leadership, policy, standards, and operational oversight. FAD works with state and field offices to ensure a safe, cost effective and efficient fire and aviation management program in support of the BLM's.

Headquartered at the National Interagency Fire Center (NIFC) in Boise, Idaho, it works with seven other federal agencies to manage wildland fire in the United States.

BLM's fire and aviation program has three organizational levels:
- the national office provides leadership and oversight, and develops policy, procedures and budgets for the fire and aviation program;
- state offices are responsible for coordinating policies and interagency activities within their state; and
- field offices are responsible for on-the-ground fire management and aviation activities, often partnering with other agencies to maximize rapid initial attack.
-

The BLM, a leader in the nation's wildland fire management efforts, undertakes a broad range of activities to safely protect the public, the natural landscape, wildlife habitat and recreational areas for America's citizens. The program includes fire suppression, preparedness, predictive services, fuels management, fire planning, community assistance and protection, prevention and education, and perhaps most significant, safety. The BLM meets these challenges by fielding highly trained and skilled professional firefighters and managers. Reducing the risk and consequence of wildland fires continues to grow in importance; however, suppression operations and safety continue to be the core of the overall fire program.

The Fire and Aviation Directorate is responsible for aircraft operation support for wildfire and resource management missions within the Bureau. BLM's aviation program is the largest within the Department of Interior's eight Bureaus. Aircraft are Bureau-owned, contracted and are obtained as Call-When-Needed (CWN) or Aircraft Rental Agreement (ARA) to fill the mission requirements to meet BLM management objectives.

Mission requirements are to support Wildland fire and prescribed fire operations, disaster response, animal census, wild horse and burro gather, habitat management, range survey, cadastral survey, law enforcement, forest management, photo mapping, search and rescue, and other uses related to public land and resource management. Types of aircraft include helicopters, Single Engine Air Tankers (SEATS), air tactical aircraft, utility aircraft, Aerial Supervision Modules (ASMI), heavy air tankers smokejumper aircraft and large transport aircraft.

Preparedness is an important step in wildland fire management. It is a continuous process that includes developing plans at the state/regional and national levels, predicting fire activity, hiring, training, and deploying wildland firefighters, evaluating performance, and improving overall operations. Preparedness takes place throughout the year, with routine evaluations of firefighters, training records, equipment, and land managers conducted before, during, and after fire season in each state.

The National Interagency Coordination Center (NICC)

The NICC is the focal point for coordinating the mobilization of resources for wildland fire and other incidents throughout the United States. It provides Intelligence and Predictive Services related-products designed to be used by the internal wildland fire community for wildland fire and incident management decision-making. Seven federal and state agencies work together to coordinate and support wildland fire and disaster operations. These agencies include the Bureau of Indian Affairs, Bureau of Land Management, Forest Service, US Fish and Wildlife Service, National Park Service, National Association of State Foresters, National Weather Service, US Fire Administration, and Aviation Management Directorate.

There are five primary components to the NICC website. The Incident Information page is designed to provide the general public with daily updates on large fires throughout the United States. The Predictive Services component provides the operational products produced by the NICC and links to outside operational activities.

Predictive Services was developed to provide decision support information needed to be more proactive in anticipating significant fire activity and determining resource allocation needs. Predictive Services consists of three primary functions;

- fire weather,
- danger/fuels
- and intelligence/resource status information.

It functions under the guidance of the National Predictive Services Subcommittee (NPSS), which is chartered under NWCG to provide leadership and direction for the program. Predictive Service staff units are located at the National Interagency Coordination Center (NICC) and the Geographic Area Coordination Centers (GACCs) across the country.

National Predictive Services Subcommittee: The committee consists of 10 members who represent the federal wildland fire agencies, the National Association of State Foresters, the National Weather Service, the Intelligence and Meteorology Working Groups (chartered under NPSS) and field managers. The goal of NPSS is to promote safe, efficient and cost effective fire management practices. Through collaborative leadership, with input from user groups at all levels, the NPSS strives to continually improve the quality, accuracy, and relevance of decision support products provided through the multi-agency coordination system to fire managers and users nationwide.

- Intelligence: The Intelligence Section provides fire management personnel, incident managers, firefighters and support staff with access to current intelligence on preparedness levels, fire situation, resources, mapping and satellite imagery, climatology, preparedness levels, resource availability, rotation schedules, and fire potential information.
- Weather: Meteorologists analyze a variety of weather products and services to provide briefings and outlooks for current and forecasted conditions, and in some cases provide spot weather and smoke forecasts. A number of innovative products and tools have been created to help fire managers assess fire potential and high risk areas.
- Fuels & Fire Danger: Wildland Fire Analysts, stationed or detailed at some locations, provide predictions and condition reports on fuels, fire danger, fire behavior, fire occurrence statistics, and resource needs.

The Logistics/Dispatch component provides operational and administrative links to the mobilization sections located in the Center. The Administrative component is designed to provide the tools, background information, and links that make Fire and Incident Operations work. And, the Related Links components provides Area and National links to other related websites.

Grazing on Public Lands

The Bureau of Land Management, which administers about 245 million acres of public lands, manages livestock grazing on 155 million acres of those lands, as guided by Federal law. The terms and conditions for grazing on BLM-managed lands (such as stipulations on forage use and season of use) are set out in the permits and leases issued by the Bureau to public land ranchers.

The BLM administers nearly 18,000 permits and leases held by ranchers who graze their livestock, mostly cattle and sheep, at least part of the year on more than 21,000 allotments under BLM management. Permits and leases generally cover a 10-year period and are renewable if the BLM determines that the terms and conditions of the expiring permit or lease are being met. The amount of grazing that takes place each year on BLM-managed lands can be affected by such factors as drought, wildfire, and market conditions.

In managing livestock grazing on public rangelands, the BLM's overall objective is to ensure the long-term health and productivity of these lands and to create multiple environmental benefits that result from healthy watersheds. The Bureau administers public land ranching in accordance with the Taylor Grazing Act of 1934, and in so doing provides livestock-based economic opportunities in rural communities while contributing to the West's, and America's, social fabric and identity. Together, public lands and the adjacent private ranches maintain open spaces in the fast-growing West, provide habitat for wildlife, offer a myriad of recreational opportunities for public land users, and help preserve the character of the rural West.

(panel)

A Brief History of Public Lands Grazing

During the era of homesteading, Western public rangelands were often overgrazed because of policies designed to promote the settlement of the West and a lack of understanding of these arid ecosystems. In response to requests from Western ranchers, Congress passed the Taylor Grazing Act of 1934 (named after Rep. Edward Taylor of Colorado), which led to the creation of grazing districts in which grazing use was apportioned and regulated. Under the Taylor Grazing Act, the first grazing district to be established was Wyoming Grazing District Number 1 on March 23, 1935. Secretary of the Interior Harold Ickes created a Division of Grazing within the Department to administer the grazing districts; this division later became the US Grazing Service and was headquartered in Salt Lake City. In 1946, as a result of a government reorganization by the Truman Administration, the Grazing Service was merged with the General Land Office to become the Bureau of Land Management.

The unregulated grazing that took place before enactment of the Taylor Grazing Act caused unintended damage to soil, plants, streams, and springs. As a result, grazing management was initially designed to increase productivity and reduce soil erosion by controlling grazing through both fencing and water projects and by conducting forage surveys to balance forage demands with the land's productivity ("carrying capacity").

These initial improvements in livestock management, which arrested the degradation of public rangelands while improving watersheds, were appropriate for the times. But by the 1960s and 1970s, public appreciation for public lands and expectations for their management rose to a new level, as made clear by congressional passage of such laws as the National Environmental Policy Act of 1969, the Endangered Species Act of 1973, and the Federal Land Policy and Management Act of 1976. Consequently, the BLM moved from managing grazing in general to better management or protection of specific rangeland resources, such as riparian areas, threatened and endangered species, sensitive plant species, and cultural or historical objects. Consistent with this enhanced role, the Bureau developed or modified the terms and conditions of grazing permits and leases and implemented new range improvement projects to address these specific resource issues, promoting continued improvement of public rangeland conditions.

(end panel)

Current Management of Public Lands Grazing

Today the BLM manages livestock grazing in a manner aimed at achieving and maintaining public land health. To achieve desired conditions, the agency uses rangeland health standards and guidelines, which the BLM developed in the 1990s with input from citizen-based Resource Advisory Councils across the West. Standards describe specific conditions needed for public land health, such as the presence of streambank vegetation and adequate canopy and ground cover. Guidelines are the management techniques designed to achieve or maintain healthy public lands, as defined by the standards. These techniques include such methods as seed dissemination and periodic rest or deferment from grazing in specific allotments during critical growth periods.

Laws that apply to the BLM's management of public lands grazing include the Taylor Grazing Act of 1934, the National Environmental Policy Act of 1969, the Endangered Species Act of 1973, the Federal Land Policy and Management Act of 1976, and the Public Rangelands Improvement Act of 1978.

Expenditures and Collections

In Fiscal Year 2014, the BLM spent $79.2 million on its rangeland management program and approximately $10 million on its Range Improvement Program, for a grand total of $89.2 million. Of that figure, the agency spent $32.8 million on grazing permit administration. The other $56.4 million covered such activities as weed management, rangeland monitoring (not related to grazing administration), planning, water development, vegetation restoration, and habitat improvement. In 2014, the BLM collected $12,117,000 in grazing fees (see section on grazing fee below). The receipts from these annual fees, in accordance with legislative requirements, are shared with state and local governments.

Federal Grazing Fee

The Federal grazing fee, which applies to Federal lands in 16 Western states on public lands managed by the BLM and the US Forest Service, is adjusted annually and is calculated by using a formula originally set by Congress in the Public Rangelands Improvement Act of 1978. Under this formula, as modified and extended by a presidential Executive Order issued in 1986, the grazing fee cannot fall below $1.35 per animal unit month (AUM); also, any fee increase or decrease cannot exceed 25 percent of the previous year's level. (An AUM is the amount of forage needed to sustain one cow and her calf, one horse, or five sheep or goats for a month.) The grazing fee for 2015 is $1.69 per AUM; the 2014 fee was $1.35.

Over time there has been a gradual decrease in the amount of grazing that takes place on BLM-managed land, and that trend continues today. Grazing use on public lands has declined from 18.2 million AUMs in 1954 to 8.5 million AUMs in 2013. In most years, the actual use of forage is less than the amount authorized because forage amounts and demands depend on several factors, such as drought, wildfire, and market conditions, as noted earlier regarding annual public land grazing levels.

Grazing, which was one of the earliest uses of public lands when the West was settled, continues to be an important use of those same lands today. Livestock grazing now competes with more uses than it did in the past, as other industries and the general public look to the public lands as sources of both conventional and renewable energy and as places for outdoor recreational opportunities, including off-highway vehicle use. Among the key issues that face public land managers today are global climate change, severe wildfires, invasive plant species, and dramatic population increases, including the associated rural residential development that is occurring throughout the West.

Livestock grazing can result in impacts on public land resources, but well-managed grazing provides numerous environmental benefits as well. For example, while livestock grazing can lead to increases in some invasive species, well-managed grazing can be used to manage vegetation. Intensively managed "targeted" grazing can control some invasive plant species or reduce the fuels that contribute to severe wildfires. Besides providing such traditional products as meat and fiber, well-managed rangelands and other private ranch lands support healthy watersheds, carbon sequestration, recreational opportunities, and wildlife habitat. Livestock grazing on public lands helps maintain the private ranches that, in turn, preserve the open spaces that have helped write the West's history and will continue to shape this region's character in the years to come.

Division of Decision, Support and Planning

To ensure the best balance of uses and resource protections for America's public lands, the BLM undertakes extensive land use planning through a collaborative approach with local, state and tribal governments, the public, and stakeholder groups. The result is a set of land use plans – called Resource Management Plans – that provide the framework to guide decisions for every action and approved use on the National System of Public Lands. The BLM currently manages over 245 million acres of surface land and 700 million acres of subsurface mineral estate.

Ensuring these plans are up-to-date is critical because so many Americans look to the public lands for a wide variety of resources, including energy, rights-of-way that support communications and energy delivery, a variety of recreational uses, and crucial habitat for species associated with the Western landscape, such as the sage-grouse and pronghorn antelope.

Land Use Planning

BLM's Resource Management Plans (RMPs) form the basis for every action and approved use on the public lands. The BLM prepares RMPs for areas of public lands, called planning areas, which tend to have similar resource characteristics. Planning emphasizes a collaborative environment in which local, state, and tribal governments, the public, user groups, and industry work with the BLM to identify appropriate multiple uses of the public lands. Plans are periodically revised as changing conditions and resource demands require.

RMPs are used by managers and the public to accomplish the following:
- Allocate resources and determine appropriate multiple uses for the public lands;
- Develop a strategy to manage and protect resources; and
- Establish systems to monitor and evaluate status of resources and effectiveness of management practices over time.

The Washington Office Planning Program establishes national planning policy and guidance, assists field offices through the plan revision process, resolves protests on proposed plans, and provides planning expertise to other Washington Office program areas.

The National Environmental Policy Act of 1969, as amended, requires federal agencies to analyze their actions in a decision-making process that is open to public review and where responsible officials take a hard look at and disclose the potential environmental effects of their actions. Compliance with NEPA is required of all federal actions including adoption of official policy, adoption of formal plans, adoption of programs, and approval of specific projects whether the action is developed by or submitted to the BLM. The NEPA compliance process within the BLM is guided by a series of federal, departmental and bureau laws, regulations and policies.

The NEPA Process
NEPA requires agencies to follow a three-step review process:
- Conduct a preliminary screening for NEPA's applicability;
- Prepare an Environmental Assessment (EA) to determine whether an Environmental Impact Statement (EIS) is required; and
- Prepare an EIS if required (an EIS is required if a proposed action may "significantly affect the quality of the human environment").

For BLM, developing or revising an RMP automatically requires an EIS. Amending an RMP requires an EA, and may or may not require an EIS.

Geospatial Program

Public land management requires knowing the location of the public lands and an understanding of the distribution and current conditions of natural resources. It also requires the ability to correlate the past, present, and future conditions of natural resources to land management activities and land use plan implementation. In addition, a wide variety of regulatory and permitting activities must also be supported. These functions all require correlating spatial locations against other variables and establishing relationships.

The BLM's Geospatial Program supports effective resource management by obtaining and providing geospatial information. The Enterprise GIS system (e-GIS) enables Bureau employees and stakeholders to access necessary data and knowledge; whenever and wherever it's needed. The Geospatial Program is currently implementing the Geospatial Services Strategic Plan, which will establish a structure for the continued governance and use of geospatial information.

The e-GIS vision it to:

Empower Bureau managers and specialists by providing access to automated, maintained, and standardized geospatial data.

Effectively integrate geospatial information into the agency's business processes.

Transform business information into corporate knowledge using geospatial applications that embody state-of-the-art spatial analysis and visualization tools.

Allow the knowledge derived from spatial analysis to be used by managers to initiate actions and effect outcomes through a defensible decision-making process.

Permit stakeholders to access the Bureau's geospatial data and information to facilitate interaction with the agency.

Socioeconomics Program

The BLM   Socioeconomics Program integrates the disciplines of anthropology, cultural geography, sociology, and economics. The BLM is required by the Federal Land Policy and Management Act to utilize "physical, biological, economic and other sciences" in its land use planning. Additionally, the National Environmental Policy Act requires federal agencies to "insure the integrated use of the natural and social sciences...in planning and decision making."

Today the BLM faces several changes in the social and economic context of its work. The Socioeconomics Program supports the Bureau's mission by participating in the resource management planning process. Furthermore, the program engages in many cross-cutting initiatives and challenges, such as addressing climate change, environmental justice, ecosystem services, and urban growth in the West.

Appropriate Dispute Resolution (ADR) Program

Collaborative stakeholder engagement and appropriate dispute resolution (ADR) processes have been recognized by the federal government as key for facing the challenges that arise in managing public lands for multiple use in an environmentally sustainable fashion.

Multiple laws and policy directives encourage or mandate the use of collaboration and ADR in the federal government. The Bureau of Land Management strives to increase public participation and government transparency through collaborative stakeholder engagement, and recognizes that appropriate use of ADR offers a valuable alternative to conventional methods of resolving disputes.

The Collaborative Stakeholder Engagement and Appropriate Dispute Resolution Program (ADR Program) supports these efforts in the field. The ADR Program consistently seeks to expand opportunities for public involvement, increasing the BLM's capacity for, and use of, collaboration and ADR through policy directives, tracking and analysis, and through program, field, and public support. Resulting reductions in protests, appeals, and litigation ensure faster and more durable outcomes as well as budget savings and increased community and employee trust.

Collaborative stakeholder engagement and appropriate dispute resolution (ADR) encompass a broad spectrum of processes for preventing, managing, or resolving conflict outside the conventional arenas of administrative adjudication, litigation, or legislation. These range from familiar processes such as direct negotiation and mediation, through stakeholder working groups, joint fact-finding, ombudsman services and many other processes and strategies for managing conflict and fostering agreement. In some cases, there may be overlap in both purpose and practice among the various processes. However, upstream collaborative processes are generally designed to prevent conflict from arising while downstream ADR processes involve managing or resolving an existing dispute, often with the assistance of a third-party neutral.

Both upstream and downstream processes can produce agreements and resolutions efficiently, cost-effectively, and cooperatively. Agreements reached this way can be more creative, satisfying, and enduring than those imposed through formal systems of redress. These processes often serve to mend or improve the overall relationship between parties because the focus is largely on interests and cooperation, while protests, appeals, and litigation are focused on positions and win/lose outcomes. When parties craft a solution themselves, they are generally more committed to the agreement than when a judge or hearing officer hands down a solution or when an agency decides on an issue without meaningful public involvement. Additionally, preventing or resolving conflict through these processes often results in savings of time, budget dollars, and public resources.

While downstream ADR processes allow the parties to develop a more flexible or creative solution than is generally possible in a court or formal hearing, Bureau policy recognizes that earlier upstream involvement amplifies these benefits and increases the likelihood of successful prevention or resolution of conflicts or disputes. In managing lands and natural resources for multiple-use, the Bureau is charged with balancing the diverse needs of myriad stakeholders. Collaborative stakeholder engagement brings interested and affected parties inside the decision-making process, increasing cooperation, understanding, and buy-in, and creating more open and transparent government decision-making.

Bureau policy is to use collaborative stakeholder engagement or ADR as standard operating practice for natural resources projects, plans, and decision-making, and for internal workplace disputes, except under unusual conditions or when constrained by law, regulation, or other mandates. All of these processes have increased success rates when initiated as early as possible (upstream), so beginning with the least formal appropriate process at the lowest possible level of the organization is encouraged. If the process fails, it is then recommended that a more downstream process be selected. It is important to recognize that many of the boundaries between the different processes are not well-defined and that many processes may contain elements of others. Any process should be adapted according to the particular circumstances of a situation, or, in some situations, these processes may not be appropriate at all. (Disputes over constitutional issues or legal precedent, for example, may be handled best in the courts. Likewise, opportunities to manage conflict at an informal level may be limited by politics or external events and constraints beyond the participants' control.)

Collaboration and ADR processes are used across the BLM: throughout renewable natural resources and land use planning, the National Landscape

Conservation System, and minerals and realty management, as well as in contracting and acquisition and internally in EEO and employee relations. Involving and engaging the public in projects and plans across the range of programs enhances the BLM's effectiveness and improves the quality of decisions. Collaboration with other agencies, with Tribal, state, and local governments, and with the communities we serve allows for shared skills, resources, and information, and increases government transparency. Providing analysis of conflict prevention and conflict management (including litigation and other conventional dispute resolution processes), and ensuring overall coordination within the Bureau, allows the BLM to adapt to new information, conditions, and direction. This helps to prevent future disputes and significantly increases the potential for reduced litigation in the future.

Division of Recreation & Visitor Services

On approximately 250 million acres of public lands, visitors enjoy countless types of outdoor adventure – participating in activities as widely varied as camping, hunting, fishing, hiking, horseback riding, boating, whitewater rafting, hang gliding, off-highway vehicle driving, mountain biking, birding and wildlife viewing, photography, climbing, all types of winter sports, and visiting natural and cultural heritage sites.

In an increasingly urbanized West, these recreational opportunities and the settings where these activities take place are vital to the quality of life enjoyed by residents of western states, as well as national and international visitors.

The Bureau of Land Management Division of Recreation and Visitor Services (BLM Recreation) is the national office in Washington DC that oversees recreation and visitor services on BLM-managed lands. The office handles a wide scope of duties that center on administering numerous National Recreation Programs.

This national focus assists BLM Field Offices improve on-the-ground recreation and visitor services management. The result is a high-quality and cost-effective recreation program that provides a broad range of benefits to users, communities, and the American public.

These national programs are briefly described below.

Accessibility Program (Access for Persons with Disabilities) – Access means freedom and the BLM is committed to providing access to its facilities, programs, services, and activities on the public lands for persons with disabilities.

Byways Program – Numerous byways, including National Scenic Byways, Backcountry Byways, and other designated routes, traverse the public lands and are recognized as part of BLM's National Scenic Byways Program.

Cave & Karst Areas Program – The BLM manages nearly 800 caves, primarily in karst (limestone) regions. Caves are a fascinating and fragile world that is an important resource for scientific and historical research and environmental education. Caves also provide habitat for bats and other wild creatures. Some caves on BLM public lands are also available for public exploration.

Heritage Resources – BLM lands contain many important archaeological and historic sites including ghost towns, ancient Puebloan villages, and rock art panels. These lands also have been home to many important fossil discoveries including dinosaur skeletons now on display in some of the Nation's great museums.

Interpretation Program – The BLM Interpretive Program serves visitors, promotes the health of the land, and enhances the public's enjoyment, understanding and appreciation of the natural and cultural resources of the public lands.

Hunting/Shooting Sports – The BLM provides opportunities to hunt and engage in shooting sports activities in a safe and environmentally sound manner that promote marksmanship, public safety, hunter education, competition, and lawful hunting. The BLM partners with state governments, local communities, interest groups, shooting clubs and other organizations to develop safe and environmentally responsible hunting and shooting sports activities.

Stewardship & Outdoor Ethics Program – BLM promotes and supports land stewardship and outdoor education as a way to enhance the visitor experience; to further appreciation and understanding of BLM-managed land resources; and to minimize recreation impacts.

Tourism & Community Services Program – BLM Recreation helps to sustain domestic tourism opportunities that provide valuable community amenities, attract new businesses, protect sensitive resources, and improve the quality of life for both visitors and residents. In turn, these efforts support sustainable economic growth, and assist with diversifying and stabilizing local communities.

Trails System – BLM manages more than 16,000 miles of multiple-use trails, including approximately 6,000 miles of trails classified within the National Trails System.

National Conservation Lands

The Bureau of Land Management's **National Conservation Lands**, also known as the National Landscape Conservation System, contain some of the West's most spectacular landscapes. They include 874 federally recognized areas and approximately 30 million acres of National Monuments, National Conservation Areas, Wilderness Areas, Wilderness Study Areas, Wild and Scenic Rivers, National Scenic and Historic Trails, and Conservation Lands of the California Desert.

The National Conservation Lands are uniquely diverse. They encompass red-rock deserts and rugged ocean coastlines, deep river canyons and broad Alaskan tundra. Many areas are remote and wild but others are surprisingly accessible. The National Conservation Lands also reveal and protect our cultural legacy. They safeguard American Indian cliff dwellings and cultural sites, and preserve the remaining traces of our Nation's historic trails and pathways. The mission of the National Conservation Lands is to conserve, protect, and restore these nationally significant landscapes that are recognized for their outstanding cultural, ecological, and scientific values.

National Conservation Lands are part of an active, vibrant landscape where people live, work and play. They offer exceptional opportunities for recreation, solitude, wildlife viewing, exploring history, scientific research, and a wide range of traditional uses. The National Conservation Lands sustain for the future - and for everyone - these remarkable landscapes of the American spirit.

National Monuments

The Bureau of Land Management's National Conservation Lands include 21 national monuments in nine western states. These national monuments encompass landscapes of tremendous beauty and diversity, ranging from rugged California coastline to vividly-hued desert canyons.

The Antiquities Act of 1906 grants the President authority to designate national monuments in order to protect "objects of historic or scientific interest." While most national monuments are established by the President, Congress has also occasionally established national monuments protecting natural or historic features. Since 1906, the President and Congress have created more than 100 national monuments. National monuments are currently managed by agencies including the National Park Service, Forest Service, Fish and Wildlife Service, or BLM.

Arizona

Agua Fria National Monument

The Agua Fria National Monument contains one of the most significant systems of late prehistoric sites in the American Southwest. Between A.D. 1250 and 1450, the region's pueblo communities were populated by as many as several thousand people. Agua Fria's ancient ruins offer insights into the lives of those who long ago inhabited this part of the desert southwest. Established by presidential proclamation in 2000, the Monument comprises approximately 71,000 acres containing at least 450 prehistoric sites.

Grand Canyon-Parashant National Monument

The Grand Canyon-Parashant National Monument is a vast, biologically diverse landscape encompassing an array of scientific and historic objects. The BLM and the National Park Service jointly manage the Monument, which was established by presidential proclamation in 2000. Valuable geological resources are located within the Monument boundaries, including relatively undeformed and unobscured Paleozoic and Mesozoic sedimentary rock layers and abundant fossils, which offer a clear view of the geologic history of the Colorado Plateau. The Monument also contains outstanding biological resources including giant Mojave yucca, trophy-quality mule deer, California condor, desert tortoise, and southwestern willow flycatcher.

Ironwood Forest National Monument

The Ironwood Forest National Monument offers quintessential views of the Sonoran Desert's ancient legume and cactus forests. The Monument, established by presidential proclamation in June 2000, encompass nearly 130,000 acres, including some of the Sonoran Desert's highest density ironwood trees stands. Ironwood trees provide, among other things, roosting sites for hawks and owls, forage for desert bighorn sheep, protection for saguaro against freezing, burrows for tortoises, flowers for native bees, dense canopy for nesting of white-winged doves and other birds, and protection against the sun for night blooming cereus.

Sonoran Desert National Monument

This Sonoran Desert National Monument is a magnificent example of untrammeled desert landscape, presenting an extraordinary array of biological, scientific, and historic resources within a functioning desert ecosystem. Encompassing nearly 500,000 acres, the Monument was established in January 2001 by presidential proclamation. The Monument's diverse plant communities, including striking saguaro cactus forests, support a wide variety of wildlife, such as desert bighorn sheep, mountain lions, Sonoran desert tortoise, and over 200 species of birds.

Vermilion Cliffs National Monument

Despite its arid climate and rugged isolation, Vermilion Cliffs National Monument is home to diverse plant and animal species as well as a long and rich human history. The Vermilion Cliffs rise 3,000 feet above the Paria Plateau to form a spectacular sandstone-capped escarpment underlain by multicolored, actively eroding layers of shale and sandstone. The Monument, established by presidential proclamation in 2000, encompasses nearly 300,000 acres. At least twenty species of raptors have been documented in the Monument, as well as a variety of reptiles and amphibians. California Condors have been reintroduced as part of a broader effort to recover this highly endangered species.

California

California Coastal National Monument

The California Coastal National Monument is a biological, scenic, and historical treasure, encompassing invaluable offshore and onshore resources. Originally established by presidential proclamation in 2000, the thousands of offshore islands, rocks, exposed reefs, and pinnacles in the Monument provide feeding, nesting, and breeding habitat for seabirds and marine mammals. On   March 11, 2014, the Monument was enlarged to include the Point Arena-Stornetta Unit, a coastal landbase that contains onshore   habitat for endangered, rare, and endemic species within the unit's bluffs, dunes, prairies, and estuary, in addition to   archaeological   artifacts   of the Central Pomo Indians.

Carrizo Plain National Monument

Full of natural splendor and rich in human history, the grasslands and stark ridges of the Carrizo Plain National Monument contain exceptional objects of scientific and historic interest. Encompassing more than 200,000 acres, the monument was established presidential proclamation in 2001. The Monument is home to the largest concentration of endangered species in all of California, in part because the remote 45-mile-long plain is an ecological "island." It is California's single largest remaining remnant of native grassland that was once abundant in the southern San Joaquin Valley.

Fort Ord National Monument

Fort Ord National Monument encompasses a sweeping landscape of vivid beauty and rich biodiversity in the heart of California's Central Coast. In addition to its biological wonders, the area is notable for its historical significance, including its role in the Spanish settlement of California and in the military training of generations of American soldiers. The monument, which was designated in 2012, is a world-class destination for hikers, mountain bikers, and outdoor enthusiasts who come to enjoy the area's history and scenic landscapes.

Santa Rosa and San Jacinto Mountains National Monument

Santa Rosa and San Jacinto Mountains of southern California contain nationally significant biological, cultural, recreational, geological, educational and scientific resources. The vistas, wildlife, land forms, and natural and cultural resources of these mountains provide a counterpoint to the highly urbanized areas of the nearby Coachella Valley. The Santa Rosa and San Jacinto Mountains National Monument Act established the unit in October 2000.

Colorado

Browns Canyon National Monument

This rugged area was set aside to protect its granite cliffs, colorful rock outcroppings, stunning mountain vistas, rivers, and backcountry forests, which have provided a home for humans for over 10,000 years. Many cultural and historical resources have been found in this landscape that are a testament to the area's Native Peoples as well as the history of more recent settlers and mining communities, and the area's unusual geology and roughly 3,000-foot range in elevation support a wide diversity of plants and wildlife.

Canyons of the Ancients National Monument

Containing the highest known density of archaeological sites in the nation, Canyons of the Ancients National Monument holds evidence of cultures and traditions spanning thousands of years. The Monument's complex landscape and remarkable cultural resources offer unparalleled opportunities to study and experience how cultures in the American Southwest lived and adapted over time. A presidential proclamation established the Monument in 2000.

Idaho

Craters of the Moon National Monument

Craters of the Moon National Monument was established on
May 2, 1924, to protect the unusual landscape of the Craters of the Moon lava field. The scientific value of the monument lies in the great diversity of volcanic features preserved within a relatively small area. A presidential proclamation   in 2000 expanded the Monument to its current size of approximately 661,000 acres, which are managed jointly by the BLM and the National Park Service.   The monument's central focus is the Great Rift, a 62-mile long crack in the earth's crust. The Great Rift is the source of a remarkably preserved volcanic landscape with an array of exceptional features. Craters, cinder cones, lava tubes, deep cracks, and vast lava fields form a strangely beautiful volcanic sea on central Idaho's Snake River Plain.

Montana

Pompeys Pillar National Monument

Pompeys Pillar is a massive sandstone outcrop on the banks of the Yellowstone River; it has been a celebrated landmark and outstanding observation point for the more than 11,000 years that humans have occupied the area. The Monument's most notable visitor, Captain William Clark of the Lewis and Clark Expedition, stopped at Pompeys Pillar on July 25, 1806, while returning from the Pacific coast. The 51-acre site was declared a Monument by presidential proclamation in 2001.

Upper Missouri River Breaks National Monument

The dramatic cliffs along the 149-mile stretch of river running through the Missouri River Breaks National Monument remain virtually unchanged since Lewis & Clark traveled through the area 200 years ago. A presidential proclamation established the 370,000-acre monument in 2001. Glaciers, volcanic activity, and erosion folded, faulted, uplifted, and sculpted the landscape into the majestic form it takes today. The Lewis & Clark National Historic Trail and the Nez Perce National Historic Trail run through the Monument.

New Mexico

Kasha-Katuwe Tent Rocks National Monument

Located in north-central New Mexico, the Kasha-Katuwe Tent Rocks National Monument is an outdoor laboratory that offers an opportunity to observe geologic processes as well as cultural and biological objects of interest. Cone-shaped tent rock formations are the products of explosive volcanic eruptions that occurred between 6 and 7 million years ago. The Monument, encompassing approximately 4,000 acres, was established in 2001 by presidential proclamation.

Organ Mountains-Desert Peaks National Monument

The Organ Mountains-Desert Peaks National Monument comprises almost 500,000 acres of public land in four distinct areas. The Organ Mountains, east of the city of Las Cruces, are characterized by steep, barren rock outcroppings rising to nearly 9,000 feet and extending for 20 miles. Northwest of Las Cruces are the mountain ranges and peaks of the Robledo and Doña Mountains and Sierra de las Uvas, which make up the Desert Peaks area. Southwest of Las Cruces are the Potrillo Mountains, a series of cinder cones with volcanic craters and basalt lava flows in an open desert landscape.

Prehistoric Trackways National Monument

Prehistoric Trackways National Monument, located in southern New Mexico's Robledo Mountains, was designated by Congress in 2009. The 5,280-acre monument includes a major deposit of Paleozoic Era fossilized footprint megatrackways. The monument also provides opportunities for recreational activities such as hiking and horseback riding.

Río Grande del Norte National Monument

Located northwest of Taos, New Mexico, the Río Grande del Norte National Monument encompasses a landscape of wide open plains, volcanic cones, and steep canyons with rivers tucked away in their depths. The area provides important wildlife habitat and is home to extraordinary archaeological and cultural resources dating from the Archaic Period to the more recent passage of Hispanic settlers. The monument, which encompasses approximately 240,000 acres of BLM land, was designated by presidential proclamation in 2013.

Oregon
Cascade-Siskiyou National Monument

Fir forests, oak groves, wildflower meadows, and steep canyons make the Cascade-Siskiyou National Monument an ecological wonder, with biological diversity unmatched in the Cascade Range. Approximately 52,000 acres comprise the Monument, which was established in 2000 by presidential proclamation. A tremendous variety of plants and animals make homes amidst the Monument's diverse landscapes. The Monument is also a bird haven, with more than 200 species identified, including the Northern Spotted Owl, the Great Gray Owl, the Peregrine Falcon, and the Willow Flycatcher.

Utah
Grand Staircase-Escalante National Monument

The vast and austere landscape of the Grand Staircase-Escalante National Monument offers a spectacular array of scientific and historic resources. Encompassing 1.9 million acres, the Monument was created in 1996 by presidential proclamation – the first monument entrusted to BLM management.   World-class dinosaur excavations have yielded more information about   ecosystem change at the end of the dinosaur era than almost any other place in the world. Among the fossil finds, paleontologists have identified dinosaurs not previously known to have inhabited this region, as well as several new species.

Washington
San Juan Islands National Monument

Situated in the northern reaches of Washington State's Puget Sound, the San Juan Islands are a uniquely beautiful archipelago of over 450 islands, rocks, and pinnacles. The San Juan Islands National Monument, which encompasses approximately 1,000 acres of BLM land, was designated by presidential proclamation in 2013. Drawing visitors from around the world, the San Juan Islands National Monument is a trove of scientific and historic treasures and a classroom for generations of Americans.

National Conservation Areas and Similarly Designated Lands

National conservation areas (NCAs) and similarly designated lands are designated by Congress to conserve, protect, enhance, and manage public lands for the benefit and enjoyment of present and future generations. The Bureau of Land Management's National Conservation Lands include 16 NCAs and five similarly designated lands in ten states. These lands feature exceptional scientific, cultural, ecological, historical, and recreational values. They differ tremendously in landscape and size, varying from the coastal beauty of California's 18-acre Piedras Blancas Light Station Outstanding Natural Area to the rugged desert vistas of Nevada's 1.2 million acre Black Rock Desert-High Rock Canyon Emigrant Trails NCA.

Wilderness Areas

The Bureau of Land Management is responsible for **221 Wilderness Areas** with 8.7 million acres in 10 Western States (3 percent of BLM's total acreage in the coterminous United States). Wilderness areas are special places where the earth and its community of life are essentially undisturbed. They retain a primeval character, without permanent improvements and generally appear to have been affected primarily by the forces of nature.

In 1964, Congress established the National Wilderness Preservation System and designated the first Wilderness Areas in passing the Wilderness Act. The uniquely American idea of wilderness has become an increasingly significant tool to ensure long-term protection of natural landscapes. Wilderness protects the habitat of numerous wildlife species and serves as a biodiversity bank for many species of plants and animals. Wilderness is also a source of clean water. It has long been used for science and education as well as for higher education purposes, providing sites for field trips, study areas for student research, and serving as a source of instructional examples. Recreation is another obvious appeal of wilderness, and wilderness areas are seeing steadily increasing use from people who wish to experience freedom from the Nation's fast-paced industrialized society.

Wilderness Study Areas

The Bureau of Land Management manages 528 Wilderness Study Areas (WSAs) containing almost 12.8 million acres located in the Western States and Alaska. The Federal Land Policy and Management Act of 1976 directed the Bureau to inventory and study its roadless areas for wilderness characteristics. To be designated as a Wilderness Study Area, an area had to have the following characteristics:

Size - roadless areas of at least 5,000 acres of public lands or of a manageable size;

Naturalness - generally appears to have been affected primarily by the forces
of nature;

Opportunities - provides outstanding opportunities for solitude or primitive and
unconfined types of recreation.

In addition, Wilderness Study Areas often have special qualities such as ecological, geological, educational, historical, scientific and scenic values.

The congressionally directed inventory and study of BLM's roadless areas received extensive public input and participation. By November 1980, the BLM had completed field inventories and designated about 25 million acres of WSAs. Since 1980, Congress has reviewed some of these areas and has designated some as wilderness and released others for non-wilderness uses. Until Congress makes a final determination on a WSA, the BLM manages these areas to preserve their suitability for designation as wilderness.

Wild and Scenic Rivers

On October 2, 1968, President Johnson signed the Wild and Scenic Rivers Act, sponsored by Senator Frank Church. The Act currently protects more than 200 rivers in 35 states and Puerto Rico. The Act's legacy is one of protecting the special character of certain rivers, while recognizing the potential for use and development.

"It is hereby declared to be the policy of the United States that certain selected rivers of the Nation which, with their immediate environments, possess outstandingly remarkable scenic, recreational, geologic, fish and wildlife, historic, cultural, or other similar values, shall be preserved in free-flowing condition, and that they and their immediate environments shall be protected for the benefit and enjoyment of present and future generations. The Congress declares that the established national policy of dam and other construction at appropriate sections of the rivers of the United States needs to be complemented by a policy that would preserve other selected rivers or sections thereof in their free-flowing condition to protect the water quality of such rivers and to fulfill other vital conservation purposes."

The Act provides three levels of protection: wild, scenic, and recreational. "Wild" rivers are free of dams, generally inaccessible except by trail, and represent vestiges of primitive America. "Scenic" rivers are free of dams, with shorelines or watersheds still largely primitive and shorelines largely undeveloped, but accessible in places by roads. "Recreational" rivers are readily accessible by road or railroad, may have some development along their shorelines, and may have been dammed in the past.

The Bureau of Land Management has the responsibility of managing 69 Wild and Scenic rivers in 7 states including more than 2,400 river miles and approximately 1,165,000 acres (19% of the national system). The Bureau's National Conservation Lands provide national level management and policy guidance for these rivers and represents the Bureau on the Interagency Wild and Scenic Rivers Coordinating Council.

National Scenic and Historic Trails

The Bureau of Land Management is one of several agencies responsible for management of National Historic or Scenic Trails. In 1968, Congress established the National Trails System and designated the first national trails. National Historic Trails are extended trails that closely follow a historic trail or route of travel of national significance. Designation identifies and protects historic routes, historic remnants, and artifacts for public use and enjoyment.

The Bureau of Land Management is responsible for over 5,343 miles of 11 National Historic Trails.

National Scenic Trails are extended trails that provide maximum outdoor recreation potential and for the conservation and enjoyment of the various qualities – scenic, historical, natural, and cultural – of the areas they pass through. The Bureau of Land Management is responsible for over 668 miles of the Continental Divide, Pacific Crest, Potomac Heritage, Arizona, and Pacific Northwest National Scenic Trails.

On March 30, 2009, the Omnibus Public Lands Management Act of March 30, 2009 (P.L.111-11) added three new trails and 40 miles to the NLCS. The new trails include the Arizona National Scenic Trail, Pacific Northwest National Scenic Trail, and the Washington Rochambeau Revolutionary Route National Historic Trail.

The BLM administers three trails and supports five national trail-related visitor centers to foster visitor enjoyment, appreciation, and learning, including California Trail Historic Interpretive Center; National Historic Oregon Trail Interpretive Center; National Historic Trails Interpretive Center; Pompeys Pillar National Monument Visitor Contact Station; and Upper Missouri River Breaks National Monument Interpretive Center.

Science on the National Conservation Lands

BLM's National Conservation Lands comprise a natural scientific laboratory that attracts scientists from around the world. Indeed, several NLCS units have been designated by Congress or the president due to their varied scientific objects and values of interest. These scientific values have opened the door for valuable research on topics ranging from geology, paleontology, archaeology, and history to biology, botany, and anthropology. For instance, researchers are discovering new species of dinosaurs, studying best practices for rangeland management, determining butterfly diversity, reintroducing endangered species, examining the dynamics of riparian areas, and so much more.

The benefits of this research are shared by both the scientists and BLM managers. The researchers get the opportunity to conduct research in great locations, and many of their scientific projects help the BLM to effectively and efficiently manage these amazing conservation lands. The results of these scientific projects provide a foundation that BLM managers are able to build upon in their decision-making process. This close, working relationship between scientists and BLM managers and staff has provided for many fruitful, mutually advantageous projects.

Many of the scientific research projects in the NLCS are conducted through partnerships with scientists and scientific organizations, including universities, government agencies, American Indian tribes, special-focus groups, and non-governmental organizations.

Take It Outside

Take It Outside was prompted by a growing national concern that children are spending significantly less time outdoors than previous generations; becoming more disconnected from nature; and increasingly showing the symptoms of an epidemic in childhood obesity.

Take It Outside is BLM's flagship youth engagement program. It was established to help ensure that young people from all backgrounds have access to outdoor recreational opportunities on public lands while fostering future generations of public land stewards. Stressing health, family, fun, and stewardship, Take It Outside provides opportunities for young people to engage in outdoor recreation, non-formal education, and volunteer projects.

BLM staff host a wide variety of Take It Outside programs and activities on BLM lands from archaeology field tours to white water rafting and camping.

National Wild Horse and Burro Program

The mid-20th century harvesting of wild horses for commercial purposes induced a Reno, Nevada, secretary – Velma Johnston – to begin a campaign that led to passage of a 1959 law to protect these iconic animals. While driving to work one day in 1950, Ms. Johnston noticed blood leaking from a livestock truck. She followed it and discovered that horses were being delivered to a slaughterhouse. Ms. Johnston responded with a massive letter-writing campaign by students to prevent other wild horses from meeting a similar end. The campaign became known as the "Pencil War" and Ms. Johnston was affectionately dubbed "Wild Horse Annie."

Follow-up efforts resulted in the enactment of the Wild Free-Roaming Horses and Burros Act of 1971, the landmark law that directs Federal management of wild horses and burros on US public lands.

The Act declares wild horses and burros to be "living symbols of the historic and pioneer spirit of the West." Under the law, the BLM and US Forest Service manage herds in their respective jurisdictions within areas where wild horses and burros were found roaming in 1971.

To help carry out its assignment, the BLM established the Wild Horse and Burro Program, through which the agency manages and protects wild horses and burros, both on and off the range, while striving to maintain rangeland health.

The BLM's goal is to ensure and maintain healthy wild horse populations on healthy public lands. To do this, the BLM works to achieve what is known as the Appropriate Management Level (AML) – the point at which wild horse and burro herd populations are consistent with the land's capacity to support them. In the context of its multiple-use mission, AML is the level at which wild horses and burros can thrive in balance with other public land uses and resources, including vegetation and wildlife.

The AML is a range of low to maximum levels that allows for population growth over a four- to five-year period. To establish AML, the BLM evaluates several years of rangeland resource and population data. Those evaluations look at information relating to vegetation, soils, weather, and water quality.

Each Herd Management Area (HMA) has its own AML. When AML is exceeded, the excess animals are gathered and then prepared for adoption or sent to long-term pastures.

This type of rangeland management is different from management of wildlife, which are controlled by hunters and natural predators, or livestock, which are controlled by grazing permits. To learn more about BLM's grazing program, click here. Because of Federal protection and a lack of natural predators, wild horse and burro herds can double in size about every four years. As of March 1, 2014, the BLM estimated that 49,209 wild horses and burros roamed BLM-managed rangelands in 10 Western states, which exceeds by more than 22,500 the West-wide AML of 26,684.

In 1971, wild horses and burros were found roaming across 53.8 million acres of Herd Areas, of which 42.4 million acres were under the BLM's jurisdiction. Today the BLM manages wild horses and burros in subsets of these Herd Areas (known as Herd Management Areas) that comprise 31.6 million acres, of which 26.9 million acres are under BLM management.

To do its work, the BLM uses qualified science and technology staff and a citizen-based advisory board. The agency also supports research to keep track of the health of wild horses and burros and the condition of the range. This includes research on population growth-suppression techniques.

The BLM protects the health and welfare of wild horses and burros from the time they are on the range, through the gather and removal process and through the adoption or sale programs to when the animal is titled as an adopter's own animal.

This comprehensive protection will receive a new emphasis and improve under the BLM's planned Comprehensive Animal Welfare Program (CAWP). The CAWP will consolidate and highlight BLM's policies and procedures for protecting animal welfare, monitor how the agency, its volunteers, and contractors handle and care for animals, address any problems or shortfalls that may occur with continuing education and training and document the BLM's ongoing commitment to protecting the health and welfare of America's wild horses and burros. This work will be documented by BLM and as always done with an emphasis on transparency. The ongoing performance of the Program will be reported on the BLM's Website and to Congress.

3

Bureau of Ocean Energy Management

The offshore areas of the United States are estimated to contain enormous quantities of resources in yet-to-be-discovered fields. The Bureau of Ocean Energy Management (BOEM) estimates of oil and gas resources in undiscovered fields on the Outer Continental Shelf (OCS) total about 89 billion barrels of oil and 398 trillion cubic feet of gas.

These volumes represent about 69 percent of the oil and 26 percent of the natural gas resources estimated to be contained in remaining undiscovered fields located in the federal OCS and State waters, and onshore areas of the continental United States and Alaska.

It is the job of the BOEM to promote energy independence, environmental protection and economic development through responsible, science-based management of offshore conventional and renewable energy and marine mineral resources.

Key functions of BOEM include:

The Office of Strategic Resources, which is responsible for the development of the Five Year Outer Continental Shelf (OCS) Oil and Natural Gas Leasing Program, oversees assessments of the oil, gas and other mineral resource potential of the OCS, inventories oil and gas reserves and develops production projections, and conducts economic evaluations that ensure the receipt of fair market value by US taxpayers for OCS leases.

BOEM handles the actual Oil and Gas Lease Sales, along with Marine Minerals negotiated agreements and official maps and GIS data.

BOEM is responsible for offshore Renewable Energy Programs. The Renewable Energy Program grants leases, easements, and rights-of-way for orderly, safe, and environmentally responsible renewable energy development activities.

BOEM's Office of Environmental Programs conducts environmental reviews, including National Environmental Policy Act (NEPA) analyses and compliance documents for each major stage of energy development planning. These analyses inform the bureau's decisions on the Five Year Program, and conventional and renewable energy leasing and development activities. Additionally, BOEM's scientists conduct and oversee environmental studies to inform policy decisions relating to the management of energy and marine mineral resources on the OCS.

BOEM is supported by three regional offices in New Orleans, Louisiana; Camarillo, California; and Anchorage, Alaska. The regional offices manage oil and gas resource evaluations, environmental studies and assessments, leasing activities including the review of Exploration Plans and Development Operations and Coordination Documents, fair market value determinations, and geological and geophysical permitting.

Oil & Gas Energy Program

The OCS is a significant source of oil and gas for the Nation's energy supply. The approximately 33 million leased OCS acres account for about 5 percent of America's domestic natural gas production and about 21 percent of America's domestic oil production. BOEM manages the nation's offshore resources to ensure that production and drilling are done in an environmentally and economically responsible manner, and that production facilities are timely removed.

BOEM is responsible for all OCS leasing policy and program development issues for oil, gas and other marine minerals and these policies and programs are directed by a five year oil and gas leasing program.

On August 27, 2012, Secretary Ken Salazar gave final approval to the schedule of lease sales set out in the Proposed Final Program (PFP). He announced and submitted the PFP and supporting analyses to the President and Congress on June 28, 2012 for a minimum of 60 days, as required under section 18. The 2012-2017 Program was effective on August 27, 2012, and will expire on August 26, 2017. The PFP decision document was the last of three documents that DOI will issue in connection with establishing the new Five Year Program. The PFP followed the January 2009 Draft Proposed Program (DPP) and the November 2011 Proposed Program (PP). The Bureau of Ocean Energy Management (BOEM) released the Proposed Final Program decision document (with supporting analyses) and the Programmatic Environmental Impact Statement (EIS) immediately after the announcement.

The OCS Oil and Gas Leasing Program for 2012-2017 establishes a lease sale schedule that is used as a basis for considering where and when oil and gas leasing might be appropriate over a five-year period.

The 2014 Annual Progress Report (issued in January, 2015) provides an overview of the activities that have occurred during the previous year, including but not limited to:

statistics of sales that have occurred in the previous year, including the number and location of lease blocks and the dollars collected on high bids

an aggregate collection of all newly enacted deferrals and mitigations

a summary of completed and ongoing safety and environmental studies

regulatory updates

a discussion of any significant new drilling activities

a summary of any significant incidents

other relevant information

As required by the OCS Lands Act, a new program—to cover the years 2017-2022—is under development.

Many different disciplines contribute to and support the overall leasing program--from the initial assessment of resources to environmental considerations to the final determination of what is actually offered for lease.

Exploration and Development Plans both require the submittal of complex information and there are many reasons that an application may not be deemed submitted or require an amendment or modification after it is deemed submitted.

Resource Evaluation Program

The Resource Evaluation Program activities support all BOEM program areas, both energy and non-energy, through critical technical and economic analysis. The primary program objective is to identify areas of the Outer Continental Shelf (OCS) that are most promising for oil and gas development including gas hydrates. Resource Evaluation Functions are carried out by personnel located at Bureau Headquarters and Regional Offices.

Resource Assessment

The objective of this component is to identify geologic plays on the Outer Continental Shelf (OCS) that offer the highest potential for the occurrence of oil and natural gas development. Resource assessment work begins with the study of an area's geology in order to determine the potential for the presence of oil and gas deposits.

Resource Evaluation Division Geoscientists will begin the resource assessment process by looking at:

Geologic history

Regional stratigraphy

Major Geologic trends

Major structural features

Source rocks

Reservoir rocks

Seals and trapping mechanism

Petroleum exploration history

In the early stages of an assessment the focus is on the regional level but gradually shifts to the prospect level as more data and information are acquired. Once a sale area has been identified, the Resource Evaluation Division focuses on the detailed mapping and analyses that is needed to more accurately estimate the resource potential of an individual prospect.

Following the identification of an individual prospect a thorough analysis of its hydrocarbon potential and economic viability is performed. Utilizing complex computer models and assessment methodologies this process incorporates a number of multi-discipline data sources including:Geologic information

Petroleum engineering data

Mathematical and statistical analyses

Risk and probability theory

Economic scenarios

Technical assumptions

Resource estimates are also developed to support critical analyses of potential impacts of policy options, legislative proposals, and industry activities affecting current and future OCS natural gas and oil activities.

Reserves Inventory Program

The Department of the Interior is required under the OCS Lands Act to "...conduct a continuing investigation...for the purpose of determining the availability of all oil and natural gas produced or located on the Outer Continental Shelf." In order to meet this requirement, BOEM is required to develop independent estimates of economically recoverable amounts of oil and gas contained within discovered fields by conducting field reserve studies. The reserve estimates are revised periodically to reflect new information obtained from development and production activities.

Reserve studies are critical inputs to resource assessments, the review and approval of royalty relief applications, as analogs for bid adequacy determinations, and in the review of industry plans and requests. The geologic and engineering information also support other program activities within DOI and cooperative efforts with the Department of Energy and its Energy Information Administration.

BOEM has adopted the Society of Petroleum Engineers' (SPE) Petroleum Resource Management System. Under this system, reserves are defined as those portions of identified oil or gas resources that can be extracted using current technology. Reserves represent quantities of hydrocarbons, which are anticipated to be commercially recovered from known accumulations from a given date forward.

The Reserves Inventory Program represents a significant part of the Resource Evaluation scope and further contributes to:

Energy supply

Forecasting;

Public policy decisions;

Independent assessment/verification;

Assuring fair value in public/private transactions.

The Reserves Inventory component of the Resource Evaluation Program assigns new producible leases to fields and establishes field limits. The Resource Evaluation Program also develops independent estimates of original amounts of natural gas and oil in discovered fields by conducting field reserve studies and reviews of fields, sands and reservoirs on the OCS. The Resource Evaluation Program periodically revises the estimates of remaining natural gas and oil to reflect new discoveries, development information and annual production.

Regulation of Pre-lease Exploration

The Geological and Geophysical (G&G) Permitting Process

The general purpose of BOEM pre-lease regulations is to ensure that pre-lease exploration, prospecting, and scientific research operations in Federal waters do not interfere with each other, with existing lease operations, or with other uses on the OCS. Pre-lease regulations also encourage data acquisition while adequately protecting the investment of data gathered and still assuring equal access and competitive balance. Adherence to these regulations will ensure that exploration and research activities will be conducted in an environmentally safe manner.

Pre-lease permits, issued individually by Region, set forth the specific details for each data-gathering activity, including the timing of activity, approved equipment and methods, and other information relevant to each specific permit.

Information required in the permit application for geophysical activities include: vessel information, a description of the energy source and receiving array, total energy output, number of impulses per linear miles, towing depth, navigation system to be used, estimate of are to be surveyed, description of final processing, estimated completion date, and a map, plat or chart showing latitude, longitude, block numbers, total line miles or blocks proposed.With respect to geological activities, the following types of information are identified in the permit application: description of drilling methods or sampling, equipment to be used, estimated bore holes or sample locations, navigation system, method of sampling, description of analyzed or processed data, estimated completion date, and a map, plat, or chart showing latitude and longitude, specific block numbers, and total number of borings and samples.

For each approved application, the operator receive a signed copy of the permit that outlines policies regarding reporting, submission, inspection, and selection of data, reimbursement, disclosure of information, possible sharing of data with affected States, and policies regarding permit modifications.

Each Region has unique environmental concerns and these are addressed through mitigating measures at the Regional level.

After data have been collected by permittees, BOEM selectively acquires data that are needed to update the existing database. Industry uses these data to determine the areas having potential for oil and gas production. Oil companies also use these data for preparing bids for lease sales. BOEM may also acquire data that have been collected for scientific research activities for which an approved permit or filing of notice is required.

Geological and Geophysical Permitting Trends

BOEM tracks G&G permits by calendar year. Total permit counts demonstrate that most OCS oil and gas activity has been in the Gulf of Mexico. The Gulf of Mexico has issued 82 percent of all permits and is followed by the Alaska Region with 9 percent. The Pacific Region has issued 7 percent of the permits, followed by the now defunct Atlantic Region with about 2 percent (since 1994 activities in the Atlantic have been assigned to the Gulf of Mexico Region). These statistics correlate extremely well with the dominant position of the Central and Western Gulf of Mexico planning areas in OCS oil and gas activities.It should be noted that since 1969, approximately 95 percent of the permits issued were for geophysical exploration and that geological exploration permits accounted for only 5 percent. While the total number of 3-D permits compared to all permits issued is rather small (8 percent) when compared with the total geophysical permits issued, over the past 10 years, 3-D permits have averaged 49 percent of all geophysical permits. Permits for deep stratigraphic test wells or COST wells account for about 2 percent of the geological permits.

The overall trends in permitting for all the Regions (i.e. Gulf of Mexico, Alaska and the Pacific) are similar and reflect fluctuations in the price and supply of petroleum. Some regional differences related to leasing moratoria, operating conditions affect hydrocarbon discoveries.

Geological & Geophysical Data Acquisition and Analysis

The main objective of the acquisition and analysis of geological and geophysical data is the development of maps identifying areas favorable for the accumulation of hydrocarbons. This is done by incorporating the data acquired through G&G surveys plus analyzing technical information develop a basic knowledge of the geologic history of an area and its effects on hydrocarbon or strategic/critical minerals generation, distribution, and accumulation within the planning area.

The primary source of the data and information used by the Resource Evaluation Program is the oil and gas industry, which conducts exploration, development, and production activities on OCS lands. BOEM issues permits to industry for collecting pre-lease as well as post-lease data. The Resource Evaluation Program approves the permits of pre-lease data acquisition and operators are required to provide certain data and information to BOEM. BOEM selectively obtains copies of data acquired in these pre-lease activities.

Permittees and lessees are normally reimbursed by BOEM for only the cost of data reproduction. However, if industry has collected data in areas not under BOEM jurisdiction, e.g., State waters or adjacent foreign waters, and BOEM selects such data, BOEM pays the significantly higher "market price" for obtaining copies of such data. The extensive amount of data and information acquired by BOEM is used by geologists, geophysicists, petroleum engineers, modelers and other specialists to perform a variety of analyses leading to Resource Assessment, Reserves Inventory and determining Fair Market Value of the auctioned tracts.

Worst Case Discharge Determination

Worst Case Discharge (WCD) for exploratory and development drilling operations is the daily rate of an uncontrolled flow of natural gas and oil from all producible reservoirs into the open wellbore. The package of reservoirs exposed to an open borehole with the greatest discharge potential is considered the worst case discharge scenario.

Operators must submit WCD calculated volumes, and associated data according to NTL 2010-N06 (Information Requirements for Exploration Plans, Development and Production Plans, and Development Operations Coordination Documents on the OCS) and the associated frequently asked questions as part of every Exploration Plan and every Development Operations Coordination Document/Development and Production Plan.

Each Region is responsible for WCD verifications and decision documentation associated with plans under their jurisdictions. Resource Evaluation geoscientists and engineers independently verify the validity of the volume calculations, assumptions, and analogs used by the operator for the WCD. The BOEM Worst Case Discharge model outputs are also used by BSEE in oil spill response plans and cap and stack or cap and containment decisions made as part of the Application for Permit to Drill process (a BSEE responsibility).

Gas Hydrates

Gas hydrates are ice-like crystalline substances occurring in nature where a solid water lattice accommodates gas molecules (primarily methane, the major component of natural gas) in a cage-like structure, also known as clathrate. These form under conditions of relatively high pressure and low temperatures, such as those found in the shallow subsurface under many of the world's deep-water oceans. One cubic foot of hydrate at reservoir temperature and pressure yields approximately 160 cubic feet of gas at atmospheric temperature and pressure. The amount of natural gas in methane hydrate worldwide is estimated to be far greater than the entire world's conventional natural gas resources.

BOEM, in conjunction with its US government partners, industry, and numerous universities, has invested significant resources to date in an effort to better understand methane hydrates. With the demand for natural gas expected to increase significantly over the next 10 to 20 years, methane gas hydrates, which are likely present on the OCS in significant quantities, may be a potential source to meet both industrial and domestic needs for natural gas.

Status of Gulf of Mexico Plans

In the wake of the *Deepwater Horizon* explosion and subsequent oil spill, the Obama Administration has put in place significant new safeguards to protect the environment beyond what has ever existed before.

When an exploration or development plan is received by the bureau, a determination is made as to whether or not a site-specific environmental assessment (SEA) is needed. This determination is based upon the identification of an Extraordinary Circumstance (EC) as set out in federal regulations 43CFR46.215(d). In an August 16, 2010, Categorical Exclusion Restriction Memorandum Bureau Director Michael R. Bromwich directed that any activity having "highly uncertain and potentially significant environmental effects or involve unique or unknown environmental risks," would be considered an EC and require the completion of a SEA.

Stronger regulations were implemented on June 8, 2010.

BOEM Economics Division

The Economics Division:
Conducts economic, statistical, engineering and cost-benefit analyses to evaluate and implement policies for the energy and minerals programs

relating to lease terms, bidding systems, auction designs, operating conditions and rulemaking.

Works to ensure receipt of fair market value for the rights to produce offshore energy and mineral resources.

Develops and maintains economic and statistical models and databases in support of sale design, resource evaluation, post-sale and operational activities, rulemaking, revenue sharing and royalty relief programs.

Generates economic assumptions and scenarios for use in post-sale tract evaluations and in applications for royalty relief.

The division comprises a team of interdisciplinary experts that provide economic analysis to other federal departments, bureaus and executive agencies in support of energy and mineral leasing policies and national energy strategies.

Five-Year Outer Continental Shelf (OCS) Oil and Gas Leasing Program

The Five-Year program for oil and gas development establishes a schedule of oil and gas lease sales proposed for planning areas of the US Outer Continental Shelf (OCS). The program specifies the size, timing, and location of potential leasing activity that the Secretary of the Interior determines will best meet national energy needs.

As required by the OCS Lands Act, a new program—to cover the years 2017-2022—is under development. The first step in the development process, a Request for Information (RFI), was published in the Federal Register on June 16, 2014, with a 45-day comment period that was extended by 15 days and closed on August 15, 2014.

The Draft Proposed Program (DPP) is the first proposal in the staged preparation process of the new program.

The DPP schedules 14 potential lease sales in 8 OCS planning areas: Ten sales in the three Gulf of Mexico (GOM) planning areas; one sale each in the Chukchi Sea, Beaufort Sea, and Cook Inlet Planning Areas, offshore Alaska; and one sale in a portion of the combined Mid-Atlantic and South Atlantic Planning Areas. The DPP was published on Jan 29, 2015, with a 60-day comment period that concluded on March 30, 2015.

The development of the 2017-2022 OCS Oil and Gas Leasing Program triggers an environmental analysis pursuant to the National Environmental Policy Act. This Programmatic Environmental Impact Statement (PEIS) will include an analysis of the potential environmental impacts of the DPP. It will also analyze reasonable alternatives to the proposed lease sale schedule and mitigation measures that may reduce or eliminate any potential impacts.

BOEM released a Notice of Intent (NOI) to prepare this PEIS in conjunction with the release of the DPP. As a part of the NOI, BOEM is seeking public input on the scope of the environmental analysis and on the alternatives and mitigation measures to be analyzed.

Risk Management

Over the past several decades, the potential for financial loss has increased as offshore structures and pipelines have aged and as operations have moved into deeper water requiring more complex engineering. At the same time, many of the operating leases have changed ownership, transferred partial ownership, or otherwise assigned operating rights through complex business agreements.

In order to address these issues, BOEM's Risk Management Program is leading an effort to revise its financial assurance protocols and standards. These updates are necessary to ensure the US Government is protected from financial loss while also promoting safe and responsible development of OCS resources.

Offshore Financial Assurance Forum

The Bureau of Ocean Energy Management (BOEM) hosted an Offshore Financial Assurance Forum on February 26th, 2105 in New Orleans, Louisiana. During this forum, BOEM presented its vision for a comprehensive offshore financial assurance framework. The framework included both near-term priorities that can be achieved through operational changes and longer-term priorities that will require updates to BOEM's regulations. This work is an extension of the 2014 Advance Notice of Proposed Rulemaking (ANPR) and a panel of BOEM speakers answered a variety of questions on Risk Management, Financial Assurance, and Loss Prevention topics.

Renewable Energy

In 2009, President Barack Obama announced the final regulations for the Outer Continental Shelf (OCS) Renewable Energy Program, which was authorized by the Energy Policy Act of 2005 (EPAct).

These regulations provide a framework for issuing leases, easements and rights-of-way for OCS activities that support production and transmission of energy from sources other than oil and natural gas.

Since the regulations were enacted, BOEM has worked diligently to oversee responsible renewable energy development.

BOEM's renewable energy program occurs in four distinct phases: (1) planning and analysis, (2) lease issuance, (3) site assessment, and (4) construction and operations. This fact sheet discusses BOEM's process for authorizing wind energy leases.

BOEM is responsible for offshore renewable energy development in Federal waters and anticipates future development on the OCS from three general sources: offshore wind, ocean wave, and ocean current energy.

Offshore Wind Energy. Wind turbines have been installed offshore a number of countries to harness the energy of the moving air over the oceans and convert it to electricity. Offshore winds tend to flow at higher sustained speeds than onshore winds, making turbines more efficient.

Ocean Wave Energy (Hydrokinetic). There is tremendous energy in ocean waves. Wave power devices extract energy directly from the surface motion of ocean waves. A variety of technologies have been proposed to capture that energy, and some of the more promising designs are undergoing demonstration testing. The Northwestern Coast of the United States has especially high potential for wave energy development, and is one of only a few areas in the world with abundant available wave power resources.

Ocean Current Energy (Hydrokinetic). Ocean currents contain an enormous amount of energy that can be captured and converted to a usable form. Some of the ocean currents on the OCS are the Gulf Stream, Florida Straits Current, and California Current. Submerged water turbines, similar to wind turbines, may be deployed on the OCS in the coming years to extract energy from ocean currents.

Regulatory Framework and Guidelines

The Energy Policy Act of 2005 (EPAct) authorized BOEM to issue leases, easements and rights of way to allow for renewable energy development on the Outer Continental Shelf (OCS). EPAct provided a general framework for BOEM to follow when authorizing these renewable energy activities. For example, EPAct requires that BOEM coordinate with relevant federal agencies and affected state and local governments, obtain fair return for leases and grants issued, and ensure that renewable energy development takes place in a safe and environmentally-responsible manner. For more information, read Section 388 of the Energy Policy Act of 2005.

In 2009, President Barack Obama and Secretary of the Interior Ken Salazar announced the finalization of regulations governing BOEM's Outer Continental Shelf (OCS) Renewable Energy Program. These regulations provide a detailed structure to govern how BOEM manages its Renewable Energy Program, ensure that BOEM meets its statutory obligations, and provide both certainty and flexibility for overseeing the nascent offshore renewable energy industry.

The **Office of Renewable Energy Programs (OREP)** oversees development of offshore renewable energy projects on the Outer Continental Shelf (OCS). This new activity in the marine environment requires an assessment of the potential environmental impacts to resources on the OCS. The Bureau's responsibilities include determining and evaluating the effects of OCS activities on natural, historical, and human resources and the appropriate monitoring and mitigating of those effects.

BOEM is working through the **Environmental Studies Program (ESP)** to collect information to be used in this assessment. The ESP was established by the **Outer Continental Shelf Lands Act**, as amended in 1978 (OCSLAA) to provide information for sound decision-making and management. BOEM is partnering with other Federal agencies including the Fish and Wildlife Service, National Park Service, Department of Energy, United States

Geological Survey, and the National Oceanic and Atmospheric Administration, to acquire the information to meet these agencies mandates. Additionally, the Bureau of Safety and Environmental Enforcement (BSEE's) **Technology Assessment Programs (TAP)** provides a research element encompassed by the BSEE Regulatory Program. TAP supports research associated with operational safety and pollution prevention. TAP (formerly known as Technology Assessment and Research (TA&R)) Program was established in the 1970s to ensure that industry operations on the Outer Continental Shelf (OCS) incorporated the use of the Best Available and Safest Technologies (BAST) subsequently required through the 1978 OCSLA amendments and Energy Policy Act of 2005.

Historic Preservation Activities of the Office of Renewable Energy Programs

The mission of the Bureau of Ocean Energy Management's **Office of Renewable Energy Programs** (OREP) is to regulate environmentally-responsible offshore renewable energy development activities. In support of that objective, the archaeologists in OREP coordinate studies and conduct Section 106 reviews under the National Historic Preservation Act, which are intended to identify and protect archaeological sites and other historic properties.

Historic properties on the Outer Continental Shelf (OCS) include historic shipwrecks, sunken aircraft, lighthouses, and pre-contact archaeological sites that have become inundated due to global sea level rise since the height of the last ice age ca. 19,000 years ago. Pre-contact archaeological sites are those that date to the time before European contact with Native Americans. Historic properties onshore (e.g., sites, buildings, and districts) are also considered where they may be affected by a proposed renewable energy project.

Section 106 of the National Historic Preservation Act (NHPA) requires federal agencies to take into account the effects of their undertakings on historic properties and afford the Advisory Council on Historic Preservation an opportunity to comment. OREP archaeologists help BOEM meets its obligations under the NHPA by conducting detailed reviews and coordinating those reviews with OREP's analyses under the National Environmental Policy Act. North Atlantic Wind Energy Areas

Guidelines for Identification of Historic Properties in Federal Waters

BOEM's regulations at 30 CFR Part 585 require renewable energy developers to provide the results of detailed site characterization surveys in order for the bureau to conduct the required technical and environmental review of an applicant's plan. Current guidelines for collecting and submitting these data, Guidelines for Providing Geological and Geophysical, Hazards, and Archaeological Information Pursuant to 30 CFR Part 585, include recommendations on the appropriate methods to identify historic properties located on the OCS. These guidelines are subject to revision as new technology develops, studies are completed, and consultations inform our scope of identification efforts. For onshore areas or areas in state waters, OREP recommends contacting the relevant State Historic Preservation Officer for guidance on the appropriate methods and level of effort to identify historic properties in these areas.

Environmental Stewardship

BOEM funds ocean research through the Environmental Studies Program to provide science in support of management decisions.

The bureau promotes energy independence, environmental protection and economic development through responsible management of these resources based on the best available science. To support this work and inform bureau policy decisions, BOEM's Environmental Studies Program (ESP) develops, funds and manages rigorous scientific research to inform policy decisions regarding OCS resource development.

These environmental studies cover a broad range of disciplines, including physical oceanography, atmospheric sciences, biology, protected species, social sciences, economics, submerged cultural resources and the environmental impacts of energy development. BOEM incorporates findings from the studies program into its environmental reviews and National Environmental Policy Act (NEPA) documents, which are used to determine steps to avoid, mitigate, or monitor the impact of energy and mineral resource development on the OCS.

Through the ESP, BOEM is a leading contributor to the growing body of scientific knowledge about the marine and coastal environment. The bureau has funded more than $1 billion in research since the studies program began in 1973. Technical summaries of more than 1,200 BOEM-sponsored environmental research projects and more than 3,400 research reports are publicly available online through the Environmental Studies Program Information System (ESPIS).

BOEM oversees scientific research conducted through contracts, cooperative agreements with state institutions or public colleges and universities in coastal states, and inter- and intra-agency agreements. These arrangements enable the bureau to leverage resources, meet national priorities and satisfy common needs for robust scientific information. The ESP regularly conducts studies with partners under the umbrella of the National Oceanographic Partnership Program, including several award-winning studies. ESP's expertise is often sought for intergovernmental and international forums.

Ongoing Environmental Studies by Region & Program

Alaska Studies

Ongoing studies in Alaska focus on protected and endangered species; physical oceanography; wildlife biology; subsistence and traditional knowledge; and economic modeling. Some take place through the BOEM/University of Alaska Coastal Marine Institute, established in 1993, to promote regional stakeholder participation. Given the current interest in oil and gas development in the Beaufort and Chukchi Seas, many studies are focused on understanding Arctic resources. The ESP actively collaborates with other federally and privately funded Arctic science programs.

Gulf of Mexico Studies

Ongoing studies in the Gulf of Mexico focus on impacts of the Deepwater Horizon oil spill, archeological and biological research, chemosynthetic communities, deepwater corals and the Loop Current. The ESP has pioneered social and economic research on the complex network of interrelationships among the energy industry and the GOM region.

Pacific Studies

The ESP has pioneered ocean research along the entire Pacific Coast of the United States. The current program includes platform biology studies, a long-standing highly acclaimed multi-agency intertidal monitoring program and in recent years, studies to support renewable energy development. In many cases, ESP studies' results represent the only research of that type ever conducted in the ocean along the coast.

Atlantic Studies

In support of the Energy Policy Act of 2005, ESP collects information to assess the environment in support of renewable energy development. This includes a suite of studies to address the distribution of birds and bats on the Outer Continental Shelf. The socioeconomic consequences of offshore wind development are also being evaluated, with studies covering space use conflicts, visual impacts, and associated economic effects. Atlantic research also informs decisions for the Marine Minerals Program for coastal restoration and shore protection in the wake of storms like Hurricane Sandy.

National Studies

At the headquarters level, the ESP develops and manages studies with bureau-wide applicability, and disseminates the findings. Studies include archiving of OCS invertebrates by the Smithsonian, renewable energy space-use conflicts, marine mammal research, and support of the Oil Spill Modeling Program.

BOEM is also tasked with managing the extraction of offshore minerals from America's Outer Continental Shelf (OCS). While the largest component of this extraction is exploration and development of oil and gas resources, the bureau is also responsible for "non-energy minerals" (primarily sand and gravel) excavated from the ocean floor.

Through research and environmental reviews, BOEM plays a key role in improving the overall scientific understanding of the potential effects of anthropogenic, or human-generated, sound on marine life.

Office of Environmental Programs

Protecting the environment while ensuring the safe development of the nation's offshore energy and marine mineral resources is a critical part of BOEM's mission. The Bureau, as with all Federal agencies, must consider the potential environmental impacts from exploring and extracting these resources.

The Environmental Assessment Division prepares program-level National Environmental Policy Act (NEPA) and Outer Continental Shelf (OCS) Lands Act reports; provides oversight, policy guidance, and direction for NEPA and other environmental laws and regulations affecting OCS activities; and participates in international conventions and treaty activities.

The Bureau must comply with numerous environmental statutes, regulations, and executive orders to carry out its mission. Some of these are listed below.

Migratory Bird Treaty Act (MBTA)

National Environmental Policy Act (NEPA)

Endangered Species Act (ESA)

Marine Mammal Protection Act (MMPA)

Coastal Zone Management Act (CZMA)

Air Quality Act (1967) or the Clean Air Act (CAA)

Federal Water Pollution Control Act (1972) or the Clean Water Act (CWA)

National Historic Preservation Act (NHPA)

Magnuson-Stevens Fishery Conservation and Management Act (FCMA)

Executive Order 12114: Environmental Effects Abroad

Executive Order 12898: Environmental Justice

Executive Order 13007: Indian Sacred Sites

Executive Order 13089: Coral Reef Protection

The BEA professional staff conducts ongoing liaison, consultation, and outreach activities with various other bureaus within DOI, agencies external to DOI, State agencies, the environmental community, industry organizations, and other groups which are directly associated with mineral and energy development. These activities are both routine in order to keep up with activities of these groups and ad hoc as special problems arise.

National Environmental Policy Act (NEPA)

The National Environmental Policy Act (NEPA) of 1969 (42 USC. 4321-4347) is the foundation of environmental policymaking in the United States. The intent of the NEPA process is to help public officials make decisions based on an understanding of environmental consequences and take actions that protect, restore, and enhance the environment. The NEPA established the Council on Environmental Quality (CEQ) to advise agencies on the environmental decision making process and to oversee and coordinate the development of Federal environmental policy. The CEQ issued regulations (40 CFR 1500-1508) in 1978 implementing NEPA. The regulations include procedures to be used by Federal Agencies for the environmental review process.

BOEM prepares Environmental Assessments (EAs) for proposals to determine if significant impacts may occur that would require preparation of an EIS. EAs are prepared for each exploration plan outside the central and western GOM. EAs are prepared for other Outer Continental Shelf (OCS) oil and gas activities on a selective basis. For example, in the central and western GOM, EAs are routinely prepared for proposals to remove structures and to operate near especially sensitive areas (e.g., the Flower Garden Banks).

BOEM prepares Categorical Exclusion Reviews (CER) to verify that neither an EA nor an EIS is needed prior to making a decision on the activity being considered for approval. A CER is the briefest form of NEPA review and are prepared mostly for exploration and development proposals in the central and western GOM and most geological and geophysical survey permit applications on all OCS areas.

Oil Spill Modeling Program

The Bureau assesses oil-spill risks associated with offshore energy activities off the US continental coast and Alaska by calculating spill trajectories and contact probabilities. These analyses address the likelihood of spill occurrences, the transport and fate of any spilled oil, and the environmental impacts that might occur as a result of the spill. The bureau's Oil-Spill Risk Analysis (OSRA) model combines the probability of spill occurrence with a statistical description of hypothetical oil-spill movement on the ocean surface.

Modeling results are used by staff for preparation of environmental documents in accordance with the National Environmental Policy Act; other Federal and State agencies for review of environmental impact statements (EISs), environmental assessments, and endangered species consultations; and oil industry specialists preparing the oil spill response plans (OSRP).

Paths of hypothetical oil spills are based on hindcasts (history) of winds, ocean currents, and ice in arctic waters, using the best available input of environmental information. Outputs of the model include tables of probable contact and GIS (Geographic Information System) representations of these probabilities, with and without the probability of the occurrence of one or more spills.

BOEM is committed to the continuous improvement of OSRA estimations and EIS analysis, and use the results of new field and modeling studies to fulfill that commitment. As offshore activity expands into deeper waters and new geographic areas, BOEM oil-spill modeling will be applied to pertinent risk assessments and validated with environmental observations.

4

Bureau of Reclamation

Established in 1902, the Bureau of Reclamation is best known for the dams, power plants, and canals it constructed in the 17 western states. These water projects led to homesteading and promoted the economic development of the West. The Bureau has constructed more than 600 dams and reservoirs including Hoover Dam on the Colorado River and Grand Coulee on the Columbia River.

Today, the Bureau is the largest wholesaler of water in the country. It brings water to more than 31 million people, and provides one out of five Western farmers (140,000) with irrigation water for 10 million acres of farmland that produce 60% of the nation's vegetables and 25% of its fruits and nuts.

Reclamation is also the second largest producer of hydroelectric power in the United States. The Bureau's 53 power plants annually provide more than 40 billion kilowatt hours generating nearly a billion dollars in power revenues and produce enough electricity to serve 3.5 million homes.

Today, The Bureau of Reclamation is a contemporary water management agency with a Strategic Plan outlining numerous programs, initiatives and activities that will help the Western States, Native American Tribes and others meet new water needs and balance the multitude of competing uses of water in the West.

Its mission is to assist in meeting the increasing water demands of the West while protecting the environment and the public's investment in these structures. Great emphasis is placed on fulfilling its water delivery obligations, water conservation, water recycling and reuse, and developing partnerships with its customers, states, and Native American Tribes, and in finding ways to bring together the variety of interests to address the competing needs for these limited water resources.

The Government Performance and Results Act (GPRA) Modernization Act of 2010

The GPRA Modernization Act modernizes the Federal Government's performance management framework, retaining and amplifying some aspects of the Government Performance and Results Act of 1993 (GPRA 1993) while also addressing some of its weaknesses. GPRA 1993 established strategic planning, performance planning and performance reporting as a framework for agencies to communicate progress in achieving their missions. The GPRA Modernization Act established some important changes to existing requirements.

The purpose of the GPRA Modernization Act is to:
- Improve the confidence of the American people in the capability of the Federal Government, by systematically holding Federal agencies accountable for achieving program results;
- Improve program performance by requiring agencies to set goals, measure performance against those goals and report publicly on progress;
- Improve Federal program effectiveness and public accountability by promoting a focus on results, service quality and customer satisfaction;
- Help Federal managers improve service delivery, by requiring that they plan for meeting program goals and by providing them with information about program results and service quality;
- Improve congressional decision-making by providing more information on achieving statutory objectives and on the relative effectiveness and efficiency of Federal programs and spending;
- Improve internal management of the Federal Government; and
- Improve usefulness of performance and program information by modernizing public reporting

The Bureau's top priorities have been categorized as follows:

- **Infrastructure.** The Department values the water, energy, and recreational services Reclamation provides at about $19.6 billion each year. It also provides about at $55 billion in economic activity and 416,000 jobs each year.
- **WaterSMART.** The S.M.A.R.T. in WaterSMART stands for Sustain and Manage America's Resources tomorrow. WaterSMART allows all bureaus of the Department to work with States, Tribes, local governments, and non-governmental organizations to pursue a sustainable water supply for the Nation by establishing a framework to provide federal leadership and assistance on the efficient use of water, integrating water and energy policies to support the sustainable use of all natural resources, and coordinating the water conservation activities of the various Interior offices.
- **Ecosystem Restoration.** To meet mission goals, a part of the programs must focus on the protection and restoration of aquatic and riparian environments influenced by its operations. It is critical that Reclamation continue to invest in eco-system restoration if the Bureau is going to continue to supply water and power reliably as it has done historically. Example: Klamath River.
- **Strengthening Tribal Nations.** The Bureau will implement Indian water rights settlements over the next 20 years. It is anticipated that Reclamation will invest between $150 and $200 million per year to fulfill this responsibility. These activities include projects and actions to implement Indian water rights settlements, technical assistance to tribes, and ecosystem restoration. Example: Navajo Gallup.
- **Renewable Energy.** Hydropower is a renewable and reliable resource providing clean energy to the western United States. It is the nation's largest renewable energy resource and the Bureau of Reclamation is the second largest producer in the United States.

WaterSMART

Water is the nation's most precious natural resource and is increasingly stressed by the demands society places on it. Adequate water supplies are an essential element in human survival, ecosystem health, energy production, and economic sustainability. Significant climate change-related impacts on water supplies are well documented in the scientific literature and scientists are forecasting changes in hydrologic cycles.

Congress recognized these issues with the passage of the SECURE Water Act, a law that authorizes federal water and science agencies to work together with state and local water managers to plan for climate change and the other threats to our water supplies, and take action to secure our water resources for the communities, economies, and the ecosystems they support.

Reclamation plays a key role in the WaterSMART program as the Department's main water management agency. Focused on improving water conservation and helping water and resource managers make wise decisions about water use, Reclamation's portion of the WaterSMART program is achieved through administration of grants, scientific studies, technical assistance, and scientific expertise.

Some recent scientific studies

Reflecting current climate projections for the western United States, a report issued by the Bureau of Reclamation in February 2015 revealed a projected shift in demand for crop irrigation across eight major river basins. The study evaluated irrigation water requirements for the second half of the 20th century and, as compared to projected demand for the second half of the 21st century, found that net irrigation water requirements in the West may be six percent higher. Another area of study revealed in the report - based on a projected temperature increase of approximately 5 degrees Fahrenheit in the region - estimates that annual evaporation at most of the 12 reservoirs modeled by the study could increase 2 to 6 inches by 2080.

The report on irrigation demand and reservoir evaporation projections is the latest in a series of West-Wide Climate Risk Assessments - analyses of overall impacts from climate change on water resources in the West through the Department of the Interior's WaterSMART Program.

In announcing the report, Reclamation Commissioner Estevan López said the study was an important piece of information about climate change imposing stresses on water resources and will ultimately help inform water planners and stakeholders in confronting future climate-related supply and demand challenges.

"Reclamation and its partners are engaged in critical work to confront a future with increasing disparity between water supply and demand in basins throughout the West," Commissioner López said. "Understanding how climate change will impact crop irrigation demand and reservoir evaporation provides vital information for the development of alternatives and solutions to meet those challenges and support the nation's economy."

Projected future irrigation demands are only estimates and provide a starting point for further analyses and discussions with customers and stakeholders. The results do not account for changing crop patterns and other socioeconomic considerations that are best addressed with stakeholder input within a basin study or other process.

Using climate projections for temperature and precipitation, scientists considered projected irrigation demand in eight major river basins: Colorado, Rio Grande, Sacramento-San Joaquin, Truckee, Columbia, Missouri and Klamath. The water evaporation model was applied to 12 reservoirs in many of those major Reclamation river basins: Lake Powell, Lake Mead, American Falls Reservoir, Lake Roosevelt, Upper Klamath Lake, Canyon Ferry Reservoir, Boysen Reservoir, Elephant Butte Reservoir, Lake Shasta, Millerton Lake, Lake Tahoe and Lahontan Reservoir.

Scientists utilized climate change data to project alterations in precipitation and temperature and to assess evaporation for 12 reservoirs within those river basins, when considering observed and projected climate change impacts. Precipitation projections are highly variable and basin dependent, and they can vary significantly within individual basins as well.

"Through these studies, Reclamation is highlighting climate change impacts and encouraging a collaborative dialogue on the effective management of our water and power resources," López said. "Facing the challenge in meeting future irrigation demands is one way we are working to underscore our commitment to a strong agricultural economy and national food security."

California predictions come true

A report released by the Department of the Interior in September 2014 found that projected changes in temperature and precipitation, combined with a growing population, will have significant impacts on water supplies, water quality, fish and wildlife habitats, ecosystems, hydropower, recreation and flood control, in California's Central Valley this century.

"These projections by Interior's Bureau of Reclamation show the importance of President Obama's Climate Action Plan to address challenges like those

California's Central Valley will face to provide a sustainable water supply for its citizens and economy," said Deputy Secretary Michael L. Connor.
"Climate change is not a problem we can leave to future generations to solve. The challenges to our water supplies illustrated in this study provide graphic examples of how acting now is an economic imperative as well as an environmental necessity."

The Sacramento and San Joaquin Basins Climate Impact Assessment projects temperatures may increase as the distance grows from the Pacific Ocean. Although most of the Central Valley may warm by 1°C in the early 21st century, a 2°C increase is projected by mid-century. Precipitation patterns indicate that there is a clear north to south decreasing precipitation trend compared to historical trends. In the northern parts of the Sacramento Valley there may be an overall increase to average annual precipitation.
"This assessment is one of several that studies climate risks to water supplies and related resources in river basins in the western United Sates," said Deputy Secretary Connor. "Although it is quite sobering to see the projections, we will follow up these assessments by continuing our work with the State of California and interested stakeholders to implement climate adaptation strategies in the Bay-Delta and other regions of the State. I am confident this ongoing collaboration along with the Climate Action Plan and the state's water action plan will help ensure that California has the necessary water supply to meet its future needs."
The study presents an overview of the current climate and hydrology over the entire Central Valley including the Sacramento, San Joaquin and Tulare Lake basins. It also evaluates how projected climatic and hydrologic changes could impact water availability, management and demands while analyzing impacts of future urban growth and changes in land-use within the Central Valley.
Some findings of the Sacramento-San Joaquin Impact Assessment that show a potential for significant implications for water management, human infrastructure and ecosystems include the following:

- Due to the warming conditions, the runoff will increase in winter and decrease in spring as more precipitation falls as rain instead of snow. Reservoirs may fill earlier and excess runoff would have to be released earlier to ensure proper flood protection is maintained. This may lead to reduced storage in reservoirs when the summer irrigation season begins.

- Water demands are projected to increase. Urban water use is expected to increase due to population increases in the Central Valley while agricultural uses are projected to decrease because of a decline in irrigated acreage and to a lesser extent the effects of increasing carbon dioxide.
- Water quality may decline by the end of the century. Sea levels are predicted to rise up to 1.6 meters in that time frame which will lead to an increase in salinity in the Delta and a decline of habitat for fish and wildlife. River water temperatures may increase because cold water availability from reservoir storage would be reduced.
- The food web in the Delta is projected to decline. Projected lower flows through the Delta and reduced cold water due to lower reservoir levels will make less water available for species, including endangered species such as migrating salmon.
- Hydropower generation is projected to decline in Central Valley Project facilities due to decreased reservoir storage. However, net power usage is also expected to decline due to reductions in pumping water and conveyance.

The climate projections utilized the Coupled Model Intercomparison Project Phase 3, CMIP3, climate projections with demographic and land use estimates based on the California Department of Water Resources Water Plan 2009.

This study supports the broader Sacramento and San Joaquin Basins Study, part of the Department of the Interior's WaterSMART Program. The basin study, which is expected to be completed in 2015, will provide additional analysis including the evaluation of adaptation strategies to mitigate impacts of climate change and meet future water demands. It will also update the climate projections using the recently-released Coupled Model Intercomparison Project Phase 5, CMIP5, climate projections and land use - demographic projections based on the recent California State Water Plan 2013 update, which were not available when the analysis was completed for this impact assessment.

"This study confirms that the current status quo for water supply in California is not sustainable," Deputy Secretary Connor said. "Reclamation and its partners in California are already developing solutions to meet the projected imbalances between future supply and demand within the Central Valley."

"The Sacramento and San Joaquin Basins Study will provide a roadmap forward for Reclamation and the State of California to ensure a sustainable water supply well into the future," Acting Reclamation Commissioner Lowell Pimley said.

Ecosystem Restoration

Supporting the Department's priority on Ecosystem Restoration is a key underpinning of Reclamation's mission. In order to meet its mission goals related to delivering water and generating power, a part of its programs must focus on the protection and restoration of the aquatic and riparian environments influenced by its operations. Ecosystem restoration involves a large number of Reclamation's activities, including Reclamation's Endangered Species Act recovery programs, which directly address the environmental aspects of the Reclamation mission.

Some restoration projects

Columbia and Snake River Salmon Recovery Project
The Federal Columbia River Power System (FCRPS) is a group of 14 hydropower projects owned and operated by the US Army Corps of Engineers and Reclamation and operated as a coordinated system. The Bonneville Power Administration markets and distributes the power from these hydropower projects to generate 24 percent of the Pacific Northwest region's firm electrical energy supply. These three agencies (Bonneville Power Administration, US Army Corps of Engineers, and Reclamation) are collectively known as the Action Agencies. Fifteen listed species of fish are affected by FCRPS operation. The US Fish and Wildlife Service (FWS) and The National Marine Fisheries Service (NOAA Fisheries) have each issued Biological Opinions (BiOps); the NOAA Fisheries Reasonable and Prudent Alternative includes a very substantial suite of required actions to ensure that threatened or endangered species are not jeopardized and their designated critical habitats are not adversely modified by the operation of the FCRPS.

In 2008, Reclamation entered, along with the other action agencies, into multiple 10-year memoranda of agreements with two States and five Tribes to support the 2008 FCRPS BiOp and anadromous fish recovery. This program also funds Reclamation actions included in those agreements.

Klamath Project

The Klamath Project stores and diverts water to provide irrigation for land in south-central Oregon and parts of north-central California. Originally built in the early 1900s, the Project provides water to approximately 1,400 individual farms and ranches, totaling approximately 200,000 irrigable acres, and contributes to a $325.0 million agriculture-dependent economy in the Upper Klamath Basin. The Project also provides water to approximately 44,300 non-agricultural acres of National Wildlife Refuges. In 2001 and 2010, severe curtailment of water for agricultural use occurred as a result of several years of below average inflows, droughts, and the legal requirements of two Endangered Species Act (ESA) biological opinions (BiOps). This action caused many adverse economic consequences to the Upper Basin's agricultural communities and stimulated efforts to improve water supply reliability, protect fish, and preserve natural resources and ecosystems through the effective use of water.

Reclamation operates the Klamath Project under a BiOp issued jointly by the US Fish and Wildlife Service and the National Marine Fisheries Service for the protection of ESA-listed shortnose and Lost River suckers as well as Coho salmon. Reclamation continues to work closely with other Federal agencies and all stakeholders to protect ESA-listed fish while managing water for the needs of agriculture and wildlife refuges and addressing Federal tribal trust responsibilities. Beyond the Department of the Interior, the Department of Commerce, US Department of Agriculture, and other state and Federal agencies continue to coordinate and prioritize Klamath Basin programs. In December 2013, The Klamath Task Force and Upper Basin Water Group completed work on an agreement in principle on Upper Basin water and economic issues. This is a major first step to address the continuing conflicts over water use in the upper basin.

Middle Rio Grande Project

The Middle Rio Grande project continues operations, maintenance and rehabilitation of project facilities; provides for flood protection; and protection and recovery of the Rio Grande Silvery Minnow and Southwestern Willow

Flycatcher. Project works are critical to delivering water to nine tribes and pueblos along the river as well as a national wildlife refuge.

The FY 2016 budget for the project includes $9.5 million for the Middle Rio Grande Endangered Species Act (ESA) Collaborative Program, composed of sixteen signatories, that establishes a forum as an alternative to litigation, that actively creates, promotes, and provides opportunities for Reclamation's participation in cooperative efforts with Federal and non-Federal partners to preserve, protect, and improve the status of endangered species while also protecting existing water uses and ensuring compliance with all applicable laws.

These collaborative activities include: studies to assess the impact and/or affect Reclamation operation and maintenance and other construction activities have on the endangered Rio Grande Silvery Minnow and Southwestern Willow Flycatcher; ESA coordination and consultation with the Fish and Wildlife Service, New Mexico Department of Game and Fish, and other stakeholders to obtain environmental clearances for proposed projects; acquisition of supplemental non-Federal water, and pumping from the low flow conveyance channel into the Rio Grande during the irrigation season to provide sufficient water supply for endangered species, irrigation, and water delivery; tasks required in the current Biological Opinion such as, population management, habitat restoration, monitoring and adaptive management, and water quality studies that are supportive of the listed species recovery plans. The project consists of El Vado Dam and Reservoir, three diversion dams, 260 miles of the Rio Grande channel infrastructure, and the 57 mile long Low Flow Conveyance Channel.

The diversion dams and 202 miles of canals, 580 miles of laterals, and 405 miles of drains are operated and maintained by the Middle Rio Grande Conservancy District under contract with the United States.

Lower Colorado River Operations Programs

The Lower Colorado River Operations Program (LCROP) is for continued development and implementation of the Lower Colorado River Multi-Species Conservation Program (LCR MSCP). This unique program provides long-term

Endangered Species Act compliance for both current and future water delivery and diversion, and power production by the Unites States and the water users. This program will provide quality habitat to conserve populations of 26 state and Federal special status species, along the lower Colorado River from Lake Mead to Mexico, including the endangered razorback sucker, bonytail chub, southwestern willow flycatcher, yellow-billed cuckoo, and Yuma clapper rail. The budget for LCROP also includes funding for river operations, water service contracting and repayment, decree accounting, and fulfilling the requirements of the Secretary's role as water master for the lower Colorado River. Funding for this program also continues the monitoring of the implementation of the historic binational Minute 319, which is emphasized as a key component of the "Manage Water and Watersheds for the 21st Century," as referenced in the Department of the Interior's Strategic Plan for FY 2014-FY 2018.

Platte River Recovery Implementation Program

The Platte River Recovery Implementation Program involves the Platte River Basin in Wyoming, Colorado, and Nebraska. In late 2006, the Governors of Colorado, Nebraska and Wyoming and the Secretary of the Interior entered into the Platte River Recovery Implementation Program (Program). The Program is a collaborative basin-wide program for endangered species in the Central Platte River in Nebraska. The Program addresses habitat for four species: the Whooping Crane, Piping Plover, Interior Least Tern, and Pallid Sturgeon. Under the Program, Reclamation received significant and essential compliance under the Endangered Species Act (ESA) for continued operations of the Colorado-Big Thompson and North Platte projects which supply water to Colorado, Nebraska, and Wyoming irrigators and municipalities. The Program, which began January 1, 2007, is authorized at $317 million, with the Federal share being $157 million (October 1, 2005 price levels). The Program requires that the Federal government provide 50 percent of the Program contributions, with the States providing at least 50 percent of the contributions ($30 million cash and $130 million in kind, cash-equivalent contributions). The first increment of this program is scheduled for completion in FY 2020.

The request continues implementation of the Platte River Recovery Implementation Program to provide ESA compliance for Reclamation projects in the North and South Platte basins. The activities planned include the continuation of the Program's participation in a water service agreement with the State of Nebraska and the Central Nebraska Public Power & Irrigation District for water from the proposed J-2 Reservoir Project. In addition, other work projects include: 1) Program Land Plan activities for Adaptive Management Plan Experimental Design activities, including sediment augmentation and flow consolidation; 2) Integrated Monitoring & Research Plan activities, including annual whooping crane monitoring during the spring and fall migration seasons, implementation of a whooping crane telemetry tracking project, annual interior least tern and piping plover monitoring (conducted May through August), geomorphology/in-channel vegetation monitoring, and flow-sediment-mechanical "proof of concept" science activities, water quality monitoring, and LiDAR/aerial photography monitoring; and 3) the Adaptive Management Plan Independent Science Review, the preparation of the ISAC's annual report on the Program, and the peer review of up to four of the Program's technical documents.

Upper Colorado Region Recovery Implementation Program

The Endangered Species Recovery Implementation Program in the Upper Colorado Region funds the Upper Colorado and San Juan River Basins Endangered Fish Recovery Programs. These two recovery programs are intended to go beyond removal of jeopardy to the recovery of four species of endangered fish while allowing the states to develop their full compact water entitlement, in compliance with interstate compacts and various laws. Work focuses on four major areas: 1) Habitat Management - providing and protecting in-stream flows; 2) Habitat Development and Maintenance - fish ladders, fish screens, levee removal, and flooded bottom land restoration; 3) Augmentation and Conservation - of Genetic Integrity - propagation facilities, and stocking efforts; and non-native and sport fish management; 4) Conservation of other aquatic and terrestrial endangered species - restoring habitat and enhancing stream flows.

The overarching goal of the program is to develop, implement, and sustain a long-term program to take actions for the preservation, conservation, and recovery of endangered, threatened, proposed, and candidate species, resident and/or migratory to habitats within the Upper Colorado River Basin. Continued funding is critical to avoid issues arising in regard to the ability to maintain Endangered Species Act compliance for Federal and non-Federal water resource use in the Upper Colorado River Basin.

Central Valley Project, Trinity River Division

The Central Valley Project, Trinity River Division, includes the development of a comprehensive monitoring and adaptive management program for fishery restoration and construction of channel rehabilitation projects at various sites along the Trinity River. An additional $1.5 million from the Central Valley Project Restoration Fund will also be used for this purpose.

In 1984 under P.L. 98-541, Congress enacted the Trinity River Basin Fish and Wildlife Management Act to provide additional authority in order to restore and maintain the fish and wildlife stocks of the Trinity River Basin to those levels existing prior to construction of the CVP Trinity River Division.

The Central Valley Project Restoration Fund was authorized in the 1992 Central Valley Project Improvement Act, Title XXXIV of P.L. 102-575. This Fund provides funding from project beneficiaries for habitat restoration, improvement and acquisition, and other fish and wildlife restoration activities in the Central Valley Project (CVP) area of California. Revenues are derived from payments by project beneficiaries and from donations.

Funding will be used for protection, restoration, and management of aquatic and riparian habitats throughout the Central Valley, water supplies for wildlife refuges, and water acquisition and other activities to benefit anadromous fish. Annual work plans coordinated by Fish and Wildlife Service and Reclamation, in conjunction with Central Valley water users, hydropower representatives, and other interested groups, continues to help ensure efficient and effective implementation of the Act.

California Bay-Delta Restoration

The Sacramento–San Joaquin River Delta (Delta) is a regional, State, and national treasure. It is an integral part of an ecosystem dependent on more than 750 wildlife species and more than 120 species of fish. As a migratory corridor, the Delta hosts two-thirds of the State's salmon and nearly half of the waterfowl and shorebirds along the Pacific flyway. The Bay-Delta system is critical to California's economy because the two rivers that flow into the Bay-Delta provide potable water for two-thirds of California's homes and businesses and irrigate more than 7 million acres of farmland on which 45 percent of the nation's fruits and vegetables are grown, part of a $43.0 billion agricultural industry.

The Federal Central Valley Project and the State Water Project play a central, coordinated role in the water management of the Bay-Delta system and throughout California. The CALFED Bay-Delta Program was established in May 1995 to develop a comprehensive long-term plan to address the complex and interrelated problems in the Delta region, tributary watersheds, and delivery areas. The Program's focus is on conserving and restoring the health of the ecosystem and improving water management.

December 15, 2010, the Interim Federal Action Plan Status Update for the California Bay-Delta: 2011 and Beyond was issued by the six Federal agencies. The updated report urges continued progress toward completion of the California Bay-Delta Conservation Plan (BDCP) and supports major elements of the plan as a promising means of addressing the critical needs of both the Bay-Delta ecosystem and the state's water delivery structure. The FY 2016 budget requests funding actions that support the Interim Federal Action Plan. The FY 2016 budget includes bill language to extend the expiration date for the program by two years to September 30, 2018.

Native American Affairs

Reclamation is committed to increasing opportunities for Indians to develop, manage, and protect their water and related resources. The activities supporting these opportunities, sometimes informally referred to collectively as the "Native American Program," is a collaborative, coordinated, integrated function in Reclamation.

The Native American Affairs Program, which is a formal program funded through the Native American Affairs line item in Reclamation's budget, is a small but integral part of the overall Native American Program. The Native American and International Affairs Office in the Commissioner's Office serves as the central coordination point for the Native American Affairs Program and lead for policy guidance for Native American issues in Reclamation.

Hydropower Program

The Bureau of Reclamation has a long and successful history providing renewable, clean, reliable, and affordable hydropower to its customers. As the operating environment has evolved over the past century, Reclamation has adapted, leveraging new technologies and partnerships to meet the nation's water and energy needs.

In total, Reclamation holds title to 76 hydroelectric power plants. Of the 76, Reclamation operates 53 hydroelectric power plants, comprising over 14 million kilowatts of installed capacity. Generation from the 53 plants rank Reclamation as the second largest producer of hydroelectric power in the US, accounting for 15 percent of the Nation's annual hydropower output.

Annually, Reclamation operated plants generate over 40 billion kilowatt hours of electricity (enough to meet the demand of 3.5 million US homes), produce nearly one billion dollars in power revenues, and offset approximately 27 million tons of carbon dioxide. Since 1909, when our first power plant started operation, power revenues have provided more than $10 billion in repayment to the US Treasury.

The remaining 23 plants are "transferred works" - the operation and maintenance of these plants is carried out by a non-federal entity, under the provisions of a formal operation and maintenance transfer contract. 5 of the 23 "transferred works" plants generate power that is marketed by Power Marketing Administrations. The 5 plants are: Deer Creek, McPhee, Towaoc, O'Neill, and San Luis.

Bureau of Reclamation Sustainable Energy Strategy

A new sustainable energy strategic plan released on November 14, 2013 will help guide the Bureau of Reclamation into the future as the agency continues its vital role in developing and supporting renewable energy production for the nation's power grid.

"Reclamation continues to successfully generate renewable, clean and affordable hydropower as energy needs consistently grow across the western United States," Commissioner Michael L. Connor said. "It is only natural that Reclamation play a key role in facilitating the additional development and integration of renewables such as hydropower, solar, wind and geothermal to help meet the western energy demands."

Six long-term strategic objectives to further Reclamation's sustainable energy mission were developed to help guide Reclamation in this important endeavor:

- Increase renewable generation from Reclamation projects.
- Facilitate non-federal development of renewable energy projects.
- Increase energy savings and conservation at Reclamation projects.
- Support integration of variable non-dispatchable renewable resources in the United States electrical grid.
- Increase benefits of renewable energy through technological innovation.
- Improve management efficiencies related to the implementation of renewable energy and energy savings projects.

Lease of Power Privilege

A Lease of Power Privilege (LOPP) is a contractual right given to a non-federal entity to use a Bureau of Reclamation facility (e.g. dam or conduit) for electric power generation consistent with Reclamation project purposes. A LOPP project must not impair the efficiency of Reclamation generated power or water deliveries, jeopardize public safety, or negatively affect any other Reclamation project purposes.

The Lease of Power Privilege (LOPP) Processes, Responsibilities, Timelines, and Charges Directive and Standard (D&S) provides clear guidance and timelines on LOPP requirements, assigns roles and responsibilities within the organization for LOPP development, sets a standard methodology across Reclamation for the LOPP charges and identifies all potential charges for developers.

The initial D&S was published in September 2012 and revised in February 2014 to incorporate Public Law 113-24 process requirements. The February 2014 revision was released as a Temporary Reclamation Manual Release with a concurrent public comment period. The current D&S, published in September 2014 incorporates internal and external comments submitted to Reclamation.

"Through these leases, Reclamation is able to work with non-federal entities and project beneficiaries to increase the amount of renewable hydropower produced in meeting the growing energy needs of the nation," said former Reclamation Commissioner Michael L. Connor. "This directive and standard provides a clear and understandable process to develop hydropower on Reclamation's dams and canals."

Bureau of Reclamation Renewable Update

Released quarterly, the Bureau of Reclamation Renewable Energy Update identifies Federal and non-Federal renewable energy projects currently online or in development on Reclamation land, facilities, and water bodies and highlights current Reclamation renewable activities. The update provides Reclamation-wide and regional summaries, renewable energy portfolios, and project updates as well as a listing of WaterSMART Grant projects that have a renewable energy component.

5

Bureau of Indian Affairs

Established in 1824, Indian Affairs (IA) is the oldest bureau of the United States Department of the Interior. It provides services to about 1.9 million American Indians and Alaska Natives in 566 federally recognized tribes and is responsible for the administration and management of 55 million surface acres and 57 million acres of subsurface minerals estates held in trust by the United States for American Indian, Indian tribes, and Alaska Natives. It provides education services to approximately 42,000 Indian students.

As a general rule, an American Indian or Alaska Native person is someone who has blood degree from and is recognized as such by a federally recognized tribe or village (as an enrolled tribal member) and/or the United States. Of course, blood quantum (the degree of American Indian or Alaska Native blood from a federally recognized tribe or village that a person possesses) is not the only means by which a person is considered to be an American Indian or Alaska Native. Other factors, such as a person's knowledge of his or her tribe's culture, history, language, religion, familial kinships, and how strongly a person identifies himself or herself as American Indian or Alaska Native, are also important. In fact, there is no single federal or tribal criterion or standard that establishes a person's identity as American Indian or Alaska Native.

There are major differences, however, when the term "American Indian" is used in an ethnological sense versus its use in a political/legal sense. The rights, protections, and services provided by the United States to individual American Indians and Alaska Natives flow not from a person's identity as such in an ethnological sense, but because he or she is a member of a federally recognized tribe. That is, a tribe that has a government-to-government relationship and a special trust relationship with the United States. These special trust and government-to-government relationships entail certain legally enforceable obligations and responsibilities on the part of the United

States to persons who are enrolled members of such tribes. Eligibility requirements for federal services will differ from program to program. Likewise, the eligibility criteria for enrollment (or membership) in a tribe will differ from tribe to tribe.

(panel)

Native Americans

When referring to American Indian or Alaska Native persons, it is still appropriate to use the terms "American Indian" and "Alaska Native." These terms denote the cultural and historical distinctions between persons belonging to the indigenous tribes of the continental United States (American Indians) and the indigenous tribes and villages of Alaska (Alaska Natives, i.e., Eskimos, Aleuts, and Indians). They also refer specifically to persons eligible for benefits and services funded or directly provided by the BIA.

The term "Native American" came into broad usage in the 1970's as an alternative to "American Indian." Since that time, however, it has been gradually expanded within the public lexicon to include *all* Native peoples of the United States and its trust territories, i.e., American Indians, Alaska Natives, Native Hawaiians, Chamorros, and American Samoans, as well as persons from Canada First Nations and indigenous communities in Mexico and Central and South America who are US residents.

(close panel)

The Bureau of Indian Affairs (BIA) mission is to:

"... enhance the quality of life, to promote economic opportunity, and to carry out the responsibility to protect and improve the trust assets of American Indians, Indian tribes, and Alaska Natives."

The Bureau of Indian Education (BIE) mission is to:

"... provide quality education opportunities from early childhood through life in accordance with the tribes' needs to cultural and economic well being in keeping with the wide diversity of Indian tribes and Alaska Native villages as distinct cultural and governmental entities. The Bureau considers the whole person (spiritual, mental, physical and cultural aspects.)"

While the role of Indian Affairs has changed significantly in the last three decades in response to a greater emphasis on Indian self-governance and self-determination, Tribes still look to Indian Affairs for a broad spectrum of services.

The US has a unique legal and political relationship with Indian tribes and Alaska Native entities as provided by the Constitution of the United States, treaties, court decisions and Federal statutes.

The Bureau of Indian Affairs offers an extensive scope of programs that covers the entire range of Federal, State and local government services. Programs administered by either Tribes or Indian Affairs through the Bureau of Indian Education (BIE) include an education system consisting of 183 schools and dormitories educating approximately 42,000 elementary and secondary students and 28 tribal colleges, universities, and post-secondary schools. Programs administered through the Bureau of Indian Affairs (BIA) include social services, natural resources management on trust lands representing 55 million surface acres and 57 million acres of subsurface minerals estates, economic development programs in some of the most isolated and economically depressed areas of the United States, law enforcement and detention services, administration of tribal courts, implementation of land and water claim settlements, housing improvement, disaster relief, replacement and repair of schools, repair and maintenance of roads and bridges, and the repair of structural deficiencies on high hazard dams, the BIA operates a series irrigation systems and provides electricity to rural parts of Arizona.

Through Indian Affairs programs, Tribes improve their tribal government infrastructure, community infrastructure, education, job training, and employment opportunities along with other components of long term sustainable development that work to improve the quality of life for their members.

A little history...

The Continental Congress governed Indian affairs during the first years of the United States – in 1775 it established a Committee on Indian Affairs headed by Benjamin Franklin. At the end of the eighteenth century, Congress transferred the responsibility for managing trade relations with the tribes to the Secretary of War by its act of August 20, 1789 (1 Stat. 54). An Office of Indian Trade was established in the War Department by an act of April 21, 1806 (2 Stat. 402) specifically to handle this responsibility below the secretarial level. It was later abolished by an act of May 6, 1822 (3 Stat. 679) which handed responsibility for all Indian matters back to the Secretary of War.

Secretary of War John C. Calhoun administratively established the BIA within the department on March 11, 1824. Congress later legislatively established the bureau and the Commissioner of Indian Affairs post via the act of July 9, 1832 (4 Stat. 564). In 1849, the BIA was transferred to the newly created Interior Department. In the years that followed, the Bureau was known variously as the Indian office, the Indian bureau, the Indian department, and the Indian service. The name "Bureau of Indian Affairs" was formally adopted by the Interior Department on September 17, 1947.

Since 1824 there have been 45 Commissioners of Indian Affairs of which six have been American Indian or Alaska Native: Ely S. Parker, *Seneca* (1869-1871); Robert L. Bennett, *Oneida* (1966-1969); Louis R. Bruce, *Mohawk-Oglala Sioux* (1969-1973); Morris Thompson, *Athabascan* (1973-1976); Benjamin Reifel, *Sioux* (1976-1977); and William E. Hallett, *Red Lake Chippewa* (1979-1981).

For almost 200 years—beginning with treaty agreements negotiated by the United States and tribes in the late 18th and 19th centuries, through the General Allotment Act of 1887, which opened tribal lands west of the Mississippi to non-Indian settlers, the Indian Citizenship Act of 1924 when American Indians and Alaska Natives were granted US citizenship and the right to vote, the New Deal and the Indian Reorganization Act of 1934, which established modern tribal governments, the World War II period of relocation and the post-War termination era of the 1950s, the activism of the 1960s and 1970s that saw the takeover of the BIA's headquarters in Washington, D.C., to the passage of landmark legislation such as the Indian Self-Determination and Education Assistance Act of 1975 and the Tribal Self-Governance Act of 1994, which have fundamentally changed how the BIA and the tribes conduct business with each other—the BIA has embodied the trust and government-to-government relationships between the US and the   tribal nations that bear the designation "federally recognized."

Today, in keeping with their authorities and responsibilities under the Snyder Act of 1921 and other federal laws, regulations, and treaties, BIA employees across the country work with tribal governments in the administration of employment and job training assistance; law enforcement and justice; agricultural and economic development; tribal governance; and natural resources management programs to enhance the quality of life in tribal communities.

The following are just some examples of what the Bureau does:

- Provide funding to and administer government program services for the federally recognized American Indian and Alaska Native tribes located in 34 states, and through them to their approximately 1.9 million members.
- Work with tribes in the administration of approximately 56 million acres of trust land, and the natural resources therein, for the use and benefit of the tribes and individual Indians.
- Maintain five law enforcement district offices nationwide to provide police protection and investigative services for both Indian and non-Indians living in Indian Country.
- Operate or fund tribally operated law enforcement programs, courts, and detention facilities in tribal communities across the US
- Build and maintain thousands of miles of roads, as well as bridges, dams, and other physical infrastructure throughout Indian Country which benefit both Indians and non-Indians alike.
- Work with other federal, tribal, state, and local emergency personnel in responses to wildland fires and other natural disasters.
- Administer the Guaranteed Indian Loan Program to stimulate, increase, and sustain Indian entrepreneurship and business development in tribal communities.
- Assist tribes in administering federal economic development and employment and training programs.
- Administer BIA programs for tribes unable or who choose not to operate those programs.
- Directly serve thousands of individual Indian trust beneficiaries by providing assistance in the probating of Indian trust estates, administering leases approved by the Secretary of the Interior, and performing other fiduciary duties.

Until 1955, the BIA's responsibilities included providing health care services to American Indians and Alaska Natives. That year, the function was legislatively transferred as the Indian Health Service to the US Public Health Service within the Department of Health, Education and Welfare, known now as the US Department of Health and Human Services (DHHS), where it has remained to this day.

Why Tribes Exist Today in the United States

From 1778 to 1871, the United States' relations with individual American Indian nations indigenous to what is now the US were defined and conducted largely through the treaty-making process. These "contracts among nations" recognized and established unique sets of rights, benefits, and conditions for the treaty-making tribes who agreed to cede of millions of acres of their homelands to the United States and accept its protection. Like other treaty obligations of the United States, Indian treaties are considered to be "the supreme law of the land," and they are the foundation upon which federal Indian law and the federal Indian trust relationship is based.

Article 1, Section 8 of the United States Constitution vests Congress, and by extension the Executive and Judicial branches of our government, with the authority to engage in relations with the tribes, thereby firmly placing tribes within the constitutional fabric of our nation. When the governmental authority of tribes was first challenged in the 1830's, U. S. Supreme Court Chief Justice John Marshall articulated the fundamental principle that has guided the evolution of federal Indian law to the present: *That tribes possess a nationhood status and retain inherent powers of self-government.*

The **federal Indian trust responsibility** is a legal obligation under which the United States "has charged itself with moral obligations of the highest responsibility and trust" toward Indian tribes (Seminole Nation v. United States, 1942). This obligation was first discussed by Chief Justice John Marshall in Cherokee Nation v. Georgia (1831). Over the years, the trust doctrine has been at the center of numerous other Supreme Court cases, thus making it one of the most important principles in federal Indian law.

The federal Indian trust responsibility is also a legally enforceable fiduciary obligation on the part of the United States to protect tribal treaty rights, lands, assets, and resources, as well as a duty to carry out the mandates of federal law with respect to American Indian and Alaska Native tribes and villages. In several cases discussing the trust responsibility, the Supreme Court has used language suggesting that it entails legal duties, moral obligations, and the fulfillment of understandings and expectations that have arisen over the entire course of the relationship between the United States and the federally recognized tribes.

A **federally recognized tribe** is an American Indian or Alaska Native tribal entity that is recognized as having a government-to-government relationship with the United States, with the responsibilities, powers, limitations, and obligations attached to that designation, and is eligible for funding and services from the Bureau of Indian Affairs.

Furthermore, federally recognized tribes are recognized as possessing certain inherent rights of self-government (i.e., tribal sovereignty) and are entitled to receive certain federal benefits, services, and protections because of their special relationship with the United States. At present, there are 566 federally recognized American Indian and Alaska Native tribes and villages.

Historically, most of today's federally recognized tribes received federal recognition status through treaties, acts of Congress, presidential executive orders or other federal administrative actions, or federal court decisions.

In 1978, the Interior Department issued regulations governing the Federal Acknowledgment Process (FAP) to handle requests for federal recognition from Indian groups whose character and history varied widely in a uniform manner. These regulations – 25 C.F.R. Part 83 – were revised in 1994 and are still in effect.

Also in 1994, Congress enacted Public Law 103-454, the Federally Recognized Indian Tribe List Act (108 Stat. 4791, 4792), which formally established three ways in which an Indian group may become federally recognized:

By Act of Congress,

By the administrative procedures under 25 C.F.R. Part 83, *or*

By decision of a United States court.

However, a tribe whose relationship with the United States has been expressly terminated by Congress may not use the Federal Acknowledgment Process. Only Congress can restore federal recognition to a "terminated" tribe.

The Federally Recognized Indian Tribe List Act also requires the Secretary of the Interior to publish annually a list of the federally recognized tribes in the Federal Register.

When tribes first encountered Europeans, they were a power to be reckoned with because the combined American Indian and Alaska Native population dominated the North American continent. Their strength in numbers, the control they exerted over the natural resources within and between their territories, and the European practice of establishing relations with countries other than themselves and the recognition of tribal property rights led to tribes being seen by exploring foreign powers as sovereign nations, who treatied with them accordingly.

However, as the foreign powers' presence expanded and with the establishment and growth of the United States, tribal populations dropped dramatically and tribal sovereignty gradually eroded. While tribal sovereignty is limited today by the United States under treaties, acts of Congress, Executive Orders, federal administrative agreements and court decisions, what remains is nevertheless protected and maintained by the federally recognized tribes against further encroachment by other sovereigns, such as the states. Tribal sovereignty ensures that any decisions about the tribes with regard to their property and citizens are made with their participation and consent.

In the United States there are three types of reserved federal lands: military, public, and Indian. A federal Indian reservation is an area of land reserved for a tribe or tribes under treaty or other agreement with the United States, executive order, or federal statute or administrative action as permanent tribal homelands, and where the federal government holds title to the land in trust on behalf of the tribe.

Approximately 56.2 million acres are held in trust by the United States for various Indian tribes and individuals. There are approximately 326 Indian land areas in the US administered as federal Indian reservations (i.e., reservations, pueblos, rancherias, missions, villages, communities, etc.). The largest is the 16 million-acre Navajo Nation Reservation located in Arizona, New Mexico, and Utah. The smallest is a 1.32-acre parcel in California where the Pit River Tribe's cemetery is located. Many of the smaller reservations are less than 1,000 acres.

Some reservations are the remnants of a tribe's original land base. Others were created by the federal government for the resettling of Indian people forcibly relocated from their homelands. Not every federally recognized tribe has a reservation. Federal Indian reservations are generally exempt from state jurisdiction, including taxation, except when Congress specifically authorizes such jurisdiction.

Other types of Indian lands are:

Allotted lands, which are remnants of reservations broken up during the federal allotment period of the late nineteenth and early twentieth centuries.

Although the practice of allotting lands had begun in the eighteenth century, it was put to greater use after the Civil War. By 1885, over 11,000 patents had been issued to individual Indians under various treaties and laws. Starting with the General Allotment Act in 1887 (also known as the Dawes Act) until the Indian Reorganization Act of 1934, allotments were conveyed to members of affected tribes and held in trust by the federal government. As allotments were taken out of trust, they became subject to state and local taxation, which resulted in thousands of acres passing out of Indian hands. Today, 10,059,290.74 million acres of individually owned lands are still held in trust for allotees and their heirs.

Restricted status, also known as restricted fee, where title to the land is held by an individual Indian person or a tribe and which can only be alienated or encumbered by the owner with the approval of the Secretary of the Interior because of limitations contained in the conveyance instrument pursuant to federal law.

State Indian reservations, which are lands held in trust by a state for an Indian tribe. With state trust lands title is held by the state on behalf of the tribe and the lands are not subject to state property tax. They are subject to state law, however. State trust lands stem from treaties or other agreements between a tribal group and the state government or the colonial government(s) that preceded it.

American Indian and Alaska Native tribes, businesses, and individuals may also own land as private property. In such cases, they are subject to state and local laws, regulations, codes, and taxation.

Congress ended treaty-making with Indian tribes in 1871. Since then, relations with Indian groups have been formalized and/or codified by Congressional acts, Executive Orders, and Executive Agreements. Between 1778, when the first treaty was made with the Delawares, to 1871, when Congress ended the treaty-making period, the United States Senate ratified 370 treaties. At least 45 others were negotiated with tribes but were never ratified by the Senate.

The treaties that were made often contain commitments that have either been fulfilled or subsequently superseded by Congressional legislation.

In addition, American Indians and Alaska Natives can access education, health, welfare, and other social service programs available to all citizens, if they are eligible. Even if a tribe does not have a treaty with the United States, or has treaties that were negotiated but not ratified, its members may still receive services from the BIA or other federal programs, if eligible.

The specifics of particular treaties signed by government negotiators with Indian tribes are contained in one volume (Vol. II) of the publication, Indian Affairs, Laws and Treaties: 1778-1883, compiled, annotated, and edited by Charles J. Kappler. Published by the United States Government Printing Office in 1904, it is now out of print, but can be found in most large law libraries and on the Internet at http://digital.library.okstate.edu/Kappler. The treaty volume has also been published privately under the title, "Indian Treaties: 1778-1883."

Originals of all the treaties are maintained by the National Archives and Records Administration of the General Services Administration.

Federal-Tribal and State-Tribal Relations

The relationship between federally recognized tribes and the United States is one between sovereigns, i.e., between a government and a government. This "government-to-government" principle, which is grounded in the United States Constitution, has helped to shape the long history of relations between the federal government and these tribal nations.

Because the Constitution vested the Legislative Branch with plenary power over Indian Affairs, states have no authority over tribal governments unless expressly authorized by Congress. While federally recognized tribes generally are not subordinate to states, they can have a government-to-government relationship with these other sovereigns, as well.

Furthermore, federally recognized tribes possess both the right and the authority to regulate activities on their lands independently from state government control. They can enact and enforce stricter or more lenient laws and regulations than those of the surrounding or neighboring state(s) wherein they are located. Yet, tribes frequently collaborate and cooperate with states through compacts or other agreements on matters of mutual concern such as environmental protection and law enforcement.

In 1953, Congress enacted Public Law 83-280 (67 Stat. 588) to grant certain states criminal jurisdiction over American Indians on reservations and to allow civil litigation that had come under tribal or federal court jurisdiction to be handled by state courts. However, the law did not grant states regulatory power over tribes or lands held in trust by the United States; federally guaranteed tribal hunting, trapping, and fishing rights; basic tribal governmental functions such as enrollment and domestic relations; nor the power to impose state taxes. These states also may not regulate matters such as environmental control, land use, gambling, and licenses on federal Indian reservations.

The states required by Public Law 280 to assume civil and criminal jurisdiction over federal Indian lands were Alaska (except the Metlakatla Indian Community on the Annette Island Reserve, which maintains criminal jurisdiction), California, Minnesota (except the Red Lake Reservation), Nebraska, Oregon (except the Warm Springs Reservation), and Wisconsin. In addition, the federal government gave up all special criminal jurisdiction in these states over Indian offenders and victims. The states that elected to assume full or partial jurisdiction were Arizona (1967), Florida (1961), Idaho (1963, subject to tribal consent), Iowa (1967), Montana (1963), Nevada (1955), North Dakota (1963, subject to tribal consent), South Dakota (1957-1961), Utah (1971), and Washington (1957-1963).

Subsequent acts of Congress, court decisions, and state actions to retrocede jurisdiction back to the Federal Government have muted some of the effects of the 1953 law, and strengthened the tribes' jurisdiction over civil and criminal matters on their reservations.

Tribal Government: Powers, Rights, and Authorities

Tribes possess all powers of self-government except those relinquished under treaty with the United States, those that Congress has expressly extinguished, and those that federal courts have ruled are subject to existing federal law or are inconsistent with overriding national policies. Tribes, therefore, possess the right to form their own governments; to make and enforce laws, both civil and criminal; to tax; to establish and determine membership (i.e., tribal citizenship); to license and regulate activities within their jurisdiction; to zone; and to exclude persons from tribal lands.

Limitations on inherent tribal powers of self-government are few, but do include the same limitations applicable to states, e.g., neither tribes nor states have the power to make war, engage in foreign relations, or print and issue currency.

For thousands of years, American Indians and Alaska Natives governed themselves through tribal laws, cultural traditions, religious customs, and kinship systems, such as clans and societies. Today, most modern tribal governments are organized democratically, that is, with an elected leadership.

Through their tribal governments, tribal members generally define conditions of membership, regulate domestic relations of members, prescribe rules of inheritance for reservation property not in trust status, levy taxes, regulate property under tribal jurisdiction, control the conduct of members by tribal ordinances, and administer justice. They also continue to utilize their traditional systems of self-government whenever and wherever possible.

Most federally recognized tribes are organized under the Indian Reorganization Act (IRA) of 1934 (25 USC. 461 et seq.), including a number of Alaska Native villages, which adopted formal governing documents under the provisions of a 1936 amendment to the IRA. The passage in 1971 of the Alaska Native Claims Settlement Act (43 USC. 1601), however, provided for the creation of regional and village corporations under state law to manage the money and lands granted to Alaska Natives by the act. The Oklahoma Indian Welfare Act of 1936 provided for the organization of Indian tribes within the State of Oklahoma.

Many tribes have constitutions, others operate under articles of association or other bodies of law, and some have found a way to combine their traditional systems of government within a modern governmental framework. Some do not operate under any of these acts, but are nevertheless organized under documents approved by the Secretary of the Interior. Contemporary tribal governments are usually, but not always, modeled upon the federal system of the three branches: Legislative, Executive, and Judicial.

The chief executive of a tribe is usually called a chairman, chairwoman or chairperson, but may also be called a principal chief, governor, president, mayor, spokesperson, or representative. The chief executive presides over the tribe's legislative body and executive branch. In modern tribal government, the chief executive and members of the tribal council or business committee are almost always elected.

A tribe's legislative body is usually called a tribal council, a village council, or a tribal business committee. It is comprised of tribal members who are elected by eligible tribal voters. In some tribes, the council is comprised of all eligible adult tribal members. Although some tribes require a referendum by their members to enact laws, a tribal council generally acts as any other legislative body in creating laws, authorizing expenditures, appropriating funds, and conducting oversight of activities carried out by the chief executive and tribal government employees. An elected tribal council and chief executive, recognized as such by the Secretary of the Interior, have authority to speak and act for the tribe as a whole, and to represent it in negotiations with federal, state, and local governments.

Furthermore, many tribes have established, or are building, their judicial branch – the tribal court system – to interpret tribal laws and administer justice.

Generally, tribal courts have civil jurisdiction over Indians and non-Indians who either reside or do business on federal Indian reservations. They also have criminal jurisdiction over violations of tribal laws committed by tribal members residing or doing business on the reservation.

Under 25 C.F.R. Part 115, tribal courts are responsible for appointing guardians, determining competency, awarding child support from Individual Indian Money (IIM) accounts, determining paternity, sanctioning adoptions, marriages, and divorces, making presumptions of death, and adjudicating claims involving trust assets. There are approximately 225 tribes that contract or compact with the BIA to perform the Secretary's adjudicatory function and 23 Courts of Indian Offenses (also known as CFR courts) which exercise federal authority. The Indian Tribal Justice Act of 1993 (P.L. 103-176, 107 Stat. 2005) supports tribal courts in becoming, along with federal and state courts, well-established dispensers of justice in Indian Country.

Congress has recognized the right of tribes to have a greater say over the development and implementation of federal programs and policies that directly impact on them and their tribal members. It did so by enacting two major pieces of legislation that together embody the important concepts of tribal self-determination and self-governance: The Indian Self-determination and Education Assistance Act of 1975, as amended (25 USC. 450 et seq.) and the Tribal Self-Governance Act of 1994 (25 USC. 458aa et seq.). Through these laws, Congress accorded tribal governments the authority to administer themselves the programs and services usually administered by the BIA for their tribal members. It also upheld the principle of tribal consultation, whereby the federal government consults with tribes on federal actions, policies, rules or regulations that will directly affect them.

The Federal Government is a trustee of Indian property, not a guardian of all American Indians and Alaska Natives. Although the Secretary of the Interior is authorized by law to protect, where necessary, the interests of minors and adult persons deemed incompetent to handle their affairs, this protection does not confer a guardian-ward relationship.

As early as 1817, US citizenship had been conferred by special treaty upon specific groups of Indian people. American citizenship was also conveyed by statutes, naturalization proceedings, and by service in the Armed Forces with an honorable discharge in World War I. In 1924, Congress extended American citizenship to all other American Indians born within the territorial limits of the United States. American Indians and Alaska Natives are citizens of the United States and of the individual states, counties, cities, and towns where they reside. They can also become citizens of their tribes or villages as enrolled tribal members.

American Indians and Alaska Natives have the right to vote just as all other US citizens do. They can vote in presidential, congressional, state and local, and tribal elections, if eligible. And, just as the federal government and state and local governments have the sovereign right to establish voter eligibility criteria, so do tribal governments.

American Indians and Alaska Natives have the same rights as other citizens to hold public office. Over the years, American Indian and Alaska Native men and women have held elected and appointed offices at all levels of federal, state, and local government. Charles Curtis, a member of the Kaw Tribe of Kansas, served in both houses of Congress before holding the second highest elected office in the nation – that of Vice President of the United States under President Herbert Hoover. American Indians and Alaska Natives also serve in state legislatures, state judicial systems, county and city governments, and on local school boards.

Any "special" rights held by federally recognized tribes and their members are generally based on treaties or other agreements between the tribes and the United States. The heavy price American Indians and Alaska Natives paid to retain certain rights of self-government was to relinquish much of their land and resources to the United States. US law protects the inherent rights they did not relinquish. Among those may be hunting and fishing rights and access to sacred sites.

They pay the same taxes as other citizens with the following exceptions:

Federal income taxes are not levied on income from trust lands held for them by the US

State income taxes are not paid on income earned on a federal Indian reservation.

State sales taxes are not paid by Indians on transactions made on a federal Indian reservation.

Local property taxes are not paid on reservation or trust land.

As US citizens, American Indians and Alaska Natives are generally subject to federal, state, and local laws. On federal Indian reservations, however, only federal and tribal laws apply to members of the tribe, unless Congress provides otherwise. In federal law, the Assimilative Crimes Act makes any violation of state criminal law a federal offense on reservations. Most tribes now maintain tribal court systems and facilities to detain tribal members convicted of certain offenses within the boundaries of the reservation.

American Indians and Alaska Natives come from a multitude of different cultures with diverse languages, and for thousands of years used oral tradition to pass down familial and cultural information among generations of tribal members. Some tribes, even if widely scattered, belong to the same linguistic families. Common means of communicating between tribes allowed trade routes and political alliances to flourish. As contact between Indians and non-Indians grew, so did the necessity of learning of new languages. Even into the 20th century, many American Indians and Alaska Natives were bi- or multilingual from learning to speak their own language and English, French, Russian, or Spanish, or even another tribal language.

It has been reported that at the end of the 15th century over 300 American Indian and Alaska Native languages were spoken. Today, fewer than 200 tribal languages are still viable, with some having been translated into written form. English, however, has become the predominant language in the home, school, and workplace. Those tribes who can still do so are working to preserve their languages and create new speakers from among their tribal populations.

American Indians and Alaska Natives live and work anywhere in the United States (and the world) just as other citizens do. Many leave their reservations, communities or villages for the same reasons as do other Americans who move to urban centers: to seek education and employment. Over one-half of the total US American Indian and Alaska Native population now live away from their tribal lands. However, most return home to visit relatives; attend family gatherings and celebrations; participate in religious, cultural, or community activities; work for their tribal governments; operate businesses; vote in tribal elections or run for tribal office; retire; or to be buried.

American Indians and Alaska Natives have a long and distinguished history of serving in our nation's Armed Forces. During the Civil War, American Indians served on both sides of the conflict. Among the most well-known are Brigadier General Ely S. Parker (Seneca), an aide to Union General Ulysses S. Grant who recorded the terms of Confederate General Robert E. Lee's surrender at Appomattox Courthouse in Virginia that ended the war, and Brigadier General Stand Watie (Cherokee), the last of the Confederate generals to cease fighting after the surrender was concluded. American Indians also fought with Theodore Roosevelt in the Spanish-American War.

During World War I over 8,000 American Indian soldiers, of whom 6,000 were volunteers, served. Their patriotism moved Congress to pass the Indian Citizenship Act of 1924. In World War II, 25,000 American Indian and Alaska Native men and women fought on all fronts in Europe and the South Pacific earning, collectively, at least 71 Air Medals, 51 Silver Stars, 47 Bronze Stars, 34 Distinguished Flying Crosses, and two Congressional Medals of Honor. Alaska Natives also served in the Alaska Territorial Guard.

Starting in World War I and again in World War II, the US military employed a number of American Indian servicemen to use their tribal languages as a military code that could not be broken by the enemy. These "code talkers" came from many different tribes, including Chippewa, Choctaw, Creek, Crow, Comanche, Hopi, Navajo, Seminole, and Sioux. During World War II, the Navajos constituted the largest component within that elite group.

In the Korean Conflict, one Congressional Medal of Honor was awarded to an American Indian serviceman. In the Vietnam War, 41,500 Indian service personnel served. In 1990, prior to Operation Desert Storm, some 24,000 Indian men and women were in the military. Approximately 3,000 served in the Persian Gulf with three among those killed in action. American Indian service personnel have also served in Afghanistan (Operation Enduring Freedom) and in Iraq (Operation Iraqi Freedom).

While American Indians and Alaska Natives have the same obligations for military service as other US citizens, many tribes have a strong military tradition within their cultures, and veterans are considered to be among their most honored members.

Bureau Offices

Indian Affairs–Office of Information Technology (IA–OIT)

IA–OIT supports the IT infrastructure that facilitates the fulfillment of the highly complex IA mission across all of its lines of business. IA–OIT supports the President's Management Agenda as aligned through the DOI and IA strategic plans. IA–OIT has established a Mission, Vision, Goals, and Objectives, Performance Measures, and Core Values. Additionally, it has aligned IT with business stakeholders in the IA organization, who oversee the various Lines of Business (LOB).

IA–OIT is responsible for providing information and technology leadership for all of Indian Affairs. The IA–OIT organization is comprised of approximately 300 staff members working throughout the nation servicing desktop computers, printers, network equipment, file/print servers, land mobile radio, Geospatial Information Systems, and other IT equipment.

Office of Congressional and Legislative Affairs - Indian Affairs (OCLA-IA)

Congressional and Legislative Affairs oversee and coordinate the legislative planning and congressional relations activities for Indian Affairs. The office provides legislative research and assistance in developing, drafting, and analyzing proposed legislation. These activities are coordinated with the Office of the Secretary to ensure consistency of Departmental communications with Congress. Legislative research and assistance are provided to program offices in developing and drafting legislation, preparing testimony, and providing legislative histories on various issues.

The Office responds to requests for information from congressional staff, the Department, other Federal Agencies, Tribal leadership, members and organizations, law firms, and the public at large, on various issues concerning American Indians and Alaska Natives. Congressional correspondence is coordinated through this office.

Office of Facilities, Environmental and Cultural Resources (OFECR)

The office is responsible for the management and administration of Indian Affairs facilities management and construction, environmental management, safety and risk management, and cultural resources management programs.

Office of Federal Acknowledgment (OFA)

The Office of Federal Acknowledgment (OFA) within the Office of the Assistant Secretary - Indian Affairs of the Department of the Interior (Department) implements Part 83 of Title 25 of the Code of Federal Regulations (25 CFR Part 83), Procedures for Establishing that an American Indian Group Exists as an Indian Tribe.

The acknowledgment process is the Department's administrative process by which petitioning groups that meet the criteria are given Federal "acknowledgment" as Indian tribes and by which they become eligible to receive services provided to members of Indian tribes. Through the Department's Office of the Solicitor, OFA makes recommendations to the Assistant Secretary - Indian Affairs (AS-IA). The AS-IA has the authority to make the decision whether to acknowledge tribal existence and establish a government-to-government relationship or to deny acknowledging a petitioning group as an Indian tribe.

By applying anthropological, genealogical, and historical research methods, OFA reviews, verifies, and evaluates groups' petitions for Federal acknowledgment as Indian tribes. OFA makes recommendations for proposed findings and final determinations to the AS-IA, consults with petitioners and third parties, provides copies of 25 CFR Part 83 and its guidelines, prepares technical assistance review letters, maintains petitions and administrative correspondence files, and conducts special research projects for the Department. OFA also performs other administrative duties that include maintaining lists of petitioners and responding to appeals, litigation, and Freedom of Information Act requests.

Since 1978, 356 groups have stated their intent to seek acknowledgment through the administrative process. Of this number, 269 groups have submitted only letters of intent or partially documented petitions, and are not ready for evaluation. The remaining 87 have submitted completed petitions. Of this number, the Department has resolved 55 and 19 have been resolved by Congress or through other means; the current OFA workload consists of 7 petitions under active consideration, while 2 petitions are ready and waiting for active consideration. Four petitioners elected suspension until revised regulations are considered. Two resolved decisions are in litigation in Federal court and two before the Interior Board of Indian Appeals.

Office of Homeland Security and Emergency Services (OHSES)

The Department of the Interior carries out its emergency management responsibilities and supports the National Response Framework (NRF) through the Office of Emergency Management and the eight constituent bureaus and agencies. The Office of Homeland Security and Emergency Services (OHSES) is responsible for overall coordination of all Indian Affairs emergency management responsibilities.

The Office was established in 2006. Its mission is to provide for a coordinated and comprehensive federal response to terrorist attacks, natural disasters or other large scale emergencies in Indian Country for the protection of its citizens, lands, critical infrastructure and key resources.

OHSES has partnered with the Department of Homeland Security to encourage tribal Law Enforcement/Homeland Security/Emergency Management officials to apply and obtain Secret Level Security Clearances from the Department of Homeland Security.

OHSES and the Department of Homeland Security are developing a Tribal Liaison Officer Program for Indian Country. This program prepares tribal officers to serve at State Intelligence Fusion centers. This program trains officer how to collect and utilize intelligence information to keep our Nation and Indian country safe from terror attacks.

OHSES is assisting with improving and maintaining the information flow between the Federal Government and Federally Recognized Indian Tribes.

The exchange of information/intelligence information on Law

Enforcement/Emergency Management/Homeland Security issues is critical to the security and safety of Indian Country and our Nation as a whole.

OHSES developed a Physical Security Inspection Program for all of Indian Affairs owned, and leased facilities. This program utilizes certified and credentialed Inspectors and collaborates with security managers and assigned officials to conduct onsite physical security assessments that insure compliance with Homeland Security Presidential Directive - 7 (HSPD-7), the National Infrastructure Protection Plan, and subsequent ancillary requirements including DOI 444 DM 1&2.

Office of Human Capital Management (OHCM)

The Office of Human Capital Management (OHCM) oversees human resources management, policy and operations for the Bureau of Indian Affairs, Bureau of Indian Education and the Assistant Secretary Indian Affairs. The Office of Human Capital Management reports to the Indian Affairs Deputy Assistant Secretary Management

Office of Indian Energy and Economic Development (IEED)

IEED's mission is to help Indian communities gain economic self-sufficiency through the development of their energy and mineral resources, application of established business practices, and co-sponsorship of innovative training programs. The office is made up of four Divisions:

Division of Energy and Mineral Development - Assists Tribes with the exploration, development, and management of their energy and mineral resources with the ultimate goal of creating jobs and sustainable tribal economies.

Division of Economic Development - Assists Tribes in creating an environment for economic progress through training, business planning, and expert consultation.

Division of Capital Investment - Manages the Indian Loan Guaranty Program to facilitate access to capital and loan financing for Indians.

Division of Workforce Development - Manages a wide variety of job placement and training programs to promote Indian employment opportunities.

Office of Indian Gaming (OIG)

The Office of Indian Gaming, under the supervision of the Deputy Assistant Secretary-Indian Affairs Economic Development and Policy, is responsible for implementing those gaming-related activities assigned to the Bureau of Indian Affairs by the Indian Gaming Regulatory Act and other Federal laws. The office develops policies and procedures for review and approval of: tribal/state compacts; per capita distributions of gaming revenues; and requests to take land into trust for purpose of conducting gaming. Work is coordinated with the National Indian Gaming Commission and with state, local, and tribal governments that may be impacted by gaming proposals.

Office of Internal Evaluation & Assessment (OIEA)

The Office of Internal Evaluation and Assessment (OIEA) provides guidance and oversight to Indian Affairs organizations to ensure that internal controls are established and maintained for all programs, organizations and functions. Additionally, OIEA assists and ensures that Indian Affairs organizations implement and comply with internal control guidelines established by the Department of the Interior, Office of Management and Budget (OMB), Government Accountability Office, etc. to include developing an annual internal control review plan, conducting internal control reviews/assessments, identifying and correcting program and operational deficiencies and developing the Indian Affairs Annual Assurance Statement for Internal Control to the Secretary of the Interior.

OIEA also provides guidance and oversight for audits of Tribal contractors and grantees and ensures Indian Affairs compliance with the Single Audit Act and OMB Circular A-133, Audits of States, Local Governments and Non-Profit Organizations. OIEA also conducts internal Indian Affairs' audits, investigations, and reviews to ensure programs achieve their intended results; resources are used consistent with agency mission; resources are protected from waste, fraud, and mismanagement; and compliance with laws, regulations, policies and procedures. The office also serves as the audit liaison/point of contact for all Indian Affairs organizations to the Department of the Interior, Assistant Secretary Policy, Management and Budget and Chief Financial Officer; Department of the Interior, Office of Inspector General; Government Accountability Office; and other agency Inspector Generals (e.g. Department of Education, Federal Communication Commission) pertaining to all audit issues to include Tribal audit matters.

Office of Planning & Performance Management (OPPM)

The Office of Planning and Performance Management (OPPM) provides guidance and technical assistance for Indian Affairs' performance management, focusing on results and the efficient delivery of those results to improve organizational effectiveness.

OPPMs role includes administering the Indian Affairs Performance Management System (IA-PMS) to manage the development, validation and verification of Indian Affairs' performance data; performance reporting to meet federal requirements such as Government Performance and Results Act (GPRA), Performance Improvement Initiative (PII), and the Performance and Accountability Report (PAR); and working to provide timely and effective guidance on the requirements, processes, and benefits of performance management.

The Vision of OPPM is to provide Indian Affairs with a set of business processes and support tools to streamline performance data collection and reporting; facilitating transparency and accountability to Congress, the public, and the Indian Affairs community.

Office of Public Affairs (OPA)

The Office of Public Affairs-Indian Affairs supports the Office of the Assistant Secretary-Indian Affairs, the Bureau of Indian Affairs and the Bureau of Indian Education by providing information on secretarial decisions and actions to news media and other entities interested in Indian Affairs via news releases, media relations, and the Indian Affairs website. It is the primary contact within Indian Affairs for journalists, writers, researchers and the public seeking general information about IA bureaus, offices, programs and activities; American Indians and Alaska Natives; federally recognized tribes; federal Indian laws and policies; and the history of federal-tribal relations as they relate to Indian Affairs.

The Office of Regulatory Affairs and Collaborative Action (RACA)

The Office of Regulatory Affairs and Collaborative Action (RACA), formerly known as the Office of Regulatory Management (ORM), is responsible for a broad range of regulatory functions that involve collaboration with all Indian Affairs (IA) bureaus, offices, tribal partners and other stakeholders, including: facilitating IA's compliance with the Administrative Procedures Act, Privacy Act, and Paperwork Reduction Act; developing and revising regulations to address statutory requirements and IA program issues; serving as the Department's regulatory contact for IA; managing the Federal Register notice process for IA; and providing guidance and assistance to facilitate the development, updating, and implementation of consistent IA policies, procedures, and handbooks. RACA also provides oversight, assistance, and implementation of the CORE PLUS dispute resolution program within IA.

Office of Self-Governance (OSG)

The Office is responsible for implementation of the Tribal Self Governance Act of 1994, including development and implementation of regulations, policies, and guidance in support of self-governance initiatives. The staff negotiates annual funding agreements with eligible tribes and consortia, coordinates the collection of budget and performance data from self-governance tribes, and resolves issues that are identified in financial and program audits of self-governance operations. The Office works with tribal governments to protect and support tribal sovereignty within a Government-to-Government partnership and to advocate for the transfer of Federal programmatic authorities and resources to tribal governments in accordance with tribal self-governance statutes and policies. The program staff work with self-governance tribes to implement and resolve issues or problems associated with self-governance agreements. Self-governance tribes represent nearly 40 percent of all federally recognized tribes nationwide. The Office provides financial management, budgeting, accounting and contracting services for an estimated $400 million in funds annually that are allocated or awarded to self-governance tribes, including reprogrammings within Operation of Indian Programs (OIP) and transfers from other Federal programs. This includes funds from Bureau of Land Management and additional manpower training funds under the Integration of Employment, Training, and Related Services Demonstration Act (Public Law 102-477).

In addition, allocation funding of $79 million from the Federal Highway Indian Reservation Roads (IRR) Program was assumed by the Office in 2007 increasing self-governance management responsibilities. The additional functions under the IRR program include new mandatory reporting requirements for Transportation Project Cost Accounting and Transportation Expenditure Processing. The office is responsible for implementing the Tribal Self-Governance Act, the Indian Self-Determination and Education Assistance Act (P.L. 93-638), and Joint Funding Simplification Act (P.L. 95-510) as they pertain to Indian Self-Determination. The Office develops and implements regulations, policies, and guidance in support of the Self-Governance initiatives; facilitate the negotiation of annual funding agreements with eligible tribes and consortia; coordinates the collection of budget and performance data from Self-Governance tribes; and resolves issues that are identified in financial and program audits of Self-Governance operations.

Bureau of Indian Education (BIE)

The BIE mission is to provide quality education opportunities from early childhood through life in accordance with the tribe's needs for cultural and economic well-being in keeping with the wide diversity of Indian tribes and Alaska Native villages as distinct cultural and governmental entities. The BIE also shall manifest consideration of the whole person by taking into account the spiritual, mental, physical, and cultural aspects of the person within his or her family and tribal or village context.

The Bureau is responsible for educating approximately 41,051 American Indian and Alaska Native children at 183 elementary and secondary schools on

64 reservations in 23 states. Of these, 58 are BIE-operated and 125 are tribally operated under BIE contracts or grants. The Bureau also funds or operates off-reservation boarding schools and peripheral dormitories near reservations for students attending public schools. The BIE also serves American Indian and Alaska Native post-secondary students through higher education scholarships and support funding for tribal colleges and universities. The BIE directly operates two post-secondary institutions: the Haskell Indian Nations University (HINU) in Lawrence, Kansas, and the Southwest Indian Polytechnic Institute (SIPI) in Albuquerque, New Mexico.

The school system employs approximately 5,000 teachers, administrators, and support personnel, while an estimated 6,600 work in tribal school systems.

The educational services the BIE provides is vital to current and future students who are their tribes' future.

Formerly known as the Office of Indian Education Programs, the Bureau of Indian Education (BIE) was renamed and established on August 29, 2006, to reflect the parallel purpose and organizational structure BIE has in relation to other programs within the Office of the Assistant Secretary-Indian Affairs. The BIE is headed by a Director, who is responsible for the line direction and management of all education functions, including the formation of policies and procedures, the supervision of all program activities and the approval of the expenditure of funds appropriated for education functions.

There have been three major legislative actions that restructured the Bureau of Indian Affairs (BIA) with regard to educating American Indians since the Snyder Act of 1921. First, the Indian Reorganization Act of 1934 introduced the teaching of Indian history and culture in BIA schools (until then it had been Federal policy to acculturate and assimilate Indian people by eradicating their tribal cultures through a boarding school system). Second, the Indian Self-Determination and Education Assistance Act of 1975 (P.L. 93-638) gave authority to federally recognized tribes to contract with the BIA for the operation of Bureau-funded schools and to determine education programs suitable for their children. The Education Amendments Act of 1978 (P.L. 95-561) and further technical amendments (P.L. 98-511, 99-99, and 100-297) provided funds directly to tribally operated schools, empowered Indian school boards, permitted local hiring of teachers and staff, and established a direct line of authority between the Education Director and the AS-IA. The No Child Left Behind Act of 2001 (P.L. 107-110) brought additional requirements to the schools by holding them accountable for improving their students' academic performance with the US Department of Education supplemental program funds they receive through the Bureau.

As stated in Title 25 CFR Part 32.3, BIE's mission is to provide quality education opportunities from early childhood through life in accordance with a tribe's needs for cultural and economic well-being, in keeping with the wide diversity of Indian tribes and Alaska Native villages as distinct cultural and governmental entities. Further, the BIE is to manifest consideration of the whole person by taking into account the spiritual, mental, physical, and cultural aspects of the individual within his or her family and tribal or village context. The BIE school system employs thousands of teachers, administrators and support personnel, while many more work in tribal school systems.

The Bureau of Indian Education (BIE), formerly known as the Office of Indian Education Programs (OIEP), is under the Assistant Secretary – Indian Affairs. It is responsible for the line direction and management of all BIE education functions, including the formation of policies and procedures, the supervision of all program activities, and the approval of the expenditure of funds appropriated for BIE education functions.

Indian Land Consolidation Program (ILCP)

The Mission of the Program is to acquire as many fractionated interests as economically feasible; to consolidate these land interests into tribal ownership to enable better tribal utilization; management, promote and enhance tribal self-determination, economic, social, and cultural development needs while reducing government administrative costs.

The Indian Land Consolidation Center (ILCC)

The ILCP Director manages the Indian Land Consolidation Program (ILCP) and coordinates the acquisition program using a systematic strategy to expand the program to reservations nationwide. The Director establishes policies, develops and implements cooperative agreements, provides technical assistance, and provides oversight, direction, monitoring, and program evaluation. The Director also coordinates with the BIA, the Department of the Interior (DOI), Office of Management and Budget (OMB), Congress, and other government entities and Tribal entities.

Benefits of Successful Consolidation:

Consolidation of fractionated ownership interests in the name of the Tribe/Band for benefit of all tribal members.

Increased opportunities for land use and business.

Creates more opportunities for land exchanges and/or partitionment with remaining owners.

Prevents loss of land and ownership from trust status

Long term savings to the government are realized through reduced administrative costs.

Office of Indian Services

Its mission is to facilitate support for tribal people and tribal governments by promoting safe and quality living environments, strong communities, self-sufficient and individual rights, while enhancing protection of the lives, prosperity and wellbeing of American Indians and Alaska Natives.

Office of Justice Services (OJS)

OJS is responsible for the protection of lives, resources, and property which lies at the heart of the BIA's law enforcement effort. BIA-OJS fully supports the Secretary's ongoing commitment to safe and healthy Indian communities. Under the direction of the Deputy BIA Director - Office of Justice Services, the Office of Justice Services (OJS) is responsible for the overall management of the Bureau's law enforcement program. Its main goal is to uphold the constitutional sovereignty of the Federally recognized Tribes and preserve peace within Indian country.

Office of Trust Services

The Office of Trust Services carries out Indian Affairs trust responsibilities to Indian tribes and individuals and oversees all headquarter activities **associated** with management and protection of trust and restricted lands, natural resources, and real estate services. The office provides land related functions to Indian trust owners including acquisition, disposal, rights-of-way, leasing and sales, and assists them in the management, development, and protection of trust land and natural resource assets. Programs administered include real estate services; land title and records; probate; natural resources; forestry and wildland fire management; irrigation, power and safety of dams. In more detail the six divisions are:

Division of Real Estate Services.

The division provides assistance, advice, policy, oversight, monitoring, and coordination for the protection, management, planning, conservation, development, and utilization of trust and restricted Federal Indian-owned lands that include acquisition, disposal, tenure, rights-of-way, permits, leasing, and sales. The division manages the Bureau's program to accept real estate on behalf of tribes under the Base Realignment and Closure Act and similar programs. The division manages the Cadastral Survey program for the determination of legal boundaries on Indian land.

Division of Land Titles and Records.

The division oversees policy development, deployment, and implementation of the title portion of the trust asset and accounting system, and oversees the administration and maintenance of title documents, document certification, title research and examination, and the determination of legal title for Federal Indian trust or restricted lands.

Division of Probate.

The division provides functional control, assistance, policy development coordination for probate programs, and monitors and evaluates probate operations. The division exercises program oversight and provides planning and scheduling of Bureau probate and assisted activities. The division coordinates the implementation of the Bureau's policies and procedures, to ensure that the probate initiatives meet the Secretary's fiduciary responsibilities and improves efficiency of services to tribes and individual Indians. The division is responsible for developing action plans and systems for probate programs and for developing and implementing improvements to the probate process. The division is responsible for management and implementation of probate-related outsourcing efforts and coordinates associated operations with other trust reform activities and other Departmental initiatives.

Division of Natural Resources.

The division provides coordination, management, planning, oversight, and monitoring for development and protection of trust natural resources, protection of Indian water rights, water development projects, litigation support, attorney's fees, and fish and wildlife resources. The Bureau's responsibilities under the Federal Power Act in re-licensing hydro-power projects that affect Indian trust resources are carried out in this division. The division provides direction and guidance for all activities related to the planning, management, conservation, development, and utilization of soil, water, farmland, rangeland, fish and wildlife resources, and endangered species. The division is responsible for the Bureau's natural resource damage assessment and restoration program.

Division of Forestry and Wildland Fire Management.

The division is responsible for providing coordination, management, planning, oversight, and monitoring for activities related to development, enhancement and protection of trust forest resources including the National Wildland Fire Program. The division exercises program oversight and provides planning and scheduling of Bureau-wide forestry activities at the national level to ensure that regulatory and policy requirements are followed and that technical standards of sound forest management are upheld. The division has staff in Washington, DC; Denver, CO; the National Interagency Fire Center in Boise, ID; and interagency fire coordination centers in Missoula, MT; Albuquerque, NM; and Oklahoma City, OK.

Division of Water and Power.

The division is responsible for irrigation construction, dam rehabilitation and the operation and maintenance of dams, irrigation, and power projects. The scope of responsibilities include, engineering management, operations and maintenance involving over 135 dams, numerous large irrigation projects, more than 100 irrigation systems and several large revenue generating power operations. The division is also responsible for flood plain management. This division is resource utilization oriented and functions as an engineering management and oversight operation. The Safety of Dams (SOD) program prepares capital asset plans for the major rehabilitation projects in accordance with the Capital Planning and Investment Control process. The SOD program, irrigation, and power programs report construction-in-progress to Bureau management officials, and conduct condition assessments to quantify the deferred maintenance backlog for budget justifications and reporting purposes.

6

Bureau of Safety and Environmental Enforcement

The Bureau of Safety and Environmental Enforcement (BSEE) was formally established on October 1, 2011 as part of a major reorganization of the Department of the Interior's offshore regulatory structure.

It works to promote safety, protect the environment, and conserve resources offshore through vigorous regulatory oversight and enforcement.

BSEE uses the full range of authorities, policies and tools to compel safety, emergency preparedness, environmental responsibility and appropriate development and conservation of offshore oil and natural gas resources. Key functions include:

an offshore regulatory program that develops standards and regulations and emphasizes a culture of safety in all offshore activities;

oil spill response preparation including review of industry Oil Spill Response Plans to ensure compliance with regulatory requirements;

environmental enforcement with a focus on compliance by operators with all applicable environmental regulations, as well as ensuring that operators adhere to the stipulations of their approved leases, plans and permits;

and funding scientific research to enhance the information and technology needed to build and sustain the organizational, technical and intellectual capacity within and across BSEE's key functions that keeps pace with industry technological improvements, innovates regulation and enforcement and reduces risk through systematic assessment and regulatory and enforcement actions in order to better carry out the BSEE mission.

The bureau maintains regional offices in Anchorage, Alaska, Camarillo, Calif., and New Orleans, La., with additional district offices along the Gulf of Mexico coast.

The Offshore Regulatory Program develops standards and regulations to enhance operational safety and environmental protection for the exploration and development of offshore oil and natural gas on the US Outer Continental Shelf (OCS).

The Oil Spill Response division is responsible for developing standards and guidelines for offshore operators' Oil Spill Response Plans (OSRP) through internal and external reviews of industry OSRPs to ensure compliance with regulatory requirements and coordination of oil spill drill activities. It also plays a critical role in the review and creation of policy, guidance, direction and oversight of activities related to the agency's oil spill response. The division oversees the Unannounced Oil Spill Drill program and works closely with sister agencies such as the US Coast Guard and Environmental Protection Agency to continually enhance response technologies and capabilities.

The newly created Environmental Enforcement Division is a first in the federal offshore energy regulatory program. This Division will provide sustained regulatory oversight that is focused on compliance by operators with all applicable environmental regulations, as well as making sure that operators keep the promises they make at the time they obtain their leases, submit their plans and apply for their permits.

BSEE is supported by three regional offices: New Orleans, La., Camarillo, Calif. and Anchorage, Alaska. The regional offices are responsible for reviewing Applications for Permit to Drill to ensure all of the recently implemented enhanced safety requirements are met and for conducting inspections of drilling rigs and production platforms using multi-person, multi-discipline inspection teams. BSEE's inspectors issue Incidents of Non-Compliance and have the authority to fine companies through Civil Penalties for regulatory infractions. Regional and field operations personnel also investigate accidents and incidents.

Strategic goals

To better fulfill its mandates from Congress and DOI and to guide its decisions toward the accomplishment of its mission, the Bureau embarked on a strategic planning effort. The BSEE FY 2012-2015 Strategic Goals focuses what has to be done through two strategies that will improve the Bureau's ability to create a robust, innovative, and stable regulatory system so that exploration and development of the Outer Continental Shelf (OCS) will be conducted safely.

In the development of this strategy, the Bureau considered not only its strengths, challenges, and recommendations from external stakeholders, but also the history and journey of its predecessors. The Deepwater Horizon disaster was the catalyst for the development of the bureau, and one it continues to learn from. The OCS is a complex environment with many challenges as well as the potential to contribute to the nation's energy future. In this plan are strategies that will position it to respond to today's challenges and prevent tomorrow's disasters.

The collective goals include instilling a stronger sense of safety and environmental responsibility among operators, while promoting compliance with regulation. It faces the challenges of keeping pace with technological and process innovations from operators and equipment manufacturers as well as developing analytic tools that will enable it to compare, assess, and identify risks earlier. To achieve these goals and overcome these challenges, it is building upon the skills of everyone at BSEE while also recruiting and retaining the best talent. This involves developing performance metrics that measure results and consistently communicate its progress.

Operators are taking action to reform their safety practices and are working with the Bureau and other federal leaders to develop and embrace safety cultures.

These goals provide the context and strategies that should enter into all decision-making for BSEE, guide the allocation of resources, and provide a basis for measuring BSEE's performance.

Strategic Goal 1

Regulate, enforce, and respond to OCS development using the full range of authorities, policies, and tools to compel safety, emergency preparedness and environmental responsibility and appropriate development and conservation of the offshore oil and natural gas resources.

- Properly define, assess, and differentiate risks
- Build clear, consistent, comprehensive and effective permitting processes
- Create, define, and expand regulatory approaches and tools
- Refine and enhance continuous offshore safety performance

Strategic Goal 2

Build and sustain the organizational, technical, and intellectual capacity within and across BSEE's key functions – capacity that keeps pace with OCS industry technological improvements, innovates in regulation and enforcement, and reduces risk through systemic assessment and regulatory and enforcement actions.

- Human capital transformation: recruiting, training, and retaining to reflect the increasing expertise needed
- technology and information management investment: revamp data systems, knowledge management, and innovation.

Divisions

Environmental Enforcement Division (EED)

EED Focus: To monitor, verify, improve, and enforce industry's compliance with environmental standards during Outer Continental Shelf (OCS) operations. These standards include, but are not limited to, environmental laws, regulations, and relevant provisions, stipulations, and conditions placed on OCS leases, plans, and permits. Its responsibilities include:

Environmental oversight in the Alaska OCS Regional Office (AKOCSR), Pacific OCS Regional Office (POCSR), and the Gulf of Mexico OCS Regional Office (GOMR);

EED policy, regulation, and program development and implementation;

Compliance with the National Environmental Policy Act (NEPA) regarding the permitting of the BSEE's OCS operations, and the monitoring of these activities;

Environmental compliance and enforcement activities;

Coordination with the Bureau of Ocean Energy Management (BOEM) and other Federal, State, and local agencies;

Public outreach efforts regarding environmental compliance; and

Support of the Alaska Region, Pacific Region and the Gulf of Mexico Region of the Outer Continental Shelf (OCS)

The Scientists and Engineers in EED carry out their responsibilities as BSEE's National Coordinators for the following Environmental Programs:

Archaeological Cultural Resources Program

A major part of BSEE's mission is protecting the environment offshore, including archaeological and cultural resources. One of the ways BSEE does this is by developing mitigation measures from consultation information as required by the National Historic Preservation Act (NHPA) and Department of the Interior Tribal Consultation Policy. These mitigation measures are developed into requirements attached to offshore energy leases, plans, and permits before they are approved. These stipulations, or conditions of approval, which generally require a Post Activity Submittal, that include surveys and videos that verify no harm came to archaeological and cultural resources.

The National Historic Preservation Act (NHPA) of 1966, as amended, is Federal legislation that mandates that the nation's historical and archaeological properties are not lost through neglect or inadvertently damaged by activities permitted or funded by Federal Bureaus and Agencies. As a federal bureau, BSEE is required by the NHPA to institute procedures to ensure that Federal plans and programs contribute to the preservation and enhancement of non-federally owned sites, structures and objects of historical, architectural, or archaeological significance.

BSEE is also responsible for preservation of archaeological properties under agency jurisdiction and control. BSEE meets this statutory obligation through its Archaeological/Cultural Resources Program and by enforcing our regulations, 30 CFR 250.194(c), which require immediate notification of the Regional Director in the event of the unanticipated discovery of an archaeological resource. In addition, BSEE works with the Bureau of Ocean Energy Management (BOEM) to ensure that archaeological sites on the Outer Continental Shelf (OCS) are not damaged during offshore energy development.

Archaeological sites are locations where past human activities are preserved for study, either prehistoric Native American sites or historic sites (offshore, these are typically historic shipwrecks).

NEPA Compliance

President Richard Nixon signed the National Environmental Policy Act (NEPA) into law on January 1, 1970. It was the first major environmental law in the United States. Congress recognized that the Federal Government's actions may cause significant environmental effects. These actions include issuing regulations, providing permits, making federal land management decisions, and many other types of actions. As such, every agency in the executive branch of the Federal Government is required to implement NEPA, including BSEE. NEPA analysis informs federal decision-makers of the potential environmental effects of a specified federal action. This analysis consists of scientific studies, public input, operational trends, and consultation and coordination with other Federal Agencies. BSEE uses the information in the NEPA analysis to develop mitigation strategies that protect our Nation's environmental resources as a part of our regulatory oversight of the Outer Continental Shelf (OCS).

Marine Trash and Debris (MT&D) Oversight

BSEE works to promote safety, protect the environment, and conserve resources offshore through vigorous regulatory oversight and enforcement.

BSEE protects the environment across the 1.7 billion acres of the US Outer Continental Shelf (OCS), including trash and debris from the offshore energy industry. The BSEE Marine Trash and Debris (MT&D) program focuses on education and regulation to minimize environmental damage on the OCS.

BSEE's Marine Trash and Debris Program is designed to eliminate debris associated with oil and gas operations on the Outer Continental Shelf (OCS). This is achieved by:

requiring safe practices for handling trash,

manifesting trash sent to shore,

displaying MT&D placards, and

providing educational training for all personnel working on offshore facilities.

There are many sources of marine trash and debris. Marine trash and debris includes any items in our oceans and coastal waters that people lose or purposely discard. Such items vary in their durability and may persist for months, years, and even for centuries. Items that are composed of organic materials (e.g., food, cotton, and paper) will decompose in weeks or months. However, inorganic items such as metals, synthetic materials, and plastics persist for very long durations and have become a significant problem in our oceans. The chart below depicts the estimated time it takes for various items of

MT&D to decompose. Glass is estimated to take up to a million years to decompose.

Plastics do not truly decompose. They do not "mineralize," which means to break down into their elemental parts, i.e., the minerals that compose them. They retain their basic structure as plastic, but just continue to break into smaller and smaller pieces. Eventually, the pieces get so small that they are the size of marine plankton. Researchers have found the concentration of plastic particles in the North Pacific Ocean currents is 45 times higher than the concentration of plankton in that area. Ocean currents concentrate floating particles, and this can be a significant problem. Animals that feed on plankton are also ingesting quantities of plastic.

Plastics in our oceans come from many sources. Land-based sources actually contribute a large portion of the MT&D to our oceans. Much debris is deposited directly into rivers and floats down to the sea. However, even debris that is deposited on the land itself can find its way into the ocean. For example, a plastic bag that held 20 pounds of ice can be lost from the back of a pick-up truck and fall into the ditch. The sun works on it and it starts breaking into smaller and smaller pieces. The next flooding rain washes the plastic pieces into the nearest creek or bayou, where it eventually finds its way into our coastal bays and into the ocean. Of course, boat traffic is another major source of debris in our oceans.

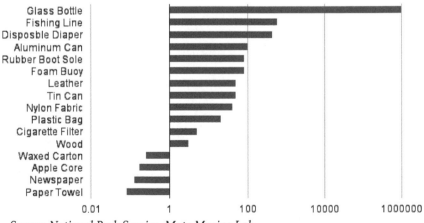

Source: National Park Service, Mote Marine Lab

Protected Species

A major part of BSEE's mission is protecting the environment offshore, including 'protected species.' BSEE does this by developing mitigation measures as a component of the National Environmental Policy Act (NEPA) analysis and incorporating information derived from biological assessments, biological opinions, and other science-based information as required by the Endangered Species Act (ESA) and Marine Mammal Protection Act (MMPA). The mitigation measures are developed into requirements attached to leases, plans, and permits as stipulations or conditions of permit approval to prevent harm from coming to our 'protected species.'

Protected species include those protected under the Endangered Species Act and the Marine Mammal Protection Act. On the Outer Continental Shelf (OCS) these include sea turtles, cetaceans, polar bears, pinnipeds, and manatees just to name a few. OCS activities that have increased protected species monitoring and mitigations include seismic surveys, drilling operations and explosive removals of offshore structures. Noise from these activities is of particular concern to marine mammals as they use sound to communicate, navigate, and detect predators and prey.

BSEE oversees oil and gas and renewable energy activities in the Alaska, Gulf of Mexico (GOM), and Pacific regions. Activities vary by region both in the amount of activity and the protected species present.

BSEE EED ensures that industry complies with all environmental laws, regulations, and relevant provisions, stipulations, and conditions placed on OCS leases, plans, and permits. There are a number of protected species requirements for industry operators when working on the OCS. These requirements are included in approvals or permits, but may also be summarized in Notices to Lessees (NTLs). Regional requirements, protected species information, stranding contacts, and other resources are provided below.

Rigs-to-Reefs (R2R) - Artificial Reef Program

Did you know?

Since December 2013, approximately 450 platforms had been converted to permanent artificial reefs in the Gulf of Mexico.

A typical eight-leg structure provides a home for 12,000 to14,000 fish, according to a study by the Coastal Marine Institute.

A typical four-leg structure provides two to three acres of habitat for hundreds of marine species.

Over the years, studies have documented a connection among fish and other marine life, fishing, and the oil and gas structures in the marine environment. Shortly after a platform is installed, it becomes habitat to marine life and communities begin to grow. Fishermen, divers, and coastal states have been concerned with the removal of these structures heavily-populated with marine life. BSEE began to work with interested parties and coastal states to address these concerns, creating Rigs to Reefs.

In 1984, the US Congress signed the National Fishing Enhancement Act (Public Law 98-623, Title II) because of increased interest and participation in fishing at offshore oil and gas platforms and widespread support for effective artificial reef development by coastal states. The Act recognizes the social and economic values in developing artificial reefs, establishes national standards for artificial reef development, provides for creation of a National Artificial Reef Plan, and provides for establishment of a reef-permitting system.

BSEE is responsible for permitting the placement and eventual removal of temporary facilities on the Federal Outer Continental Shelf (OCS). When an OCS Lease expires and/or development and production operations cease, companies are obligated to decommission and remove their facilities (30 CFR §250.1725(a)) and clear the seabed of all obstructions (30 CFR §250.1740). BSEE responded to coastal states' concerns about losing the marine life that had developed on and around these temporary oil and gas structures by adopting a national Rigs to Reefs policy.

The current BSEE Rigs to Reefs Policy began by first compiling a database of information to help understand and interpret ancillary uses of oil and gas structures and to inform decisions about the role of these structures in fisheries conservation and development.

BSEE initially negotiated an interagency agreement with the National Marine Fisheries Service (NMFS) in order to conduct studies with the participation of other participants such as Texas A&M University and the oil and gas industry.

Five objectives were identified in this cooperative agreement:

Develop a national policy that recognized the artificial reef benefits of oil and gas platforms

Prepare a Rigs to Reefs program plan for the Gulf of Mexico

Establish standard procedures to ensure and facilitate timely conversion of obsolete platforms as reefs

Identify research and studies necessary to optimize the use of platforms as reefs

Identify legal restrictions that could prevent using obsolete platforms as reefs

NMFS laid the foundation for Federal endorsement of offshore artificial reefs projects in 1985 when it developed and published the National Artificial Reef Plan under Title II of the National Fishing Enhancement Act of 1984 (33 USC 2101). Since 1985 BSEE has supported and encouraged the reuse of obsolete oil and gas platform jackets as artificial reef material and will grant a departure from removal requirements under 30 CFR §250.1725(a) and applicable lease obligations provided that:

The structure becomes part of a State reef program that complies with the National Artificial Reef Plan;

The State agency acquires a permit from the US Army Corps of Engineers and accepts title and liability for the reefed structure once removal/reefing operations are concluded;

The operator satisfies any US Coast Guard navigational requirements for the structure; and

The reefing proposal complies with BSEE engineering and environmental reviewing standards.

Rigs to Reefs At Work

First, a coastal state has to have an approved, state-specific artificial reef plan. All five Gulf of Mexico coastal states have approved artificial reef plans: Alabama, Florida, Louisiana, Mississippi, and Texas. All five Gulf States have incorporated decommissioned platforms into their artificial reef programs; however, Louisiana and Texas are the primary participants in Rigs to Reefs since the majority of platforms are installed offshore the two states.

Each state has an artificial reef coordinator, who assesses the state's interest in accepting an obsolete structure. The state coordinator identifies offshore areas which are suitable for reefing, whether existing or newly proposed reef sites, works with the operator to develop a reefing proposal and secures the required permit from the US Army Corps of Engineers.

When the proposed structure and reef site have been permitted, the state and operator negotiate the terms of an agreement for a donation from the operator to the state. In most cases, half of the cost benefits to the operator are donated to the state's artificial reef program. If decommissioning a structure costs $800,000 to remove, transport and scrap on shore, and reefing the structure will cut costs to $400,000, the operator would donate $200,000 to the state to assist with the management of their artificial reef program.

Concurrently, the operator submits an application for removal to BSEE, which includes the reefing proposal. A reef team reviews the proposal to ensure that all reefing requirements are met. These include the structure being sound, stable, clean, and overall beneficial to the environment, while protecting the Gulf of Mexico's natural resources.

After the state receives the Corps of Engineers' permit, and the proposal meets BSEE requirements, BSEE can grant the operator approval to convert the structure into an artificial reef. The title and liability for the structure is transferred from the operator to the state, once the operator converts the structure to a permanent artificial reef and has complied with all permits and donation agreements.

Three general methods are used for removing and "reefing" a retired structure: 1) tow-and-place, 2) topple-in-place, and 3) partial removal.

Tow-and-place involves severing the structure from the sea floor either using explosives or mechanical cutting techniques and then towing it to the selected reef for deployment.

Topple-in-place also detaches the structure from the seabed. The detached structure is then toppled onto its side.

Partial removal generally does not use explosives. The top portion of the structure is severed at a permitted navigational depth, typically 85 feet deep, and placed on the sea floor next to the base of the remaining structure.

Platform size, complexity, structural integrity and location are key considerations in evaluating its reefing potential. Complex, stable, durable and clean platforms are generally candidates for reefing. Platforms toppled due to structural failure are not candidates for reefing.

Benefits include:

For the environment, repurposing obsolete structures saves fuel emissions that otherwise would be expended transporting and disposing of the structure. It also enriches the marine life in the area.

For oil and gas companies, repurposing obsolete structures saves them the costs of removing, transporting, and disposing of them onshore. BSEE regulations require that, within one year of a lease's expiration, the obsolete structure must be removed.

For states, the artificial reefs attract marine life that enhance fisheries and contribute to the economy by attracting recreational and commercial fishing and diving.

For divers and recreational and commercial fishers, artificial reefs create a rich diversity of marine life.

For marine species, the artificial reefs provide habitat, shelter, food, and other necessary elements for biodiversity and a productive ocean.

The natural bottom of the Gulf of Mexico is a flat plain of clay, mud, and sand, offering very little natural hard bottom and reef habitat. Artificial reefs provide habitat that supports marine life.

Office of Offshore Regulatory Programs

The Office of Offshore Regulatory Programs (ORP) manages rules, standards, and compliance programs governing oil, gas, and mineral operations on the Outer Continental Shelf (OCS). ORP is responsible for
OCS regulations and the associated policy documents
Safety management programs
Safety and pollution prevention research
Technology assessments
Inspection and enforcement policies
Accident investigation practices
Development and execution of the agency's technical training program
ORP coordinates Bureau of Safety and Environmental Enforcement (BSEE) operational and safety programs with the US Coast Guard, other Federal and State agencies, industry groups, and international regulatory partners.

The ORP **Emerging Technologies Branch** (ETB) is charged with the identification, development and incorporation of new or emerging technologies into the BSEE regulatory program. The ETB works with accredited laboratories, standards organizations, and technical experts to evaluate the Best Available and Safest Technologies (BAST) suitable for use on an OCS facility.

The ORP **Safety and Environmental Management Systems Branch** (SEMS) provides guidance to assist the OCS industry in evaluating and improving their overall safety management systems. The SEMS program promotes an operator-driven system that continually improves safety culture and safety practices within the oil and gas industry. Recent achievements of the SEMS Program include publication of the SEMS II final Rule, the final Safety Culture Policy Statement, and the announcement of Safety Culture Public Workshops. BSEE implements practices of the SEMS Program and demonstrates a robust internal safety culture by promoting employee safety awareness through a variety of Bureau safety activities.

The ORP **Regulations and Standards Branch** directs the national program in the assessment, development, and promulgation of regulations and standards for the exploration and development of oil, gas, sulfur, and other minerals on the OCS.

The ORP **Offshore Safety Improvement Branch** is responsible for oversight of the Bureau's programs for inspection, aviation management, incident investigation and data analysis, and systems reliability.

The ORP **Offshore Training Branch** (OTB) develops and designs training and professional development opportunities for all BSEE employees. A primary focus of the OTB is to enhance the qualifications and capabilities of inspectors and engineers to enforce compliance with environmental laws and regulations, promote safety, and encourage proper stewardship and conservation of our nation's offshore resources.

The ORP **Civil Penalties and Enforcement Support Team** oversees the BSEE Civil Penalty and Enforcement Program. The goal of the OCS Civil Penalties Program is to assure safe and clean operations on the OCS. Through the pursuit, assessment, and collection of civil penalties, the program is designed to encourage compliance with OCS statutes and regulations.

Oil Spill Preparedness Division

The Bureau of Safety and Environmental Enforcement (BSEE) oversees oil spill planning and preparedness for US facilities located in both state and federal waters seaward of the coastline that handle, store or transport oil. This authority is granted through the Oil Pollution Act of 1990 and Executive Order 12777. All functions related to BSEE authorities in oil spill research, planning, preparedness and response are now handled through the National Oil Spill Program which is administered by the Oil Spill Preparedness Division (OSPD).

OSPD is headquartered in Herndon, Virginia, with regional offices located in New Orleans, Louisiana; Camarillo, California; and Anchorage, Alaska.

OSPD is responsible for carrying out BSEE authorities related to oil spill research, planning, preparedness, and response. Some of these functions include:

Reviewing and approving oil spill response plans.

Funding and dissemination of oil spill response research

Supporting the National Response Team, Regional Response Teams, Area Committees, and the Interagency Coordinating Committee on Oil Pollution Research (ICCOPR)

Providing subject matter expertise to the Federal On-Scene Coordinator during oil spills from regulated offshore facilities

Engaging with the international community to improve oil spill planning, preparedness, and response

Conducting government initiated unannounced exercises

Verifying that spill response resources are at optimal performance levels.

National Offshore Training Program

The National Offshore Training Program provides comprehensive, multi-tiered, professional development opportunities for BSEE inspectors and engineers. Its focus is to enhance the capabilities of these BSEE professionals to enforce safety and environmental regulations. In 2014, BSEE Professionals attended 23,396 hours of training.

The Program's mission is to develop and promote a culture of safety across BSEE at all levels, at all times to:

Reduce vulnerabilities by designing and delivering programs that meet the unique and varied needs of BSEE inspectors and engineers

Provide structured training opportunities that integrate the latest technical expertise and practices of industry with prudent and rigorous safety and compliance mandates.

Offer a world-class training program that serves as a model of professional development and continuing education.

The Bureau of Safety and Environmental Enforcement (BSEE) is a recognized world leader in offshore oil and gas regulation, research and technical assistance. Through various multilateral and bilateral relationships, BSEE is helping to set the standard for safety and environmental protection across a global industry. Bureau experts are routinely sought after to provide technical assistance and training to other nations who are working to develop their offshore energy resources in a safe and environmentally responsible manner.

BSEE engages in a range of bilateral, multilateral, and regional activities and discussions to promote safety and environmental protection in offshore energy activities. Efforts can range from information sharing with other offshore regulators to participation in multilateral venues and agreements. These include:

International Regulators Forum (IRF) is comprised of regulatory agencies with responsibilities for offshore facility safety. The first meeting was held in Houston in 1994, and annual meetings have been held subsequently. Currently, representatives from the US, the United Kingdom, Brazil, Norway, Canada, the Netherlands, Australia, New Zealand, and Mexico participate in the IRF. Participants share information on technological advances, safety issues, accident investigations, regulatory policies, international standards and conventions, performance measurement, and research. Members may also exchange personnel, and establish reciprocal agreements.

International Forum of Offshore Petroleum Environmental Regulators (IOPER) is an international forum of offshore petroleum environmental regulators dedicated to the common cause of raising offshore environmental performance. Membership flows from the older International Regulators Forum (IRF). IOPER is similar to IRF, but focuses on environmental performance. IOPER members represent major oil and gas producing countries. IOPER is focused on regulatory issues associated with environmental impacts rather than the International Regulator's Forum safety and health concerns. Information shared between members and discussions can potentially affect the decision-making of the member regulatory agencies. IOPER does not aim to drive international regulatory or policy actions, but to encourage cross feed of ideas.

International Oil Spill Conference provides a vital forum for professionals from the international response community, private sector, government, and non-governmental organizations to come together to tackle oil spill challenges with sound science, practical innovation, social engineering and imagination. This conference is an ideal environment for government agencies, contractors, researchers, industry, and other stakeholders to work together toward mutual objectives, through the exchange of ideas and lessons learned from actual spill responses and research around the world.

Memorandum of Understanding Regarding Cooperation Between BSEE and the National Energy Board of Canada.

BSEE and Canada's National Energy Board (NEB) signed a Memorandum of Understanding (MOU) in February, 2013 to share regulatory best-practices and to mutually work together to benefit workplace safety in offshore oil and gas exploration and production. Prior to the MOU with the NEB, Canada and the US had formal agreements since 1986.

US Mexico Transboundary Hydrocarbon Agreement

Some oil and gas reserves below the Gulf of Mexico cross the international maritime boundary between the two countries. The Agreement provides a mechanism to facilitate the safe and efficient exploration and exploitation of hydrocarbon resources along the maritime boundary and provides new opportunities for US companies. The Agreement is designed to enhance North American energy security and support the United States' and Mexico's shared duty to exercise responsible stewardship of the Gulf of Mexico. It is built on a commitment to the safe, efficient, and equitable exploitation of transboundary reservoirs. The Mexican Senate ratified the Agreement the following April, and Mexican President Calderon issued a final decree on May 22, 2012. On December 26, 2013, authority to implement the agreement was granted to the Secretary of the Interior Public Law No: 113-67.

International Committee on Regulatory Authority Research and Development (ICRARD) The offshore oil and gas industry is an international organization. Major companies operate in many countries, and in each, certain organizations assess and ensure the use of sound technological developments. ICRARD's purpose is to coordinate research activities, to exchange information, and to promote research cooperation between these organizations. The ICRARD is open for membership to any country interested.

The **Energy Governance and Capacity Initiative (EGCI)** is a US Department of State-led, US inter-agency effort to provide a wide range of technical and capacity building assistance to the host governments of select countries that are on the verge of becoming the world's next generation of oil and gas producers. The countries receiving EGCI assistance have world class hydrocarbon resource potential and expect to receive sizable, near-term financial windfalls from the development of their oil and gas resources. EGCI's core objective is to help these countries establish the capacity to manage their oil and gas sector revenues wisely and in a manner that maximizes the value of the resource development for the government. Although EGCI's goals are country-specific in nature, the program broadly tries to ensure sound and transparent energy sector governance for the benefit of national economic development. EGCI also supports a broad range of US foreign policy objectives, including ensuring the security of global oil and gas supplies, supporting clean energy goals by maximizing the efficiency of oil and gas resource development, furthering political and economic stability in developing countries, promoting democracy and human rights, and combating corruption.

Interagency Collaboration

BSEE's responsibilities for the regulation of offshore energy development on the US Outer Continental Shelf (OCS) often overlap with the responsibilities and regulations of other federal agencies. The Bureau works closely with our partners to ensure we approach this shared regulatory space in an efficient and consistent manner. The Bureau also leverages its limited resources through agreements with federal partners and other agencies through memoranda of understanding or agreement (MOU, MOA) and interagency agreements.

7

National Park Service

Did You Know?

The largest National Park is Wrangell-St. Elias National Park and Preserve, in Alaska covering 13.2 million acres, and the smallest is Thaddeus Kosciuszko National Memorial, Pennsylvania at just 0.02 acres.

The National Park service employs 22,000 permanent, temporary and seasonal staff supported my more than 221,000 volunteers.

Every Year our National Parks attract more than 292,800,082 visitors.

Our National parks contain many of the nation's most treasured landscapes, from the majestic mountain ranges of Alaska to the vast sawgrass prairies of the Everglades.

The national park system comprises 407 areas covering more than 84 million acres in every state, the District of Columbia, American Samoa, Guam, Puerto Rico, and the Virgin Islands. These areas include national parks, monuments, battlefields, military parks, historical parks, historic sites, lakeshores, seashores, recreation areas, scenic rivers and trails, and the White House.

To safeguard these treasures, the National Park Service has a budget of $3.65 billion (FY 2015) and combines the best available science with innovative education and stewardship programs, such as Biodiversity Discovery, the Climate Change Youth Initiative, and Geoscientists-in-Parks.

A little history

The idea of a "national park" must have jarred strangely the nineteenth century intellects upon which the words of a Montana lawyer fell as he spoke from the shadows of a campfire in the wilderness of the Yellowstone one autumn night 70 years ago. For Cornelius Hedges addressed a generation dedicated to the winning of the West. He spoke at a time when stout hearted pioneers had their faces determinedly set toward the distant Pacific as they steadily pushed the frontier of civilization and industrialization across prairie and mountain range to claim the land for a Nation between the coasts. His plan was presented to men cast of that die-men whose courage and enterprise characterized the era in which they lived.

But Cornelius Hedges had looked deeply into American character and was not disappointed. He counted upon the altruism which marked that character, and planted in it the ideal which instantly took root and has since flowered as one of America's greatest treasures: the national park system.

The man who broached the national park idea to those men of courageous spirit who comprised the Washarn-Langford-Doane Expedition for exploration of the Yellowstone was indeed the most courageous of all. This expedition of 1870 had set out at its own expense to investigate once and for all the incredible stories of natural wonders which had been coming out of the region for years, from the time the first scouts of fur trading companies blazed their trails across the fantastic wonderland. They found that all of it was true, and that the tallest yarns of the wildest spinners of tales (except perhaps the notorious Jim Bridger, who later simply embellished what nature had already provided) could hardly outstrip what the eye itself beheld. Here were the geysers shooting their columns of boiling water and steam into the sky; here were the hot pools, the mud volcanoes, and other strange phenomena. Here were the gigantic falls of the Yellowstone River in its gorgeously tinted canyon a thousand feet deep. Here were the forests and the abundance of wildlife in every form native to the region. Here, indeed, was a fairyland of unending wonders.

As they sat around their campfire the night of September 19, 1870 near the juncture of the Firehole and Gibbon Rivers (now called Madison Junction), the members of the party quite naturally fell to discussing the commercial value of such wonders, and laying plans for dividing personal claims to the land among the personnel of the expedition. It was into this eager conversation that Hedges introduced his revolutionary idea. He suggested that rather than capitalize on their discoveries, the members of the expedition waive personal claims to the area and seek to have it set aside for all time as a reserve for the use and enjoyment of all the people. The instant approval which this idea received must have been gratifying to its author, for it was a superb expression of civic consciousness.

As the explorers lay that night in the glow of dying embers, their minds were fired with a new purpose. In fact, some of them later admitted that prospects of the campaign for establishment of the Nation's first national park were so exciting that they found no sleep at all.

This, then, was the birth of the national park idea. The idea became a reality, and the reality developed into a system which, through the years, has grown to embrace 21,011,778.58 acres of land and water including 25 national parks, 80 national monuments, and 45 national historical parks, national battlefields and other various classifications of areas.

The advocates of the national park idea lost no time in following their plan through. First steps for carrying out the project to create Yellowstone National Park were taken at Helena, Montana, principally by Cornelius Hedges, Nathaniel P. Langford, and William H. Clagett. Fortunately for the plan, Clagett had just been elected delegate to Congress from Montana and was in a splendid position to advance the cause. In Washington he and Langford drew up the park bill which was introduced in the House of Representatives by the Montana delegate on December 18, 1871.

During the preceding summer, the U. S. Geological Survey had changed its program of field work so as to give attention to the wonders described by the civilian explorers. Two Government expeditions, one under Dr. F. V. Hayden and the other under Captains Barlow and Heap of the Engineer Corps of the Army, had traveled together in making Yellowstone studies. W. H. Jackson, who continues to this day to serve as a collaborator on national park studies, was a member of the Hayden party. He obtained a remarkably fine series of Yellowstone photographs, samples of which Dr. Hayden placed on the desks of all Senators and Congressmen.

In other ways, Dr. Hayden joined Clagett and his Montana constituents in influencing the passage of the National Park Act. Finally a copy of it was carried personally by Mr. Clagett to the Senate where it was introduced by Senator Pomeroy of Kansas. In response to a request from the House

Committee on Public Lands for his opinion, the Secretary of the Interior endorsed the bill. The measure was put through after perhaps the most intensive canvass accorded any bill, in which all the members of Congress were personally visited and, with few exceptions, won over to its support. It was adopted by the House on January 30, 1872, passed by the Senate on February 27, and received the signature of President Grant on March 1.

For the first time the Government had acted to conserve land for a new purpose. The term "conservation," so commonly applied to coal, iron, or other raw materials of industry, was now applied to mountains, lakes, canyons, forests and other great and unusual works of nature, and interpreted in terms of public recreation.

Early Growth and Administration

The United States had a system of national parks for many years before it had a National Park Service. Even before establishment of Yellowstone National Park in 1872 as "a public park or pleasuring-ground for the benefit and enjoyment of the people," the Government had shown some interest in public ownership of lands valuable from a social use standpoint. An act of Congress in 1852 established the Hot Springs Reservation in Arkansas (which became a national park in 1921), although this area was set aside not for park purposes, but because of the medicinal qualities believed to be possessed by its waters. It was not until 1890 that action was taken to create more national parks. That year saw establishment of Yosemite, General Grant, and Sequoia National Parks in California, and nine years later Mount Rainier National Park was set aside in Washington.

Soon after the turn of the century the chain of national parks grew larger. Most important since the Yellowstone legislation was an act of Congress approved June 8, 1906, known as the Antiquities Act, which gave the President authority "to declare by public proclamation historic landmarks, historic and prehistoric structures, and other objects of scientific interest that are situated

upon the lands owned or controlled by the Government of the United States to be national monuments."

In these early days the growing system of national parks and monuments was administered under no particular organization. National parks were administered by the Secretary of the Interior, but patrolled by soldiers detailed by the Secretary of War much in the manner of forts and garrisons. This, of course, was quite necessary, in the early days, for the protection of areas situated in the "wild and woolly" West. it is a fact that in this era highwaymen held up coaches and robbed visitors to Yellowstone National Park, and poachers operated within the park boundaries. The national monuments were administered in various ways. Under the Act of 1906 monuments of military significance were turned over to the Secretary of War, those within or adjacent to national forests were placed under the Department of Agriculture, and the rest—and greater number—were under the jurisdiction of the Department of the Interior. Chickamauga-Chattanooga National Military Park, established in 1890 as the first Federal area of its type, was administered by the War Department.

Under this disjointed method of operation, national parks and monuments continued to be added to the list until 1915 when its very deficiencies exposed the plan as unsatisfactory and inefficient. The various authorities in charge of the areas began to see the need for systematic administration which would provide for the adoption of definite policies and make possible proper and adequate planning, development, protection, and conservation in the public interest.

National Park Service Created

Realizing the specialized nature of national park work and the desirability of unifying the parks into one integrated system, Secretary of the Interior Franklin K. Lane in 1915 induced the late Stephen T. Mather to accept appointment as his assistant to take charge of park matters. A keen lover of the out-of-doors, Mr. Mather accepted the appointment because he saw in it an

opportunity to devote his energies to the furtherance of national parks. Under his efficient leadership the work was coordinated and expanded, and, on August 25, 1916, President Wilson signed a bill creating the National Park Service as a separate bureau of the Department of the Interior. The Service was organized in 1917.

Senator Reed Smoot of Utah and Representative William Kent of California sponsored the bills in Congress which resulted in establishment of the Service. Representative Kent's bill was passed by the House on July 1, 1916, and the Smoot bill was passed by the Senate as amended, August 5, 1916. (Mr. Kent had previously introduced three similar bills, and one had also been introduced in the House by Representative John E. Raker of California.) The Senate amendments were disagreed to by the House, and conferees were appointed to consider them. The conference report was made and agreed to in the Senate on August 15, and in the House on August 22.

Efforts to obtain the necessary legislation for establishment of the Service had, in fact, been carried on for many years. President Taft sent a special message to Congress on February 2, 1912, in which he said: "I earnestly recommend the establishment of a Bureau of National Parks. Such legislation is essential to the proper management of those wondrous manifestations of nature, so startling and so beautiful that everyone recognizes the obligations of the Government to preserve them for the edification and recreation of the people." As the movement grew it involved the active support of many civic leaders interested in the conservation of lands for parks and recreation. Prominent among these was Dr. J. Horace McFarland of Harrisburg, Pennsylvania, who is now a member of the Board of Directors of the American Planning and Civic Association. As president for 20 years of the former American Civic Association, which he founded, Dr. McFarland focused public opinion upon the need for a Government bureau to take charge of national parks. The act creating the Service was largely the result of consultation between officials of the Department of the Interior and Dr. McFarland, Frederick Law Olmsted, and the late Henry A. Barker, representing the American Civic Association.

Dr. McFarland's efforts began as early as 1908 when he addressed a conference of governors called by President Theodore Roosevelt to consider

measures for conservation of the country's natural resources. He alone, among speakers at the conference, urged the conservation of scenery. Said he:

"The scenic value of all the national domain yet remaining should be jealously guarded as a distinctly important natural resource, and not as a mere incidental increment. In giving access for wise economic purposes to forest and range, to valley and stream, the Federal Government should not for a moment overlook the safeguarding to the people of all the natural beauty now existing. That this may be done without preventing legitimate use of all the other natural resources is certain."

The American Civic Association continued its support of the national park movement, devoting its 1911 and 1912 annual meetings to that subject. When Mr. Lane became Secretary of the Interior in President Wilson's cabinet, Dr. McFarland called on him to urge the establishment of a bureau to administer the national parks. During the period preceding enactment of the bill to create the Service, Dr. McFarland, Mr. Olmsted and others carried on negotiations for keeping Congress informed, and worked untiringly through the American Civic Association for passage of the bill.

Merged in 1935 with the National Conference on City Planning to form the American Planning and Civic Association, the organization founded by Dr. McFarland continues its active support of the national parks.

Mr. Mather became the first director of the National Park Service, and put into his work all the energy and enthusiasm possible for a true lover of nature and one who appreciated the importance of proper control of park areas in order to permit use without damage or destruction. He even spent large sums from his personal fortune to acquire needed additions of land for parks, or to further necessary development operations. He was forced by ill health to tender his resignation on January 8, 1929.

Mr. Mather was succeeded by Horace M. Albright, who had come into the new Bureau as assistant to the Director. Mr. Albright had also served for nine and one-half years as superintendent of Yellowstone National Park, and thus was well grounded in the work when he assumed the directorship. Under his leadership the Service established a Branch of Research and Education and expanded its landscape architectural work. The national park system grew with the addition of three national parks and ten national cemeteries during his regime, and, under an Executive Order by the President, was given jurisdiction over park and monument areas formerly administered by the Departments of War and Agriculture.

Mr. Albright resigned as director, effective August 9, 1933, to become vice-president and general manager of the United States Potash Company, after 20 years of service in the Department of the Interior. He left behind him the most advanced ideas and ideals in conservation of natural resources for recreation, and still maintains his interest in park work as president of the American Planning and Civic Association, and a director of the National Conference on State Parks.

Arno B. Cammerer, the present director of the National Park Service, was appointed to succeed Mr. Albright. He also carried to the office a broad background in park work, having been acting director on many occasions. He entered the Federal Service in 1904 as an expert bookkeeper in the Treasury Department, and was promoted through numerous higher positions to that of private and confidential clerk to several assistant secretaries of the Treasury. In 1916 he was chosen assistant secretary to the National Commission of Fine Arts, serving at the same time as first secretary of the Public Buildings Commission of Congress. In that period he served in various confidential capacities with officers in charge of Public Buildings and Grounds in connection with the parkway system of Washington, the Rock Creek and Potomac Parkway, and the construction of the Lincoln Memorial and various other monumental structures in the National Capital.

Mr. Cammerer joined the National Park Service in 1919 when Mr. Albright resigned the assistant directorship to become superintendent of Yellowstone National Park. The present director was selected by Mr. Mather and Secretary Lane to succeed Mr. Albright as assistant director. Later, as the activities of the Service expanded, he was made associate director.

Outstanding has been Director Cammerer's work in the interest of the eastern park projects, including the Great Smokies, Shenandoah, Mammoth Cave, and Isle Royale. He represented the Secretary of the Interior personally in negotiations between the Federal Government and the states and various organizations engaged in acquiring the lands necessary for the establishment of these parks, worked out the park boundaries with the various state commissions, and in other ways assisted in bringing the projects materially nearer consummation.

From its beginning, the National Park Service has been as fortunate in the caliber of men attracted to its ranks as in the fidelity of the friends of national parks who worked for the establishment of the Service and have since supported its program.

One of the most valuable men who entered the Service soon after its organization was Roger W. Toll, superintendent of three national parks, who met death in an unavoidable automobile accident in 1936. Mr. Toll's wide knowledge of and experience in mountaineering, engineering, and general park problems made him especially valuable to the Service in the study of areas proposed for national park status, and several months each year he represented the Director in the investigation of such areas.

At the time of the accident which caused his death and the death of George M. Wright, chief of the Wildlife Division, Mr. Toll was serving with his companion as a member of a commission of six appointed by the Secretary of State, at the request of the Secretary of the Interior, and with the approval of the President, to meet a similar committee appointed by the Mexican Government, for the purpose of studying possibilities of international parks and wildlife refuges along the international boundary between the United States and Mexico.

Mr. Wright, although only 32 years old, had also had a distinguished career in the Service. While studying forestry at the University of California, he accompanied Joseph S. Dixon, at that time economic mammalogist of the University, on an expedition to Mount McKinley, Alaska, where he discovered the nest of the surf bird. After graduation, he held positions as ranger and junior park naturalist in Yosemite National Park, and became chief of the Wildlife Division when it was established on May 3, 1933.

Various acts of Congress and regulations set up by the Department and the Service have, during the years, become resolved into general policies for the protection, conservation, and administration of the national park and monument system. These policies were best set forth by Louis C. Cramton, special attorney to the Secretary of the Interior, the results of whose studies were incorporated in the annual report of the Director to the Secretary for the fiscal year ended June 30, 1932.

They are:

- A national park is an area maintained by the Federal Government and "dedicated and set apart for the benefit and enjoyment of the people." Such Federal maintenance should occur only where the preservation of the area in question is of national interest because of its outstanding value from a scenic, scientific, or historical point of view. Whether a certain area is to be so maintained by the Federal Government as a national park should not depend upon the financial capacity of the state within which it is located, or upon its nearness to centers of population which would insure a large attendance therefrom, or upon its remoteness from such centers which would insure its majority attendance from without its state. It should depend up on its own outstanding scenic, scientific, or historical quality and the resultant national interest in its preservation.

- The national-park system should possess variety, accepting the supreme in each of the various types and subjects of scenic, scientific, and historical importance. The requisite national interest does not necessarily involve a universal interest, but should imply a wide-spread interest, appealing to many individuals, regardless of residence, because of its outstanding merit in its class.

- The twin purposes of the establishment of such an area as a national park are its enjoyment and use by the present generation, with its preservation unspoiled for the future; to conserve the scenery, the natural and historical objects and the wild life therein, by such means as will insure that their present use leaves them unimpaired. Proper administration will retain these areas in their natural condition, sparing them the vandalism of improvement. Exotic animal or plant life should not be introduced. There should be no capture of fish or game for purposes of merchandise or profit and no destruction of animals except such as are detrimental to use of the parks now and hereafter. Timber should never be considered from a commercial standpoint but may be cut when necessary in order to control the attacks of insects or disease or otherwise conserve the scenery or the natural or historic objects, and dead or down timber may be removed for protection or improvement. Removal of antiquities or scientific specimens should be permitted only for reputable public museums or for universities, colleges, or other recognized scientific or educational institutions, and always under department supervision and careful restriction and never to an extent detrimental to the interest of the area or of the local museum.

- Education is a major phase of the enjoyment and benefit to be derived by the people from these parks and an important service to individual development is that of inspiration. Containing the supreme in objects of scenic, historical, or scientific interest, the educational opportunities are preeminent, supplementing rather than duplicating those of schools and colleges, and are available to all. There should be no governmental attempt to dominate or to limit such education within definite lines. The effort should be to make available to each park visitor as fully and effectively as possible these opportunities, aiding each to truer interpretation and appreciation and to the working out of his own aspirations and desires, whether they be elementary or technical, casual or constant.

- Recreation, in its broadest sense, includes much of education and inspiration. Even in its narrower sense, having a good time, it is a proper incidental use. In planning for recreational use of the parks, in this more restricted meaning, the development should be related to their inherent values and calculated to promote the beneficial use thereof by the people. It should not encourage exotic forms of amusement and should never permit that which conflicts with or weakens the enjoyment of these inherent values.

- These areas are best administered by park-trained civilian authority.

- Such administration must deal with important problems in forestry, road building and wild life conservation, which it must approach from the angles peculiar to its own responsibilities. It should define its objectives in harmony with the fundamental purposes of the parks. It should carry them into effect through its own personnel except when economy and efficiency can thereby best be served without sacrifice of such objectives, through cooperation with other bureaus of the Federal Government having to do with similar subjects. In forestry, it should consider scenic rather than commercial values and preservation rather than marketable products; in road building, the route, the type of construction and the treatment of related objects should all contribute to the fullest accomplishment of the intended use of the area; and, in wild life conservation, the preservation of the primitive rather than the development of any artificial ideal should be sought.

- National park administration should seek primarily the benefit and enjoyment of the people rather than financial gain and such enjoyment should be free to the people with out vexatious admission charges and other fees.

- Every effort is to be made to provide accommodations for all visitors, suitable to their respective tastes and pocketbooks. Safe travel is to be provided for over suitable roads and trails. Through proper sanitation the health of the individual and of the changing community is always to be protected.

- Roads, buildings, and other structures necessary for park administration and for public use and comfort should intrude upon the landscape or conflict with it only to the absolute minimum.

- The national parks are essentially noncommercial in character and no utilitarian activity should exist therein except as essential to the care and comfort of park visitors.

- The welfare of the public and the best interests of park visitors will be conserved by protective permits for utilities created to serve them in transportation, lodging, food, and incidentals.

- The national interest should be held supreme in the national-park areas and encroachments conflicting therewith for local or individual benefit should not be permitted.

- Private ownership or lease of land within a national park constitutes an undesirable encroachment, setting up exclusive benefits for the individual as against the common enjoyment by all, and is contrary to the fundamental purposes of such parks.

- National parks, established for the permanent preservation of areas and objects of national interest, are intended to exist forever. When under the general circumstances such action is feasible, even though special conditions require the continuance of limited commercial activities or of limited encroachments for local or individual benefit, an area of national-park caliber should be accorded that status now, rather than to abandon it permanently to full commercial exploitation and probable destruction of its sources of national interest. Permanent objectives highly important may thus be accomplished and the compromises, undesired in principle but not greatly destructive in effect, may later be eliminated as occasion for their continuance passes.

- In a national park the national laws and regulations should be enforced by a national tribunal. Therefore, exclusive jurisdiction of the Federal Government is important.

- National monuments, under jurisdiction of the Department of the Interior, established to preserve historic landmarks, historic and prehistoric structures, and other objects of scientific or historical interest, do not relate primarily to scenery and differ in extent of interest and importance from national parks, but the principles herein set forth should, so far as applicable, govern them.

Since its establishment as a bureau of the Department of the Interior for the care and administration of the national park system, the duties and responsibilities of the National Park Service have been steadily extended by acts of Congress and Executive Orders. One of the most important of these was President Franklin D. Roosevelt's Executive Order of June 10, 1933 which effected consolidation, two months later, of all Federal park activities under the Service.

This Order provided:

"All functions of administration of public buildings, reservations, national parks, national monuments and national cemeteries are consolidated in an Office of National Parks, Buildings, and Reservations in the Department of the Interior, at the head of which shall be a Director of National Parks, Buildings, and Reservations; except that where deemed desirable there may be excluded from this provision any public building or reservation which is chiefly employed as a facility in the work of a particular agency. This transfer and consolidation of functions shall include, among others, those of the National Park Service of the Department of the Interior, and the National Cemeteries and Parks of the War Department which are located within the continental limits of the United States. National cemeteries located in foreign countries shall be transferred to the Department of State, and those located in insular possessions under the jurisdiction of the War Department shall be administered by the Bureau of Insular Affairs of the War Department.

"The functions of the following agencies are transferred to the Office of National Parks, Buildings, and Reservations of the Department of the Interior, and the agencies are abolished:
Arlington Memorial Bridge Commission
Public Buildings Commission
Public Buildings and Public Parks of the National Capitol
National Memorial Commission
Rock Creek and Potomac Parkway Commission

"Expenditures by the Federal Government for the purposes of the Commission of Fine Arts, the George Rogers Clark Sesquicentennial Commission, and the Rushmore National Commission shall be administered by the Department of the Interior."

National monuments formerly administered by the United States Forest Service were included in these transfers.

Although this Order designated the Service as the Office of National Parks, Buildings and Reservations, the original name "National Park Service" was restored in recognition of its prestige in the field of conservation, in the Act making appropriations for the Department of the Interior for the 1935 fiscal year. This was accomplished through the interest of Senator Carl Hayden of Arizona, chairman of the Senate Subcommittee of the Senate Appropriations Committee, which had charge of the bill.

In accordance with the President's Executive Order, the Service was charged with maintenance of most of the Federal buildings in the National Capital, with the exception of certain buildings such as the Capitol, the main Treasury Building, Library of Congress, Government Printing Office, Supreme Court Building, and the National Bureau of Standards building. The Service also maintained a few Federal buildings outside the District of Columbia.

In order to fulfill these additional responsibilities, the Service separated the functions of the former Office of Public Buildings and Public Grounds into two distinct units, the Branch of Buildings Management and the office of National

Capital Parks. The Branch of Buildings Management was coordinate with the other administrative branches of the Service, while National Capital Parks is a field unit comparable to the various national park units outside the District of Columbia.

On July 1, 1939, the Branch of Buildings Management was discontinued when the Public Buildings Administration was established under the Federal Works Agency to handle the operation of buildings.

Another important piece of legislation affecting the activities of the Service was the Act of Congress approved August 21, 1935, empowering the Secretary of the Interior, through the National Park Service, to conduct a Nation-wide survey of historic American sites, buildings, objects, and antiquities. This Act also made provisions for cooperative agreements with states and local and private agencies in the development and administration of historic areas of national interest, regardless of whether titles to the properties were vested in the United States.

A discussion of progress in historical conservation achieved under the Historic Sites Act will be given later. Prior to passage of the Historic Sites Act of 1955, the Historic American Buildings Survey was initiated, in December 1953, as a Civil Works Administration project, under agreement between the Secretary of the Interior and the Civil Works Administrator. Later authorized by Congress, it has been conducted in cooperation with the American Institute of Architects and financed successively by FERA, WPA, and PWA funds. The Survey has resulted in the collection of exact graphic records of more than 5,000 antique buildings and other structures, important historically or architecturally. This material is being filed by special arrangement with the Library of Congress among the pictorial American archives of the Library.

Extension of National Park Service activities into the field of cooperation with the states and local governments in the planning of recreational areas, facilities and programs was authorized by the Park, Parkway and Recreation Study Act approved June 25, 1956. Under this Act the Service is conducting the Park, Parkway and Recreational-Area Study (discussed in detail under the heading "State Cooperation").

So widespread have the activities of the Service become, particularly since cooperation with the states began under the CCC and emergency relief programs in 1933, that an administrative system of four regions has been established. Each region is in the charge of a Regional Director, as follows: Region I, Miner R. Tillotson, regional director, Richmond, Virginia; Region II, Thomas J. Allen, regional director, Omaha, Nebraska; Region III, John R. White, regional director, Santa Fe, New Mexico; Region IV, Frank A. Kittredge, regional director, San Francisco, California.

One of the most important aspects of the extended activities of the Service is the fact that although the Service is working in new fields and with funds coming from several sources, its enlarged personnel is no less a part of the organization in the traditional sense. This realization on the part of later appointees comes with the knowledge that the Service is a permanent bureau of a regularly established Department of the Government, and that no matter what phase of the program the individual is working on, it is an integral part of the whole program of the National Park Service.

Development of the Educational Program

Although Congress authorized establishment of the first national park as a "pleasuring ground," growth of the system by the addition of many areas of truly outstanding importance as living laboratories of natural history made it obvious that the parks offered superb educational opportunities. It was logical, then, that a program of research and education should be developed along with a program of recreational use.

The educational advantages of the parks were recognized early by individuals and university groups, and at the turn of the century teachers were leading classes into these reserves for field study. In 1917 Director Mather launched his plans for an educational program by appointing Robert Sterling Yard as chief of the educational division. Immediately the Service introduced educational material into its booklets of information on the parks. At the same time, individuals without the Service—notably John Muir of the Sierra Club, C. M. Goethe and Joseph Grinnell of California—were attracting interest in the educational opportunities of the parks and stimulating in many persons a desire to study the geologic and biologic features of these areas.

A national park educational committee was organized by Dr. Charles D. Walcott of the Smithsonian Institution in June of 1918. About a year later this group, consisting of 75 university presidents and representatives of leading conservation organizations, merged into the National Parks Association, and Mr. Yard left the National Park Service to become associated with this new organization.

It was at this time that the concept of nature guiding, developed in a world survey which brought the idea from Europe to America, was being well demonstrated in Yosemite, where Dr. Harold C. Bryant, educational director of the California Fish and Game Commission, was delivering a number of lectures, and where trips afield for nature study were offered. By 1920 Mr. Mather and certain of his friends had become so convinced of the effectiveness of this work that they supported it with private funds. In that year Dr. Bryant and Dr. Loye Holmes Miller offered guided field trips and gave lectures in Yosemite to lay the foundation for later work.

The naturalist staff was not represented in the Washington Office until the Branch of Research and Education was established in 1930. Following the resignation of Dr. Wallace W. Atwood, Jr., as assistant in charge of work relating to earth sciences, Earl A. Trager was appointed in March 1932, to take charge of this section of the work. The following year the Naturalist Division was organized with Mr. Trager as Chief.

The Naturalist Division consists of a staff located in the Washington Office, in Regional Offices and in the parks and monuments. The duties of the staff are:

1. To interpret the inspirational and educational features of the parks to the public through the medium of trips afield and lectures.

2. To advise on all matters pertaining to the educational use of or the conservation of the natural or scientific features within the national parks and monuments.

3. To assemble complete data on all scientific and esthetic features of the park area as the basis for both the interpretation and general administrative program of the park.

The staff in the Washington Office consists of executive and technical personnel; the staff in the field consists of technical personnel whose administrative duties are limited to those necessary to accomplish the field work program.

The naturalists' program of conservation and interpretation involves work in the biological and geological fields. The technical assistance required in biology is supplied by the Wildlife Division. The technical assistance required in geology is furnished by geologists attached to the Naturalist Division.

Coincident with the development of a "free nature guide service" in Yosemite, the Service began the interpretation of park phenomena through museum exhibits. Ansel F. Hall, previously in charge of information at Yosemite, was made park naturalist and developed a museum. In Yellowstone M. P. Skinner, under the direction of the Superintendent, organized a museum program. Nature guide service was established in other parks in the next few years, and in 1923 Director Mather appointed Mr. Hall as chief naturalist to extend the field of educational development to other parks. In the same year Dr. Carl P. Russell was appointed park naturalist in Yosemite and Mr. Hall devoted his efforts to the educational program in all the parks.

By this time it was seen that a definite plan of operation was needed, and Director Mather appointed Dr. Frank R. Oastler to investigate the educational work and, in collaboration with Chief Naturalist Hall, to draw up a general policy. An organization plan was prepared after Dr. Oastler had spent four and one-half months in the field in 1924. This outline defined the duties of the chief naturalist and the park naturalists, and advocated the development of an "educational working plan" for each park which would set forth the qualifications and training of the staff, an outline of each educational activity, plans of necessary buildings and equipment, and the required budget. Of special importance was the recommendation in this report that "each park should feature its own individual phenomena rather than try to cover the entire field of education."

Another survey of educational opportunities of the parks was made in 1924 by the American Association of Museums, of which C. J. Hamlin was president, and definite plans looking toward the establishment of natural history museums in some of the larger parks were suggested. On the basis of this study the Laura Spelman Rockefeller Memorial donated funds for construction of an adequate, fireproof museum building with necessary equipment and important accessories, in Yosemite.

Even before the Yosemite museum installations had been opened to the public, demonstration of the effectiveness of the institution as headquarters for the educational staff and visiting scientists convinced leaders in the American Association of Museums that further effort should be made to establish a general program of museum work in national parks. Additional funds were obtained from the Laura Spelman Rockefeller Memorial and new museums were built in Grand Canyon and Yellowstone National Parks. Dr. Hermon C. Bumpus, who had guided the museum planning and construction in Yosemite, continued as the administrator representing the Association and Rockefeller interests, and Herbert Maier, now Associate Regional Director, Region IV, was architect and field superintendent on the construction projects.

It was Dr. Bumpus who originated the "focal point museum" idea so well represented by the several small institutions in Yellowstone, each one concerned with a special aspect of the park story, and so located as to tell its story while its visitors were surrounded by and deeply interested in the significant exhibits of the out-of-doors. The trailside exhibits now commonly used in many national parks and first tried at Obsidian Cliff in Yellowstone were an out-growth of the focal point museum idea.

When the museums of, Yosemite, Grand Canyon, and Yellowstone had demonstrated their value to visitors and staff alike, they were accepted somewhat as models for future work, and upon the strength of their success; the Service found it possible to obtain regular government appropriations with which to build more museums in national parks and monuments. When PWA funds became available, further impetus was given to the parks museum program and a Museum Division of the Service was established in 1935, embracing historic areas of the East as well as the scenic national parks.

Research and Information

In 1925 the Secretary of the Interior approved Director Mather's plan for establishment of headquarters of the Educational Division at Berkeley, California, under Mr. Hall. Administration of the program was handled from that point until establishment of the Service's Branch of Research and Education under Dr. Bryant in Washington, D. C., on July 1, 1930. During this period administrative plans were developed for the educational activities of each park, in cooperation with the park superintendents and naturalists.

Simultaneously, a plan of administration for the educational service as a whole was worked out, and its approval by the Director on June 4, 1929 formed the basis of operation and administration in the field.

The principal study of educational program needs in the national park system was made by a committee appointed by the Secretary of the Interior in 1929, which operated with funds provided by the Laura Spelman Rockefeller Memorial. Its personnel included Dr. John C. Merriam, chairman, and Drs. Hermon C. Bumpus, Harold C. Bryant, Vernon Kellogg, and Frank R. Oastler. These men made field trips in the summer of 1928 and reported many practical suggestions for development of the program.

Acting on the recommendation of this committee, the Secretary of the Interior, in 1929, invited several eminent scientists and educators to serve on a National Park Service Educational Advisory Board. This group consisted of those already on the educational committee with the exception of Dr. Bryant, and in addition Drs. Clark Wissler, Wallace W. Atwood and Isiah Bowman. The committee on study of educational problems was also enlarged to include Dr. Atwood and Dr. Wissler.

Further field investigations were conducted in 1929 and 1930 by the committee and its members rendered individual reports on the areas they visited. The committee submitted its final report to the Secretary of the Interior on November 27, 1929. In this report, it was recommended hat the position of educational director of the Service should be filled by a man "of the best scientific and educational qualifications," that headquarters of the educational division should be a part of the central organization in Washington, and that two assistants be appointed who, together with the head, should represent the subjects of geology, biology, anthropology, and history.

With the establishment of the Branch of Research and Education in 1930, Dr. Harold C. Bryant, a biologist, was appointed assistant director in charge of this work. Dr. Wallace W. Atwood, Jr., was made assistant in charge of work relating to earth sciences, and a year later Verne E. Chatelain was appointed assistant in charge of historical and archeological developments. With these steps having been taken, the main work of the educational committee was completed, and the group was disbanded in 1931.

Now called the Branch of Research and Information, this branch is charged with the task of interpreting to the public the natural phenomena within the national parks and monuments, conducting or sponsoring such research as is necessary to that program, and the protection and conservation of the natural resources therein. The planning and administration of the work of the Branch, which is comprised of three divisions, the Naturalist, the Wildlife (assigned to National Park Service duty from the Biological Survey), and the Museum Division, is under the direction of a Supervisor, Dr. Carl P. Russell, who was appointed to fill the vacancy caused by the transfer of Dr. Bryant to the Superintendency of Grand Canyon National Park in February 1939.

Several main policies have been followed in the development of the educational program, and important among these are:

1. Simple, understandable interpretation of the major features of each park to the public by means of field trips, lectures, exhibits, and literature.

2. Emphasis upon leading the visitor to study the real thing rather than to utilize second-hand information. Typical academic methods are avoided.

3. Utilization of a highly trained personnel with field experience in geological and biological sciences able to interpret to the public the laws of the universe as exemplified in the parks, and able to develop concepts of the laws of life useful to all.

4. A research program in the natural sciences which will furnish a continuous supply of dependable facts suitable for use in connection with the educational program and for guidance in shaping National Park Service policy.

5. Promotion of library facilities and practice throughout the national park system.

Wildlife

The National Park Service is entrusted by the American people with protection, conservation, and proper management of characteristic portions of the country as it was seen by the early explorers. In fulfilling this stewardship, the Service is responsible for the protection of the animals which constitute the wildlife population of the parks.

The wildlife management policies of the Service are based upon three points:

1. That the wildlife of America exists in the consciousness of the people as a vital part of their natural heritage.

2. That in its appointed task of preserving characteristic examples of primitive America, the National Park Service faces an especially important responsibility for the conservation of wildlife. This is emphasized by the wholesale destruction which has decimated the fauna in nearly every part of the land outside of the park areas.

3. That the observation of animals in the wild state contributes so much to the enjoyment derived by visitors that this is becoming a park attraction of steadily increasing importance.

After wiping out vandalism and poaching in the parks, the Service realized that mere protection of the wildlife would not accomplish what was desired and necessary, and that an actual program of management was needed, to restore and perpetuate the fauna in its pristine state by combatting the harmful effects of human influence.

The problem of wildlife management was aptly set forth in Fauna of the National Parks of the United States—No. 1, by George M. Wright, Joseph S. Dixon, and Ben H. Thompson: "The unique feature of the case is that perpetuation of natural conditions will have to be forever reconciled with the presence of large numbers of people on the scene, a seeming anomaly. A situation of parallel circumstances has never existed before."

In considering its responsibility for the conservation of wildlife, the Service realized that mere protection was not enough. The need to supplement protection with constructive wildlife administration became evident with a steady increase of biological problems in many of the national parks and monuments. In 1929 a wildlife survey was undertaken in an effort to concentrate greater interest on the fundamental aspects of wildlife administration throughout the national park system. This survey involved a reconnaissance of the park system, to analyze and delineate the existing status of wildlife in the parks, to assist park superintendents in solving urgent biological problems, and to develop a well-defined wildlife policy for the national park system. The results of this survey, together with proposed wildlife policies which have since been adopted by the Service, were published in the Fauna Series 1 and 2.

For two years, from 1929 to 1931, this work was financed entirely by the late George Wright who personally paid the salaries of two men while contributing his own services. In 1931 and 1932 the Government began contributing toward the budget, although Mr. Wright continued his support of the work. In 1933 the Government took over the financing entirely. It was in that year that a Wildlife Division was formally established within the Branch of Research and Education for the purpose of directing all activities pertaining to conservation and management of park wildlife. Prior to 1934 the staff consisted of a chief, a field naturalist and a supervisor of fish resources. In 1934 this staff was increased with trained biologists employed under the Emergency Conservation Work program. Wildlife technicians are assigned to each regional office and are assisted by technicians of the associate, assistant, and junior grades. In November 1939, the Wildlife Division was transferred to the Biological Survey, which bureau immediately assigned all staff members to the same Park Service duties which they had been performing.

The wildlife policies of the Service were recognized by the Biological Survey and subscribed to in the new inter-bureau relationships.

They follow:

Relative to areas and boundaries—

1. That each park shall contain within itself the year-round habitats of all species belonging to the native resident fauna.

2. That each park shall include sufficient areas in all these required habitats to maintain at least the minimum population of each species necessary to insure its perpetuation.

3. That park boundaries shall be drafted to follow natural faunal barriers, the limiting faunal zone, where possible.

4. That a complete report upon a new park project shall include a survey of the fauna as a critical factor in determining area and boundaries.

Relative to management—

5. That no management measure or other interference with biotic relationships shall be undertaken prior to a properly conducted investigation.

6. That every species shall be left to carry on its struggle for existence unaided, as being to its greatest ultimate good, unless there is real cause to believe that it will perish if unassisted.

7. That, where artificial feeding, control of natural enemies, or other protective measures, are necessary to save a species that is unable to cope with civilization's influences, every effort shall be made to place that species on a self-sustaining basis once more; whence these artificial aids, which themselves have unfortunate consequences, will no longer be needed.

8. That the rare predators shall be considered special charges of the national parks in proportion to the extent that they are persecuted elsewhere.

9. That no native predator shall be destroyed on account of its normal utilization of any other park animal, excepting if that animal is in immediate danger or extermination, and then only if the predator is not itself a vanishing form.

10. That species predatory upon fish shall be allowed to continue in normal numbers and to share normally in the benefits of fish culture.

11. That the numbers of native ungulates occupying a deteriorated range shall not be permitted to exceed its reduced carrying capacity and, preferably, shall be kept below the carrying capacity at every step until the range can be brought back to normal productiveness.

12. That any native species which has been exterminated from the park area shall be brought back if this can be done, but if said species has become extinct, no related form shall be considered as a candidate for reintroduction in its place.

13. That any exotic species which has already become established in a park shall be either eliminated or held to a minimum provided complete eradication is not feasible.

Relative relations between animals and visitors—

14. That presentation of the animal life of the parks to the public shall be a wholly natural one.

15. That no animal shall be encouraged to become dependent upon man for its support.

16. That problems of injury to the persons of visitors or to their property or to the special interests of man in the park, shall be solved by methods other

than those involving the killing of the animals or interfering with their normal relationships, where this is at all practicable.

Relative faunal investigations—

17. That a complete faunal investigation, including the four steps of determining the primitive faunal picture, tracing the history of human influences, making a thorough zoological survey and formulating a wild-life administrative plan, shall be made in each park at the earliest possible date.

18. That the local park museum in each case shall be repository for a complete study skin collection of the area and for accumulated evidence attesting to original wild-life conditions.

19. That each park shall develop within the ranger department a personnel of one or more men trained in the handling of wild-life problems, and who will be assisted by the field staff appointed to carry out the faunal program of the Service.

Plans and Design

One of the chief responsibilities of the Service in its administration of the national park and monument system is to bring about a proper compromise between (1) preservation and protection of the landscape, and (2) developments for making park areas accessible and useful to the public. A delicate balance of conservation, calling for the exercise of sound judgment, is indicated in the correct adjustment of these seemingly opposing objectives.

From the very beginning, the Service recognized this responsibility as a serious one to be discharged through careful professional planning. The first landscape architect was employed by the Service in 1918 more or less as a field adviser in the western parks. Thomas C. Vint, the present chief of planning, came into the Service in 1922, with headquarters in Yosemite National Park, California. In 1923 the office was moved to Los Angeles, and thence to San Francisco in 1927. The present Branch of Plans and Design was so designated in 1933. From 1927 until 1935 the Branch grew in personnel from three or four to a total of 120 employees, including architects and landscape architects. In 1936, when the Branch assumed additional responsibilities in connection with state park work, a total of 220 men in the professional classifications were employed. These, of course, did not include foremen assigned to CCC camps to do a considerable amount of work of the same nature.

The main function of the Branch of Plans and Design is to serve as adviser to the Director and park superintendents on all matters of general policy and individual problems, covering physical improvements, development, preparation of plans and designs of an architectural or landscape architectural nature; and to design and prepare all architectural and landscape architectural plans and specifications for buildings constructed by the Government in the park and monument areas.

The Branch prepares and keeps up to date a master plan showing the general scheme for physical development of each park and monument area, and supervises the preparation and revision of other master plans for areas being developed under the direction of the Service. It advises the Director on the location of parkways, and collaborates with the Public Roads Administration in the preparation of plans, construction and inspection of parkways, and the location, design and construction of major roads in park and monument areas, in accordance with the "Inter-bureau Agreement." It also collaborates with the Branch of Engineering in the construction of minor roads and trails in the areas of the system.

Representing the Director, the Branch recommends approval or disapproval of landscape and architectural plans prepared by park operators and other concessionaire agencies, and consults and collaborates with them in the preparation of their plans. One of its chief functions is to maintain a construction program for each park, correlated with the master plan. It directs the activities of the Historic American Buildings Survey, supervising the preparation of drawings and supporting data, and keeping records of all other operations incidental to the successful operation of this program.

The making of location surveys (of proposed parkways) is the responsibility of this Branch, and this involves the collection of data, maps and other information for proper presentation of reports and recommendations on parkways proposed. Another duty is the preparation of right-of-way plans for roads and parkways proposed or constructed by the Service.

Engineering

Making the areas of the national park and monument system available for public use has always presented problems in the proper design of structures and facilities. The earliest efforts in this direction demonstrated clearly the necessity for professional engineering services in planning developments in the park.

The first real engineering undertaking in any park was, in fact, the famous Hayden Geological Survey Expedition into the Yellowstone in the '70's, made primarily for the purpose of collecting accurate geological and geographical data on the region. During the early years after establishment of Yellowstone National Park, no funds were available for development and there was little or no need for engineering services. When Congress finally appropriated money for road construction in the park in the '80's, engineering was placed under the U. S. Corps of Engineers. In 1883 Captain D. C. Kingman of the Corps became the first officer to be detailed for such work in Yellowstone, and thus was the first national park engineer.

The first engineering structure in a national park was, undoubtedly, a log and timber bridge constructed over the Yellowstone River just below Tower Falls and not far from the present bridge across the stream. It was built by private interests who also constructed a road through the park to the Cooke City mining district just outside the park boundaries at the northeast corner. This structure was named Baronett Bridge and was built about 1870 or shortly thereafter. It became of historical interest when used by General O. O. Howard's command when he was pursuing the Nez Perce Indians under Chief Joseph through the park in 1877.

Early engineering activities in the national parks consisted almost entirely of the construction of roads, bridges and trails. After the National Park Service was established, the needs for water and sewer systems, power plants, communication service, and other essentials were developed. The early operators, or concessionaires in the parks, were required to construct and maintain their own utilities in connection with the operation of hotels, camps and other types of accommodations.

Road building was continued in Yellowstone and afterward in other national parks under the U. S. Corps of Engineers and immediate supervision of successive engineers until about 1917. Most prominent of the Army engineers of that era was General Hiram M. Chittenden who was assigned to Yellowstone National Park after the close of the Spanish-American War in 1899 and remained for a number of years. He accomplished the most in Yellowstone road building and also became the author of "The Yellowstone National Park," an historical and descriptive volume which is one of the best sources of authentic information on the history and phenomena of the Yellowstone.

Through his efforts Congress appropriated upwards of a million dollars during the three years 1902 to 1905 for reconstruction of roads in Yellowstone to provide an excellent system of horse stage roads. A new road was built from the Canyon around to Mammoth Hot Springs by way of Dunraven Pass and Tower Falls to provide a loop making it unnecessary for tourists to travel any portion of the route a second time. This system of roads sufficed for horse stage travel and later for auto bus and automobile travel until the early '20's when small yearly appropriations became available for reconstructing some of the most dangerous sections and widening other sections to permit two-way travel.

As new areas were brought into the system from time to time in the '90's and after the turn of the century, the engineering activities were placed generally in the charge of the U. S. Corps of Engineers. There was, apparently, little correlation of methods and standards between the engineers in the various parks. After the National Park Service was created and took over administration of the system, the Corps of Engineers continued in charge of engineering work until April 1917 when George E. Goodwin was appointed the first civilian engineer of the Service, with the title of civil engineer. He made his first headquarters in Portland, Oregon, with an assistant in each of the larger parks. In 1921 Mr. Goodwin was made chief engineer, in general charge of all engineering in the national parks. After Congress passed the Roads and Trails Act of 1924 and appropriated funds for the building of roads, trails and bridges in national parks, the chief engineer's organization was considerably expanded in personnel for making surveys and plans, and for supervising construction activities. In July 1925, however, Mr. Goodwin retired from the Service and all major road building activities were turned over to the Bureau of Public Roads. Bert H. Burrell was appointed acting chief engineer pending this transfer and a decision on the future of the chief engineer's office.

The Portland office was discontinued in the spring of 1926, some of the personnel being released and others being transferred to park engineering positions. The acting chief engineer, with a few employees, moved to Yellowstone to await developments.

In the summer of 1927, Frank A. Kittredge was appointed chief engineer, and in September of that year the office and small organization were moved from Yellowstone to San Francisco to occupy joint space with the Landscape Division, since renamed the Branch of Plans and Design. The activities and personnel of the Branch of Engineering were rapidly increased to keep pace with the growing needs for engineering services in practically all the national parks and monuments. Except for four of the larger parks—Yellowstone, Glacier, Grand Canyon and Yosemite, where permanent park engineers were located—the chief engineer's organization had charge of the design and construction of all engineering activities except major roads. In the next few years they designed and constructed many important engineering structures such as the Kaibab Trail Bridge over the Colorado River in Grand Canyon National Park, the Carlsbad Caverns elevators, and the Yellowstone hydroelectric plant. The four permanent park engineers operated technically under the supervision of the chief engineer, and engineering personnel was assigned to all park areas as needed for making general and topographical surveys and for supervising all construction activities except major roads, and generally supervising the maintenance of park roads.

Prior to 1930, the only national park in the east was Acadia, in Maine. Very little engineering service from the central organization was given this area, and such as was given was furnished by the chief engineer in San Francisco or the Bureau of Public Roads. In view of the prospect of establishment of additional eastern areas (with bills pending for establishment of George Washington's Birthplace National Monument, Colonial National Monument and the acquisition of land for an establishment of Great Smoky Mountains National Park, Shenandoah National Park, and Mammoth Cave National Park, which were authorized in 1926) Oliver G. Taylor was transferred in May 1950 from Yosemite National Park, where he had been resident engineer for ten years, to a field position in the Washington office.

Engineering work in eastern areas gradually increased until 1933 when there was a great increase in the number of eastern areas due to the transfer of public buildings and parks, national military parks and monuments and other areas from various Federal agencies to the National Park Service. This caused a tremendous increase in engineering responsibilities. These duties were first placed under Mr. Taylor as assistant chief engineer and later as deputy chief engineer, operating independently of the chief engineer's office in the west and reporting directly to the Director. The entire engineering organization of public buildings and parks came over to the National Park Service, but no engineering personnel was transferred with the military parks and monuments. It therefore became necessary to take on much additional engineering assistance.

In August 1937, when the Service was reorganized on a regional basis, the office of the chief engineer was transferred from San Francisco to Washington where it assumed charge of all engineering work in the national park and monument system. At that time Mr. Kittredge was appointed regional director of Region IV, with headquarters in San Francisco, and Mr. Taylor was appointed chief engineer.

Operations

Functions of administration and personnel, budget, fiscal control, operators' accounts, and mails and files came into the picture at once, upon establishment of the National Park Service, and these matters were first placed immediately under the Director.

Although the present Branch of Operations was not established until July 1, 1930, the various steps leading up to this began with the appointment of A. E. Demaray (now associate director) as senior administrative assistant on July 1, 1924. At that time Mr. Demaray was in charge of administrative work assigned by the Director, and supervised the editorial, mapping and drafting work, and the travel and informational work. On March 3, 1925 his title was changed to assistant in operations and public relations. On June 1, 1927 he was appointed as assistant to the director in charge of the preparation of estimates, administrative responsibility for road work in the park system, approval and control of expenditures, and approval of the rates of public operators. On October 11, 1929, Mr. Demaray was designated assistant director in charge of what was then called the Branch of Budget, Fiscal Control and Public Relations, and the Accounts Section was transferred from the Chief Clerk's Office to this new branch. On July 1, 1930 Mr. Demaray was appointed senior assistant director, and the name of the branch was changed to Branch of Operations, with responsibility for budget, accounting, and personnel work, embracing the following units: Division of Administration and Personnel, Division of Park Operators' Accounts, Division of Accounts, and Control Section.

Hillory A. Tolson was appointed assistant director in October 1933 and placed in charge of the Branch of Operations. At present the Branch is composed of five divisions with the following functions:

Budget and Accounts Division—Preparation of estimates of appropriations, including justifications and supporting data for use in defending them before the Budget Bureau and committees of Congress. Preparation of allotment advices pursuant to the provisions of appropriation acts or allocations making funds available. Supervision over preparation and compilation of financial and statistical data; accounting; auditing of expenditures; revision of the Accounting Manual; installation of approved systems of accounting to regulate fiscal operations; and receipt of revenues. Preparation of communications concerning accounting, budgeting, auditing and estimating of appropriations. Negotiation with representatives of General Accounting Office and other Governmental agencies concerning accounting and budget matters.

Safety Division—Supervision over building fire protection and accident prevention programs. Preparation of fire protection and safety standards for use by those responsible for building and water system designs. Review of park operators' plans for fire protection and safety measures. Analysis of building fire and employees' injury reports. Training of park employees in fire hazard and accident hazard inspections. Preparation and dissemination of information regarding building fires and injuries and accident prevention and fire hazards. Chief of Division serves as Chairman of Safety Committee composed of representatives of the different Service branches.

Public Utility Division—Furnishing of expert advice in the management and operation of public utility facilities (water, electricity, telephone, incineration, sewage) within the field areas administered by the Service. Conduct of rate analysis, valuations, and operating cost studies for determination of rate schedules for such public utility services. Preparation of plans, specifications, and estimates of new installations, extensions, improvements, and equipment purchases. Assistance to the Washington branches and field offices in connection with special utility problems.

Personnel and Records Division—Supervision and coordination of all personnel matters for adherence to civil service rules and regulations and to the policies and procedure of the Department. Maintenance of appropriate personnel records. Compilation of information, statistics, and reports relating to personnel. Handling of receipt and dispatching of all mail. Maintenance of the general files. Preparation of instructions for guidance of field officers. Review of reports regarding irregularities by the Division of Investigations and Service auditors. Advice to Service officials concerning personnel problems, policies, and procedure. Control of expenditures from contingent and printing and binding appropriations. Negotiation with officials of the Department regarding personnel policies and procedure, establishment of positions, and purchase of office supplies and equipment.

Park Operators Division—Supervision over field examinations of accounts and records of public service operators in areas administered by the Service. Prescribes bases on which amounts due the Government under franchise contracts shall be computed. Verification of correctness of amounts due under contracts and permits. Devises park operators' accounting requirements and procedure of reporting. Analysis of park operators' accounts and records for data to determine rates. Furnishing of data to officials to determine policies in exercising supervision and control over park affairs.

Law

Supervision over all legal matters of the Service is the responsibility of the Office of Chief Counsel. This Office is an outgrowth of the position of Assistant Attorney in the Secretary's Office held by former Director Horace M. Albright before establishment of the National Park Service in 1916, when the national parks were administered directly by the Secretary.

With the organization of the Service in 1917, Mr. Albright was appointed assistant director under former Director Stephen T. Mather. The position of assistant attorney formerly held by Mr. Albright was supplanted by that of "law clerk" authorized under the organic act of 1916. The position of "law clerk" advanced steadily in responsibility and volume of work as the Service grew from a small organization of some 25 employees in the Washington Office, to its present size. The designation of the position, accordingly, changed progressively to "assistant attorney," "legal officer," "assistant to the director," "assistant director," and finally to "chief counsel." All of these changes have taken place during the incumbency of the present Chief Counsel, George A. Moskey, who entered the Service in 1923.

The Office of Chief Counsel was established October 24, 1938, when the former Branch of Land Acquisition and Regulation, headed by Mr. Moskey as assistant director, was abolished. This change, made at the time a number of revisions were effected in branch names and functions, was considered advisable in view of the fact that the Branch handled not only matters pertaining to land acquisition and regulation, but all legal matters for the Service.

The Office is composed of a chief counsel and a force of assistants, principally attorneys. In addition, the Office also includes engineers, land appraisers and buyers, and specialized clerks. The functions of the Office of Chief Counsel are as follows: Supervision over all legal matters of the Service, rendition of administrative-legal advice, supervision over land acquisition, establishment of title to water rights, legislation affecting the national park system, and regulation of the various uses of these areas, and the acquisition of parkway rights-of-way. The Office renders assistance in formulating policies to govern various commercial activities in the national park system necessary for the accommodation and convenience of the visiting public. It acts as consultant to cooperating state and private agencies in technical matters relating to the establishment of new park or monument areas authorized by Congress.

From this description, it will be seen that the functions of the Office of Chief Counsel are not limited to legal work. They are approximately 75 per cent administrative in nature, and include the responsibility of carrying on and supervising important programs of the Service's work, principally those with incidental legal aspects. For instance, a land purchase program is an administrative function. In the consummation of a purchase of land, however, legal questions are involved and must be dealt with and answered. The rendering of legal opinions and advising administrative officers on strictly legal phases of the Service work constitutes the other 25 per cent of the work of the Office.

The duties and responsibilities of the Chief Counsel are thus distinguished from those of the Solicitor of the Department who is the chief legal officer of the Department, whose functions are essentially legal in nature, and to whom all legal questions requiring Departmental decision or approval are referred. With the great administrative responsibilities of the Office of Chief Counsel, it is not equipped with attorneys or personnel to undertake exhaustive research and investigations with a view to bringing out a legal issue. Its personnel is barely sufficient to carry on its programmed activities and the giving of legal guidance to administrative officers of the Service on current problems. Therefore, when situations confront the Service which require extended investigation or research as to facts before incidental legal questions are developed, field officers and administrative officers directly dealing with the problem are required to provide necessary reports from which the facts may be ascertained.

Historic Conservation

Historic conservation has been part of the conservation program of the Department of the Interior since 1906, and of the National Park Service since its establishment. The National Park Service Act itself named historic conservation as an important responsibility of the organization. Pursuant to the American Antiquities Act of 1906, the Department of the Interior, as early as 1916, had under its jurisdiction seven national monuments of historic and archeologic interest, as well as Mesa Verde National Park, which possesses the best preserved cliff dwellings in the United States. These areas were placed under the National Park Service on its establishment and formed the nucleus of its system of historic sites.

In the period between 1916 and 1931, the number of historic and archeologic areas administered by the Service steadily increased, and by the latter year totaled 19, among which were such important areas as George Washington Birthplace National Monument and Colonial National Monument (now a national historical park), commemorating the establishment of Jamestown, the first permanent English settlement in the United States, and the decisive American victory at Yorktown over Lord Cornwallis in 1781. Under the personal guidance of Mr. Albright, a program was evolved and a definite basis was laid for historical development.

The growing importance of historic areas in the system of national parks and monuments, and the wide variety of questions new to the Service that these areas presented, led, in 1931, to the creation of an historical division in the Branch of Research and Education to study problems relating to historic conservation. Verne E. Chatelain was appointed head of this division and under his supervision significant progress was made in formulating policies and methods of procedure. The necessity for specialized study of historical problems was greatly emphasized two years later when, by Executive Order, the 59 historic and archeologic areas administered by the War Department and the Department of Agriculture were transferred to the Department of the Interior. Included in the transferred areas were such outstanding battlefields of the War Between the States as Gettysburg and Vicksburg. Through this development, the National Park Service became the recognized custodian of all legally designated historic and archeologic monuments of the Federal Government.

As the historical and archeological program continued to broaden, it was recognized that it was desirable to extend the system to include most historic sites of national importance and to integrate the various pre-Columbian, colonial, military and other historically significant areas into a unified system which would tell the story of the United States from the earliest times. In order to facilitate the achievement of these objectives, the Branch of Historic Sites was established July 1, 1935, with Mr. Chatelain as acting head. The administration of scenic parks and historic sites, although involving many common problems, yet required such different methods of treatment that a separate branch to care for the broader planning and development of the historical program was essential. The functions of the branch were defined as the formulation of general policies, the supervision and coordination of the administrative policy and the interpretative and research programs of the different areas, and the Nation-wide survey of historic sites to determine which are of national importance.

In November 1934, with a view to formulating a national policy for historic conservation, Secretary of the Interior Ickes appointed J. Thomas Schneider to survey the progress made in this field in the United States and to study the legislation of the leading foreign countries.

It was largely on the basis of Mr. Schneider's recommendations that the Historic Sites Act of August 21, 1935 (49 Stat. 666), was framed. This Act, a landmark in historic conservation in the United States, greatly strengthened the legal foundation of the work of the Federal Government in this field. It declared as a national policy the preservation of historic American sites, buildings, objects and antiquities of national significance for the benefit and inspiration of the people, and empowered the Secretary of the Interior, through the National Park Service, to effectuate this policy. The Act authorized a survey of historic and archeologic sites to determine which possessed exceptional value historically, and empowered the Secretary to make cooperative agreements with states and other political units, and with associations and individuals to preserve, maintain, or operate a historic site for public use, even though title to the property did not rest in the United States.

Since the Historic Sites Act provided for a large measure of inter-bureau and inter-departmental cooperation, as well as for outside assistance, the National Park Service has taken advantage of this fact to obtain technical advice from a variety of organizations and institutions. Many invaluable benefits have been derived from the advice and assistance of the Smithsonian Institution, the National Archives, the Library of Congress and the staffs of numerous university departments of history and archeology. Through a constant interchange of ideas with these groups and with the assistance of its own Advisory Board, the National Park Service has developed a body of policies governing the survey, development and operation of historic sites, which constitutes the underlying basis for a national program of historical and archeological conservation.

Mr. Chatelain, who had been an important factor in the passage of the Historic Sites Act, and who had been acting head of the Branch of Historic Sites since its establishment on July 1, 1935, resigned in September 1936 and was succeeded by Branch Spalding, superintendent of the Fredericksburg and Spotsylvania County Battlefield Memorial National Military Park. Under Mr. Spalding, the architectural and archeological work of the Branch was broadened, and important steps were taken toward establishing a permanent organization.

In May 1938, Ronald F. Lee was made head of the Branch. Under him, the technical services of the Branch have been greatly strengthened, notably in the field of archeology, and a system of cooperation was worked out with the Library of Congress, the Smithsonian Institution and the National Archives whereby these institutions give technical advice to the National Park Service and assist in research problems.

Land Planning

Ever since the national parks and monuments were brought under the administration of one agency there has been a steady demand for the addition of numerous areas of many types to the system. This demand results from an increased public consciousness of the need for preserving areas of outstanding scenic, scientific and recreational values.

For more than a decade the investigation of proposed new areas was made by the Director or by officers of the Service designated by him, including field men. It finally became necessary and advisable to concentrate this work under one office, and in 1928 the Branch of Lands was established under the late

Washington Bartlett Lewis as assistant director. Mr. Lewis had been superintendent of Yosemite National Park from 1916 to 1928. The Branch of Lands had charge of the investigation of proposed new parks, extensions to existing areas, land acquisition, and the drafting work.

A reorganization of these activities brought about the establishment of the Branch of Planning in 1931. Conrad L. Wirth, who had been associated with the National Capital Park and Planning Commission in the acquisition of land for the park system of Washington, D. C., was named assistant director in charge of the new unit, which took over the functions of the former Branch of Lands with the exception of land acquisition, which was transferred to Office of Chief Counsel.

Through several stages of growth, the Branch of Planning has been assigned additional functions during the years, and is now called the Branch of Recreation, Land Planning and State Cooperation. It has charge of the advance land planning of the national system, and to it are referred, for investigation and report, all proposals for additions or extensions to the system. In making these studies the Branch usually calls upon other branches of the Service to collaborate on wildlife, historical, forestry, or other phases of the investigations.

As a basis for the selection of areas for addition to the national park system, studies are conducted in the recreational use of land primarily to determine their relative values from a national standpoint. This involves research, field investigations and the assembling and analysis of data regarding scenic or landscape values, physiography, vegetation, wildlife, history, archeology, and geology as factors in the outdoor recreational environment. On the basis of findings through these general preliminary studies, investigations, of specific areas are conducted by the Branch, or caused to be conducted by other branches. From the assembled data recommendations are made for areas to be established as national parks, international parks, national battlefield parks, national historical parks, national military parks, national monuments, national battlefield sites, national historic sites, national cemeteries, national memorials, national seashores, national parkways and extensive trail systems, and additions to or abandonment of such existing areas.

Upon the approval of a specific recommendation, the necessary data are assembled, the plan of action is outlined and presented to the Office of Chief Counsel for the handling of the necessary legal procedure. When an area is authorized by Congress for addition to the system, negotiations are directed for the final adjustment of boundaries within the limits authorized, and cooperation is given to the Office of Chief Counsel in the acquisition of lands.

All advance planning programs, master plans and development plans pertaining to the national park system are reviewed for conformance with planning policies of the service. If such plans conform to Service policies they are concurred in by the Supervisor of Recreation and Land Planning (whose title was changed from assistant director) and referred to the Director for approval.

It is also the duty of the Branch to study and negotiate proposed changes in nomenclature in the areas administered by the Service, in cooperation with the U. S. Board of Geographical Names.

Information and data are assembled by the Branch concerning national parks of other countries for comparative study. This information is obtained direct from the foreign countries or by cooperation with the Department of State.

The National Park Service Today

Today, roughly 60% of the 397 park areas administered by the National Park Service have been set aside as symbols and evidence of our history and prehistory. Many of our natural parks contain historic places that represent important aspects of that history. Collectively, these places present an American history textbook, a textbook that educates us about the people, events, buildings, objects, landscapes, and artifacts of the American past and about the aspirations and actions that produced those tangible survivors.

The National Park Service's history web site represents varying aspects of this history. It emphasizes the educational value of historic places and the importance of the stories that connect us to them. Our goal is to offer a window into the historical richness of the National Park System and the opportunities it presents for understanding who we are, where we have been, and how we as a society, might approach the future. This collection of special places also allows us to examine our past—the contested along with the comfortable, the complex along with the simple, the controversial along with the inspirational. We hope, in addition, that these pages will contribute to a national discussion of history and its importance to contemporary society.

The Park History Program, begun in 1931, preserves and protects our nation's cultural and natural resources by conducting research on national parks, national historic landmarks, park planning and special history studies, oral histories, and interpretive and management plans. Our staff helps evaluate proposed new parks, and we support cultural resources personnel in parks, regional offices, and Washington in all matters relating to the history and mission of the Park Service.

Located in Washington and led by the chief historian, the program offers a window into the historical richness of the National Park System and the opportunities it presents for understanding who we are, where we have been, and how we as a society, might approach the future.

Park History Program Areas

Directory of Oral History in the National Park Service

For the National Park Service oral history has long been an invaluable way to document the history of individual parks and the people and events the parks commemorate. Interviews also safeguard the collective memory and expertise of the people who have shaped the Park Service over the years. The Directory of Oral History in the National Park Service describes how scores of parks use oral history interviews to:

    document the people and events they commemorate;
    capture multiple perspectives on past events;
    enhance museum exhibits;
    manage cultural and natural resources;
    make interpretive and educational programs more relevant to visitors;
    connect with new audiences through the Web; and

record the history of individual parks and Park Service personnel.

Park National Register Documentation

Listing in the sister programs of the National Register of Historic Places (NRHP) and National Historic Landmarks (NHL) is central to preserving the significant cultural resources found in national parks. The documents created in support of NRHP and NHL designation are foundational to park resource planning, management, and facility maintenance, and are central to interpretive and educational programs for visitors in person and online. Sections 110 and 106 of the National Historic Preservation Act of 1966, which authorized the Register, require all federal agencies to maintain programs to identify, evaluate, and nominate to the Register any historic properties they own or control and to consider the effects of their actions on such properties. The Chief Historian, manager of the Park History Program, is the NPS's Deputy Federal Preservation Officer, and as such the program serves as the nominating authority for the listing and documentation of National Park Service properties.

Documenting properties with NRHP and NHL nominations is an ongoing process. Historical park units are administratively listed in the Register upon their authorization or establishment, although the accompanying documentation is usually not completed at that time. However, the property's significance and the need for compliance with Sections 106 and 110 are conferred with the Congressional or Presidential designation. Therefore, the NPS must address a continuing need for documentation for historical park units such as Fort Monroe National Monument as they are added to the system.

All cultural resources, no matter where they are located, require continued stewardship. Many older nominations need revision and updating to reflect current scholarship or boundary adjustments. In another category are the historic and prehistoric structures, and cultural landscapes and archeological sites for which no nominations exist whatsoever. Many of these are in non-historical units, which are not automatically listed. For any resources not properly identified and inventoried, resource managers' ability to preserve them is severely constrained.

In support of park and regional efforts to comply with Sections 106 and 110, the Park History Program reviews all park nominations prior to submission to the NRHP and NHL programs and works with nomination authors to ensure all NRHP regulations and guidelines are followed. Staff is available to assist with training sessions or webinars on NRHP preparation, or to provide pre-nomination guidance on boundaries, photo and mapping requirements, historic contexts, and other questions authors or researchers may have as they begin the documentation process.

The Maritime Heritage Program

This program documents and protects National Park Service and nationally significant maritime resources. It also administers the National Maritime Heritage Grant Program that provides matching funds for maritime preservation, restoration and education.

For centuries, Americans have used waterways for commerce, transportation, defense, and recreation. The Maritime Heritage Program works to advance awareness and understanding of the role of maritime affairs in the history of the United States. Through leadership, assistance, and expertise in maritime history, preservation, and archeology the program helps to interpret and preserve the nation's maritime heritage by maintaining inventories of historic US maritime properties, providing preservation assistance through publications and consultation, educating the public about maritime heritage through its website, sponsoring maritime heritage conferences and workshops, and funding maritime heritage projects when grant assistance is available.

Maritime-Related National Parks

The United States' long maritime heritage is found along oceans, rivers, lakes, and manmade waterways. Ships, lighthouses, life-saving stations, coastal fortifications, canals, and other physical resources are important parts of this history and heritage, as are the diverse arts, trades, cultures, and societies that developed along American waterways. Within the national park system, maritime history and heritage can be explored in many ways, ranging from New Bedford Whaling National Historical Park in Massachusetts to

Kaloko-Honokōhau National Park in Hawaii, and the Lewis & Clark National Historic Trail, which passes through eleven states on its route from Illinois to Oregon.

Few images are as evocative as a lighthouse standing sentry on a rocky shore, the guardian of mariners and passengers as they navigate the formidable currents, fierce storms, and shifting shoals of America's coastal and inland waterways. Since the establishment of the first lighthouse in America at Boston Harbor in 1716, lighthouses have played a critical role in providing safe passage for all maritime activities. Although their form and appearance vary according to region or the body of water they guard, the lighthouse remains one of the most recognizable images of the maritime world.

National Historic Lighthouse Preservation Act of 2000

The National Historic Lighthouse Preservation Act of 2000 (NHLPA) (54 USC 305101-305106) (formerly at 16 USC 470w-7), an amendment to the National Historic Preservation Act of 1966, provides a mechanism for the disposal of Federally-owned historic light stations that have been declared excess to the needs of the responsible agency.

The NHLPA recognizes the cultural, recreational, and educational value associated with historic light station properties by allowing them to be transferred at no cost to Federal agencies, State and local governments, nonprofit corporations, educational agencies, and community development organizations. These entities must agree to comply with conditions set forth in the NHLPA and be financially able to maintain the historic light station. The eligible entity to which the historic light station is conveyed must make the station available for education, park, and recreation, cultural, or historic preservation purposes for the general public at reasonable times and under reasonable conditions.

Only those light stations that are listed, or determined eligible for listing, in the National Register of Historic Places can be conveyed under this program. The nomination for listing, or determination of eligibility, is prepared by the US Coast Guard (USCG) following guidelines set forth in 36 CFR 60.9(c) and 36 CFR 63, respectively, as part of their responsibilities prior to the property being transferred to the GSA inventory for disposal. Light stations that are not eligible for listing will be disposed of through other processes. Prior to the NHLPA, historic lighthouses could be transferred to state or local agencies through the National Park Service's Historic Surplus Property Program or the Federal Lands to Parks Program.

Historic Life-Saving Stations

Assisting shipwrecked mariners from shore-based stations was first undertaken in the United States by volunteers, beginning with the Massachusetts Humane Society in 1786. The Federal government began to provide provisions and funds for life saving operations in 1848, and the United States Lifesaving Service was created in 1878. Stations were organized into three categories: lifesaving, lifeboat, and houses of refuge. Beginning in 1915, the US Coast Guard operated and maintained active stations. Today, many historic stations that are no longer active have been re-purposed for museum or commercial activities.

Science in the National Parks

Air Quality

Air quality is important for human health, as well as natural resources. Air pollution includes gases and particles in the air that are emitted by power plants, factories, automobiles, and other sources. This can have serious effects on air quality, wildlife, vegetation, lakes, streams, soils, and visibility. Air pollution can come from local sources or may be transported long distances—even internationally—by winds.

Air pollution impacts all National Park Service (NPS) areas. This is a challenge for the NPS, who's mission is to manage and protect resources unimpaired for the enjoyment of future generations. Understanding where air pollution comes from, what it is made of, and how it affects parks and park resources is key to protecting NPS areas.

The Biological Resources Division (BRD)

The Division provides scientific expertise and technological assistance to support the sound management, protection, and preservation of biological resources and related ecosystem processes in our national parks. BRD staff work with individual parks, the park system as a whole, and National Park Service leadership. Efforts focus on Ecosystem Restoration and Management, Human Dimensions of Biological Resource Management, Integrated Pest Management, Invasive Species, Landscape Ecology and Conservation, Threatened and Endangered Species, Vegetation Inventory, Wildlife Health, Wildlife Management, and Exotic Plant Management.

When you visit a park and reflect on the trees, rocks, landscapes, and incredible views, you are viewing and appreciating ecosystems. Ecosystems are collections of plants, animals, and micro-organisms interacting among themselves and with their habitat. While most ecosystems are hard to define and draw rigid boundaries around, scientists characterize them by their rock and soil types, by water features such as streams and ponds, and by the common plant and animal species which make their homes within these areas.

Ecosystem management brings an integrated perspective to natural resource management. It takes a "big-picture" approach, replacing short term, single species management with multi-species, long-term and large-scale approaches. For example, instead of managing for deer and elk to maximize viewing opportunities, the National Park Service manages for the entire ecosystem, considering not only deer, elk and other herbivore populations, but also vegetation, water flow, and predators and rare species. Ecosystem management also recognizes the influence of natural disturbances such as fire and windstorms, accepting that natural ecosystems are dynamic and change over time.

Logging, grazing, mining, and other human activities have left a legacy of non-native vegetation, eroded soils, and altered fire patterns in our national parks. Some former park management techniques, such as fire suppression and elimination of predators, have led to declines in the integrity of the original ecosystems. In addition, invasive species, pollution, and climate change continuously threaten these systems.

The goal of ecosystem restoration is not to replace a static picture of the past. Instead, the National Park Service works to remove the barriers to ecosystem recovery. These barriers include biological or chemical contaminants, drained wetlands, channelized rivers, alteration of fire patterns, or lack of species to re-populate areas of parks. Whole-ecosystem approaches to management ensure not only the survival of species and scenic vistas, but also allows these systems to continuously evolve and change.

Climate Change and Your National Parks

Our national parks are a testament to the reality of climate change. Disappearing glaciers, shifting migration patterns for alpine birds, coastal erosion of historic places ... these are many ways that we see the effects of climate change. Our national parks are laboratories for good science and informed management decisions and also for educating the public about how climate change affects us by impacting places we care about. National parks teach us how climate change worked in the past and how it affects us today and can give us insight into ways to protect these special places in the future.

The Environmental Quality Division

This Division supports the nearly 400 units of the National Park System, which include national parks, monuments, battlefields, military parks, historical parks, historic sites, lakeshores, seashores, recreation areas, and scenic rivers and trails. The division assists in management planning, coordinates spill response activities, helps in damage assessment and restoration of injured park resources, provides social science expertise, and coordinates reviews of other federal agency actions that may impact park resources. These environmental services help ensure that the National Park Service meets its mission to preserve park resources and values for the enjoyment of future generations.

National Park Geologic Resources

Many parks were established to protect significant geological features, landforms, and viewsheds that frame the natural and cultural heritage of our nation.

Park geological features include the world-renowned sculptured depths of Grand Canyon, the ancient fossils of Dinosaur National Monument, the longest recorded cave system in the world at Mammoth Cave National Park, the greatest density of arches in the world in Arches National Park, the world's largest and most colorful collections of petrified wood at Petrified Forest National Park, and over half of the known geysers in the world in Yellowstone National Park.

Scientifically important fossil deposits are found in 243 parks, 81 parks contain 4,900 known caves, and another 40 parks have known karst systems. Ninety-seven parks protect 7,500 miles of shoreline, 52 parks contain geothermal systems, 38 parks have volcanoes as a major feature, and 37 have active glacial features. Park museum collections have more than 35,000 geological specimens and nearly 475,000 paleontological specimens.

Inventory & Monitoring Program (I&M)

The primary goals of the I&M Program are to:
- Inventory the natural resources under National Park Service stewardship to determine their nature and status.
- Monitor park ecosystems to better understand their dynamic nature and condition and to provide reference points for comparisons with other, altered environments.
- Establish natural resource inventory and monitoring as a standard practice throughout the National Park system that transcends traditional program, activity, and funding boundaries.
- Integrate natural resource inventory and monitoring information into National Park Service planning, management, and decision making.
- Share National Park Service accomplishments and information with other natural resource organizations and form partnerships for attaining common goals and objectives.

More than 270 parks with significant natural resources have been grouped into 32 I&M networks, which have been determined based on geography and shared natural resource characteristics. The network organization facilitates collaboration among parks, information sharing, and economies of scale in natural resource inventory and monitoring. Parks within each of the 32 networks work together and share funding and professional staff to plan, design, and implement an integrated long-term monitoring program.

The vision behind the vital signs monitoring program is to provide each network of parks with consistent annual funding and approximately 5 to 7 full-time staff to develop a core, long-term program. Each network leverages these core resources with existing personnel, funding from other sources, and partnerships with other agencies and organizations, to build a single, integrated monitoring program that best addresses the needs of the parks in that network.

Natural Resource Inventories

The I&M Program provides guidance, funding, and technical assistance for National Park Service (NPS) to complete a set of 12 baseline natural resource inventories. Natural resource inventories are extensive point-in-time surveys to determine the location or condition of a resource, including the presence, class, distribution, and status of biological resources such as plants and animals, and abiotic resources such as air, water, soils, landforms, and climate. Inventories are designed to contribute to our knowledge of the condition of park resources and establish baseline information for subsequent monitoring activities.

Monitoring Natural Resources

The NPS has initiated a long-term ecological monitoring program, known as "Vital Signs Monitoring," to provide the minimum infrastructure needed to track the overall condition of natural resources in parks and to provide early warning of situations that require intervention. The scientifically sound information obtained through this systems-based monitoring program will have multiple applications for management decision-making, park planning, research, education, and promoting public understanding of park resources.

Park vital signs are a subset of physical, chemical, and biological elements and processes of park ecosystems that are selected to represent the overall health or condition of park resources, known or hypothesized effects of stressors, or elements that have important human values.

National Natural Landmarks Program

The National Natural Landmarks (NNL) Program recognizes and encourages the conservation of sites that contain outstanding biological and geological resources, regardless of landownership type. It is the only natural areas program of national scope that recognizes the best examples of biological and geological features in both public and private ownership. NNLs are owned by a variety of land stewards, and participation in the program is voluntary.

National Natural Landmarks are selected for their outstanding condition, illustrative value, rarity, diversity, and value to science and education. Sites are designated by the Secretary of the Interior, with landowner concurrence, and to-date, nearly 600 landmarks have received the NNL designation within the United States, American Samoa, Guam, Puerto Rico, and the US Virgin Islands.

The National Park Service administers the program, reports on the condition of the NNLs, acts as an advocate for the protection of designated sites, and raises public awareness of our Nation's natural heritage. Ongoing partnerships with public and private landmark owners allow participants to share information, solve problems cooperatively, and conserve outstanding sites that illustrate the rich and diverse tapestry of the country's natural landscape.

Natural Sounds and Night Skies

America's national parks contain many cherished treasures; among them are captivating natural sounds and awe-inspiring night skies. The joy of listening to the quiet symphony of nature or the beauty of seeing the Milky Way stretching overhead have become rare experiences in our lifetimes, but they can still be found in many of our national parks. Natural sounds and natural darkness, though often overlooked, are essential in keeping our national treasures whole. They are magnificent in their own right, but also inspirational to the visitors who come to national parks, vital to the protection of wilderness character, fundamental to the historical and cultural context, and critical for park wildlife.

The Natural Sounds and Night Skies Division uses science, engineering, and technology to understand and better manage these spectacular resources. The NPS pioneers innovative techniques to measure the impact of noise and light pollution, develop new approaches to safeguard natural sounds and natural darkness, and identify management solutions to restore these public resources.

The Natural Sounds and Night Skies Division works to protect, maintain, or restore acoustical and dark night sky environments throughout the National Park System. It works in partnership with parks and others to increase scientific understanding and inspire public appreciation of the value and character of soundscapes and star-filled skies. Whether it's simply talking a little softer or turning off an outdoor light, you too can make a difference in the protection of these vital resources.

Social Science Branch

The role and functions of the Social Science Branch are to:
provide leadership and direction to the social science activities of the NPS
coordinate social science activities with other programs of the NPS
act as liaison with the USGS Biological Resources Discipline and other federal agencies on social science activities
provide technical support to parks, regions, and program offices
support a program of applied social science research related to national research needs of the NPS

The Water Resources Division (WRD)

The WRD is one of eight divisions that make up the Natural Resource Stewardship and Science (NRSS) Directorate of the National Park Service. WRD was established to provide service wide program management and specialized advice and assistance to parks in the protection and management of water resources. The division is comprised of four branches: Aquatic Systems, Ocean & Coastal Resources, Planning & Information, and Water Rights.

The Water Resources Division (WRD) exists to ensure that current and future generations can experience healthy aquatic ecosystems in the National Park System. WRD provides assistance, expertise, and guidance for aquatic ecosystem stewardship. WRD provides its services directly to parks through a broad range of programs in the areas of fisheries, natural resource condition assessments, information management, hydrology, planning, ocean & coastal resources, wetlands, water quality, and water rights.

8

Office of Surface Mining and Reclamation Enforcement

Did You Know?

Wyoming is the largest coal producer in the US; 9 of the top 10 producing coal mines in the US are in WY.

West Virginia is the largest coal producer in the Appalachian coal region and 2nd largest coal-producing state in the US. Almost 29% of the coal produced in the US comes from the Appalachian coal region.

More than half the coal produced in the US comes from the Western coal region which has some of the largest coal mines in the world.

The electric power sector accounted for about 93.2% of the total US coal consumption in the first quarter of 2014.

Advances in surface mining technology have allowed the amount of coal produced by one miner in one hour to triple since 1978.

Not all coal is used for electricity. Coal is used in the production of plastics, fertilizers, medicines, synthetic fibers, and is used in the process for producing steel.

Coal is the state rock of Utah, and is found in 17 of Utah's 29 counties.

Coal is the state mineral of Kentucky.

Bituminous coal is the state rock of West Virginia.

The Office of Surface Mining Reclamation and Enforcement (OSMRE) is responsible for establishing a nationwide program to protect society and the environment from the adverse effects of surface coal mining operations, under which OSMRE is charged with balancing the nation's need for continued domestic coal production with protection of the environment.

Vision Statement

In regulating active coal mining, we will maintain compliance at high levels and ensure that all mines are properly operated and promptly reclaimed to the standards established under the Act. We will emphasize prevention and ensure that long-term environmental problems do not occur. We will ensure that the pre-mining productivity of the land is restored.

OSMRE was created in 1977 when Congress enacted the Surface Mining Control and Reclamation Act. OSMRE works with states and tribes to ensure that citizens and the environment are protected during coal mining and that the land is restored to beneficial use when mining is finished. OSMRE and its partners are also responsible for reclaiming and restoring lands and water degraded by mining operations before 1977.

OSMRE is organized with Headquarters located in Washington DC, and three regional offices – the Appalachian, Mid-Continent, and Western Regional Offices. The Regional Offices are composed of Area and Field Offices.

In its beginning, OSMRE directly enforced mining laws and arranged cleanup of abandoned mine lands. Today, most coal states have developed their own programs to do those jobs themselves, as Congress envisioned. OSMRE focuses on overseeing the state programs and developing new tools to help the states and tribes get the job done.

OSMRE also works with colleges and universities and other state and Federal agencies to further the science of reclaiming mined lands and protecting the environment, including initiatives to promote planting more trees and establishing much-needed wildlife habitat. Each year, OSMRE trains hundreds of state and tribal professionals in a broad range of needed skills.

Although a small bureau, OSMRE has achieved some impressive results by working closely with those closest to the problem: the States, Tribes, local groups, the coal industry and communities.

Its mission is to carry out the requirements of the Surface Mining Control and Reclamation Act (SMCRA) in cooperation with States and Tribes and its primary objectives are to ensure that coal mines are operated in a manner that protects citizens and the environment during mining and assures that the land is restored to beneficial use following mining, and to mitigate the effects of past mining by aggressively pursuing reclamation of abandoned coal mines.

In reclaiming abandoned mine lands, it aggressively pursues reclamation with a primary emphasis on correcting the most serious problems related to public health, safety, and the general welfare. It also ensure maximum public benefit through the prompt and fair distribution of public funds.

In cooperating with State regulatory authorities, the primary enforcers of SMCRA, and with Tribes, it promotes a shared commitment to the goals of the Act. The Office also develops comprehensive understandings about the fairness, effectiveness, and efficiency of SMCRA programs, provides constructive program reviews, oversight monitoring, and technical assistance that focus on results. It also acts independently to protect the public interest in situations of imminent harm or when a State does not implement an approved regulatory program.

In dealing with those who are affected by mining and reclamation, the Office ensures the protection of citizens from abusive mining practices, is responsive to their concerns, and allows them full access to information needed to evaluate the effect of mining on their health, safety, general welfare, and property.

In its relations with the coal industry, it has clear, fair, and consistently applied policies that respect the importance of coal production as a source of our Nation's energy supply.

By demonstrating leadership in mining and reclamation, it seeks to promote the development of the highest quality technical information and research and the transfer of that technology to those who would benefit.

Programs

Reclaiming Abandoned Mine Lands – Restoring the Environment

The Abandoned Mine Land Reclamation Program is OSMRE's largest program and one of OSMRE's primary responsibilities under SMCRA. Since SMCRA's enactment in 1977, the AML program has collected over $10.1 billion in fees from present-day coal production and distributed more than $7.6 billion in grants to states and tribes, mandatory distributions to the UMWA and OSMRE's operation of the national program to reclaim land and waters damaged by coal mining before the law's passage.

Despite remarkable achievements, more than $3 billion worth of High Priority health and safety coal-related abandoned sites remain in OSMRE's inventory. Millions of Americans live less than a mile from abandoned coal mines. OSMRE and its state and tribal partners are also aware of areas overlying deep mines that are not listed in the inventory because they do not currently present a danger to life or property. These sites may become reclamation priorities as the old mines deteriorate and subside in the future.

In the early years, the AML program focused on the physical reclamation of hazards affecting coalfield communities. More recently, the program began working to reclaim the vitality of communities left impoverished and degraded by past coal mining. OSMRE employees are doing this in concert with watershed and community groups by assisting them with a variety of improvement projects to address local challenges.

Regulating Coal Mines – Protecting the Environment

The Surface Mining Control and Reclamation Act (SMCRA) balances the need to protect the environment from the adverse effects of surface coal mining with the Nation's need for coal as an essential energy source. It ensures that coal mining operations are conducted in an environmentally responsible manner and that the land is adequately reclaimed during and following the mining process. Most coal-mining states now have the primary responsibility to regulate surface coal mining on lands within their jurisdiction, with OSMRE performing an oversight role. OSMRE also partners with states and Indian tribes to regulate mining on Federal lands and to support states' regulatory programs with grants and technical assistance.

Technology Development and Transfer Program

One of the ways that the Office of Surface Mining Reclamation and Enforcement balances coal production with environmental protection is by providing resources for technical assistance, training, and technology development. These activities support and enhance the technical skills that states and tribes need to operate their regulatory and reclamation programs in order to effectively implement the Surface Mining Control and Reclamation Act.

Divisions

Division of Administration

The Division of Administration (DA) develops OSMRE's administrative policies and procedures and implements the Bureau's administrative support activities in the following program areas:
Acquisition and Procurement;
Property and Fleet Vehicles;
Leased Space;
Continuity of Operations Planning;
Safety and Occupational Health;
OSMRE Directives;
General Services Budget Accounts;

Printing and Publications; and

FAIR Act (Competitive Sourcing)

Recognizing that the Division is a customer-focused and service-oriented organization, it strives to provide personal and exceptional customer service. Tenets of its customer service philosophy include: respect; maximizing personal interaction; communicating with confidence and assertion; appreciating the customer's constraints; respecting the customer's time; and soliciting and receiving feedback in an environment of continuous learning and improvement. Division of Administration employees are empowered to make decisions.

Division of Compliance Management

The Division of Compliance Management (DCM) audits coal mining operations to determine if they are in compliance with Public Law 95-87, Section 402, and implementing Federal regulations reclamation fee requirements. Reclamation fees must be reported quarterly on Form OSMRE-1. The permittee/operator of a mine must maintain records and books for a period of at least six years from the end of the calendar quarter in which the fee was due or paid, whichever is later, and make these records available to the auditors. These books and records should be current and should substantiate the tonnages, moisture deductions, and fee calculations reported on the OSMRE-1 Form.

Division of Financial Management (DFM)

DFM's mission is to provide excellent financial management services, in an environment where all employees contribute, learn and grow, and are valued and respected.

It is responsible for the financial operations of the Office of Surface Mining (OSMRE), which includes everything from the collection of fees from coal operators to the disbursement of grants for abandoned mine reclamation work and just about everything in between. DFM has been recognized for its financial management best practices and holds the best record in the Department of Interior for "clean audit" opinions.

It is organized into four branches.

Fee, Accounting and Collections Branch (FACB)

The Fee Accounting and Collection Branch (FACB) manages the collection of coal reclamation fees from the mining industry. This enables OSMRE to achieve one of its mission objectives of reclaiming abandoned mine lands. The FACB also collects civil penalties related to mining violations. FACB also maintains and reviews mining permit information, coal production reports and results of OSMRE audits of coal company records. For fiscal year 2013, FACB collected $214 million in fees with a collection rate of 99.9% on quarterly AML fees. Over 98% of fees and coal production were reported electronically using OSMRE's E-filing website. And the majority of the fees were also paid electronically. OSMRE's user friendly e-filing system makes it easier for coal mine operators to report quarterly coal production and pay the related reclamation fees.

Payments Branch (PAB)

The Payment Branch makes all payments to vendors, intra-governmental agencies, and all non-payroll payments to employees. The Payments branch is responsible for:

Working with the Acquisitions department to ensure timely payments to vendors

Payments made through the IPAC system (Intra-government Payment & Collection System)

Registration, training, support, and monitoring of the Integrated Charge Card Program

Registration, training, support, and monitoring of the GovTrip travel program

Payments made for employee relocations (permanent change of station (PCS))

FBMS vendor support

Accounting and Financial Information Branch (AFIB)

The Accounting and Financial Information Branch (AFIB) prepares regulatory reports, management reports, and audited Financial Statements for

OSMRE. From 1990 to 2006, AFIB published OSMRE's own Audited Financial Statements. It has received 16 consecutive "clean" audit opinions which is the best record in the Department of the Interior. Beginning with fiscal year 2007, AFIB prepares OSMRE's financial statements that are published by the Department of the Interior as part of the Department's Consolidated Financial Statements. AFIB is also responsible for:

OSMRE's financial management internal control program

Grant disbursements: Funds that are appropriated by Congress to states and tribes through grants for reclamation programs

Investments: The $2.4 billion AML fund balance is invested in US Treasury securities. The interest earned provides health benefits to miners through the United Mine Workers Association (UMWA) Health and Retirement Benefits Fund

General Ledger accounting

Financial data integrity

Cost accounting

Property

Personnel/payroll

Cash management

Financial and Administrative Systems Branch (FASB)

The Financial and Administrative Systems Branch (FASB) provides system operations, maintenance, and support services for computer systems that are classified as mission critical for OSMRE. This includes, the Coal Fee Collection Management System (CFCMS). CFCMS handles accounting and collection of accounts receivables related to quarterly coal reclamation fees paid by coal companies, audits of coal company reporting, and civil penalties issued by OSMRE inspectors and Division of Compliance Management auditors.

FASB provides production lead responsibilities for the Financial and Business Management System (FBMS). FBMS is the cornerstone to the Department of the Interior's (DOI) future. FBMS is a key to the Department's financial management modernization strategy and meeting future business needs. DFM plays a key role in the phased implementation and support of FBMS.

Division of Human Resources

The Division of Human Resources develops and implements policies, standards and systems for the effective use of human resources to accomplish the overall mission of OSMRE. Specifically, the human resources program provides managers and employees with advice and technical assistance on the full range of human resources programs in accordance with OSMRE, DOI, OPM and other federal policies and guidelines.

The division provides processing and record keeping on recruitment, staffing and hiring; conducts position classification and organizational analysis; administers pay and compensation programs for general schedule and senior executive service positions; advises and processes employee and retirement benefits; oversees performance management, awards and recognition programs; manages ethics and financial disclosure holdings programs; implements the personnel security (HSPD-12) process for both federal and contractor staff; provides mandatory employee development and training assistance; and provides guidance on employee relations and workplace issues including disciplinary actions.

The Division of Human Resources continually expands its technical systems, updates its internal website, and streamlines its personnel processes in order to effectively provide the most current information to OSMRE staff.
Special ongoing initiatives this office is working on under the Departmental Human Resource Plan are highlighted below:
Recruitment
Strategic Management of Human Capital
Work Force Planning
Automated On-line Recruitment
Strengthening Partnerships with Hiring Managers
Consulting and Training Sessions on Human Resources Matters
Increased Service Delivery (Streamlined Processes)
Enhanced Customer Service
Enhanced Use of Non-Competitive Appointments
Electronic Official Personnel Folder (EOPF)
Workforce Transformation and Tracking System (WTTS)

Hiring Manager Tool Kits
Entrance On Duty System (EODS)

Ethics Office

OSMRE's ethics program's purpose is to strengthen the public's confidence that OSMRE business is conducted with impartiality and integrity. The public trusts our employees to make decisions that are in the best interest of the public. Therefore, beyond government-wide ethics regulations, our employees follow ethics rules that are specific to OSMRE, such as 30 USC. 1211(f), 30 C.F.R. Part 706, 43 C.F.R. 20.402 and 5 C.F.R. 3501.104(a). All OSMRE employees are prohibited from having any financial interests in surface or underground coal mining operations under these rules, for instance.

A collection of statutes, executive orders, and regulations applicable to all Federal employees underscores the notion that public service is a public trust. The criminal bribery and conflict of interest statutes (18 USC. 201 and 202-209, respectively) are the core of the ethics program governing Federal employees. These statutes are implemented, in large part, by the Standards of Ethical Conduct for Employees of the Executive Branch, 5 C.F.R. Part 2635.

Information Resources Office

The Information Resources Officer provides advice and assistance to the Deputy Director and other senior OSMRE officers to ensure that information technology is acquired and information resources are managed for the bureau in a manner that is consistent with the requirements of the Information Technology Management Reform Act of 1996, the Government Information Security Reform Act of 2000, and Chapter 35 of Title 44 USC and industry best practices.

This Office is responsible for OSMRE's information technology (IT) management. Major functions include:

Provides advice and assistance to management and employees on IT policy, applicable laws, regulations, and directives;

Establishes a management framework for and coordinates OSMRE's nationwide IT capital planning and investment control activities, including approval of IT expenditures within OSMRE; and

Develops and implements IT strategic planning to ensure that all of OSMRE's electronic information systems are administered and developed in accordance with policies, long-range systems and strategic planning;

In addition, the Office manages other aspects of OSMRE's IT including enterprise architecture, security management, records management, inventory and asset management, telecommunications, project management, and IT career/skills management.

Office of Communications (OC)

This Office plans, coordinates, produces, distributes, and manages the following under the direction of the Director:

Publications

Audiovisuals

Fact sheets

OSMRE Website

Reports

Photos

Exhibits

News releases

Mine Reclamation Awards

Freedom of Information Act (FOIA) Requests

Congressional Inquiries

The Office provides information about OSMRE programs, policies, and activities for use by the public, the coal industry, and citizen groups, among others. In addition, the OC responds to specific requests for information from Congress, the news media, and the public.

The OC also functions as the principal point of contact for scheduling OSMRE briefings with key officials; provides direction for the bureau's public-facing website; maintains a correspondence tracking system to manage official correspondence; handles Freedom of Information Act requests; coordinates OSMRE's annual awards recognizing excellence in reclaiming active and abandoned mines, as well as a separate annual award honoring an individual who has made significant contributions to the spirit of SMCRA; and handles certain aspects of internal communications.

Office for Equal Opportunity

This Office is responsible for promoting equal employment opportunities for all OSMRE employees. The Office:

Provides for the prompt, fair and impartial processing of complaints of discrimination;

Provides technical assistance and advice to employees and managers on all EO issues;

Communicates the bureau's equal employment opportunity policy and program and its employment needs to all sources of job candidates without regard to race, color, religion, sex, national origin, age or handicap;

Ensures that a reasonable accommodation program is in place and is implemented in a fair and timely manner. The DOI Reasonable Accommodation Policy link is http://www.doi.gov/pmb/eeo/upload/DM-Chapter-on-Reasonable-Accommodation-Sep-05.pdf.

Ensures that an alternative dispute resolution program is available for both the pre-complaint process and the formal complaint process;

Ensures that a bureau-wide affirmative employment and EEOC-MD-715-01 Report objectives are developed and implemented; and

Maintains a Civil Rights Compliance program for federally assisted and conducted programs.

In addition, the office is responsible for Special Emphasis programs and assists the bureau in creating a model equal employment program which ensures that all OSMRE employees and applicants for employment have equal access. It is responsible for implementing initiatives in response to Executive Orders of the President, which provides for agencies to work more closely with Historically Black Colleges and Universities, Hispanic Serving Institutions and Tribal Colleges and Universities in an effort to enhance opportunities for minority higher education institutions to participate and benefit from programs related to surface coal mining and reclamation activities. As an example of outreach to minority higher education institutions, OSMRE has formed the Minority Higher Education Program. The focus of the program will be to lay the foundation for long term relationships with minority higher education institutions that were identified as having degree programs in OSMRE's mission related interest. Also, the office assists the bureau in the implementation of the Department's "Strategic Plan for Achieving and Maintaining a Highly Skilled and Diverse Workforce."

Office of Planning, Analysis, and Budget

This Office is responsible for nationwide planning and analysis, and budgetary functions for OSMRE, including the integration of organizational performance measures into the budget process. The major functions of the Office include:

Develops and maintains OSMRE's strategic plan in coordination with Departmental and OSMRE management;

Performs trend analyses and modeling to identify changing national and regional needs; and analyzes policy proposals for new initiatives and modifications to existing programs; and

Carries out the formulation, presentation, execution, and analysis of OSMRE's budget; providing policy, central coordination, uniform budget procedures and controls; and manages OSMRE's interface with OMB and Congressional committees on appropriations and other budget-related matters.

In addition, the Office coordinates internal control and other program assessment reviews, in accordance with Executive Orders and Departmental initiatives; and monitors implementation of recommendations from evaluations and reports conducted internally and externally.

9

US Fish and Wildlife Service (FWS)

The National Wildlife Refuge System, managed by the US Fish and Wildlife Service, is the world's premier system of public lands and waters set aside to conserve America's fish, wildlife and plants. Since President Theodore Roosevelt designated Florida's Pelican Island as the first wildlife refuge in 1903, the System has grown to more than 150 million acres, 551 national wildlife refuges and other units of the Refuge System, plus 37 wetland management districts.

Under the Fisheries program it also operate 70 National Fish Hatcheries, 65 fishery resource offices and 86 ecological services field stations. Its programs are among the oldest in the world dedicated to natural resource conservation.

The vast majority of fish and wildlife habitat is on non-Federal lands. The Partners for Fish and Wildlife, Partners in Flight, Sport Fishing and Boating Partnership Council, and other partnership activities are the main ways FWC fosters aquatic conservation and assist voluntary habitat conservation and restoration.

The Service employs approximately 9,000 people at facilities across the US The Service is a decentralized organization with a headquarters office in Washington, D.C., with regional and field offices across the country.

Its objectives are:
- Assist in the development and application of an environmental stewardship ethic for the nation, based on ecological principles, scientific knowledge of fish and wildlife, and a sense of moral responsibility.
- Guide the conservation, development, and management of the Nation's fish and wildlife resources.

233

- Administer a national program to provide the public opportunities to understand, appreciate, and wisely use fish and wildlife resources.

It achieves its mission by:
Enforcing federal wildlife laws,
Protecting endangered species,
Managing migratory birds,
Restoring nationally significant fisheries,
Conserving and restoring wildlife habitat such as wetlands,
Helping foreign governments with their international conservation efforts, and
Distributing hundreds of millions of dollars, through its Wildlife Sport Fish and Restoration program, in excise taxes on fishing and hunting equipment to State fish and wildlife agencies.

A little history

•1871: US Commission on Fish and Fisheries created. Charged with studying and recommending solutions to decline in fisheries. Commission was given an initial appropriation of $5000. Spencer Fullerton Baird (1823-1887) is the first Fish Commissioner.

•1872: Fish hatcheries authorized by Congress for propagation of food fishes, initial appropriation is $15,000. Baird Station in northern California used to collect, fertilize and ship salmon eggs by rail to East coast. Deep-sea exploring vessel Albatross launched August 19 to survey offshore fishing, serves as an ocean-going marine biology laboratory for 39 years.

•1885: Office of Economic Ornithology created in Department of Agriculture with a $5000 appropriation. C. Hart Merriam (1855-1942) heads new section and begins survey of geographic distribution of nation's birds and mammals. Early work centers on role of birds in controlling agricultural pests.

•1896: Division of Biological Survey was formed out of Division of Economic Ornithology and Mammalogy. In 1905, it was renamed the Bureau of Biological Survey.

• 1900: Lacey Act passed.

•1900: Division of Biological Survey is given responsibility of enforcing the Lacey Act preventing illegal shipment or importation of wildlife. Beginning of law enforcement role for agency. American Ornithologist's Union hires first "wardens" to foil plumage hunters. Audubon National committee formed to coordinate efforts.

•1903: President Theodore Roosevelt establishes nation's first wildlife refuge on March 14 at Pelican Island National Bird Reservation. Pelican Island is assigned to the Division of Biological Survey. American Ornithologist's Union agrees to pay warden, Paul Kroegel. Commission on Fish and Fisheries renamed Bureau of Fisheries and moved into new Department of Commerce and Labor.

•1905: The Bureau of Biological Survey established in the Department of Agriculture, replacing the old Division of Economic Ornithology and Mammalogy. The new bureau becomes responsible for managing new bird and mammal reservations and "set-aside" areas.

• 1906: Game and Bird Preserves Protection Act (Refuge Trespass Act) gives regulatory authority for public uses on reservation.

• 1909: President Roosevelt establishes 26 Bird Reservations, Mount Olympus National Monument in Washington for elk, and Fire Island, Alaska for moose. The Yukon Delta Bird Reservation in Alaska is 15 million acres.

• 1913: The Federal Migratory Bird Law gives federal government authority over hunting of migratory birds and the first migratory bird hunting regulations were adopted

• 1916: Treaty signed between US and Great Britain (representing Canada) to protect migratory birds.

• 1920s: Bird banding programs started (When were flyways officially designated?)

• 1918: Migratory Bird Treaty Act passed by US Congress implementing the convention between the US and Great Britain (Canada) for the protection of migratory birds.

• 1920s: Bird banding programs started (When were flyways officially designated?)

• 1924: Upper Mississippi River Wildlife and Fish Refuge established by Congress

• 1929: Bear River Migratory Bird Refuge established by Congress

• 1929: Migratory Bird Conservation Act passed authorizing the appropriation of $7.9 million for the purchase or lease of refuges for waterfowl and establishing a Migratory Bird Conservation Commission to approve areas recommended by the Secretary for acquisition with migratory bird conservation funds.

• 1931: Animal Damage Control Act provides broad authority to control predators, rodents and birds under US Department of Interior.

• 1933: Aldo Leopold (1886-1948) writes Game Management.
• 1933: Civilian Conservation Corps crews and Works Progress Administration employees build infrastructure and improve habitat on over 50 national wildlife refuges and fish hatcheries throughout the 1930s.

• 1934: Original Fish and Wildlife Coordination Act authorized the Secretaries of Agriculture and Commerce to "provide assistance to and cooperate with Federal and State agencies" on issues involving the protection and production of fish and wildlife.

• 1934: Thomas Beck, Aldo Leopold, and Jay "Ding" Darling are appointed to a special Presidential Committee on Wildlife ("Beck Committee") to make recommendations to improve national wildlife resources.

- 1934: President Franklin Roosevelt appoints "Ding" Darling to head the Bureau of Biological Survey. Darling and his Chief of Refuges, J. Clark Salyer II, expand the Refuge System to nearly 14 million acres over the next 20 years.

- 1934: Congress passes the Migratory Bird Hunting and Conservation Stamp Act (Duck Stamp Act) providing a source of funding for the acquisition and management of waterfowl habitat.

- 1934: Division of Game Management was created in the Bureau of Biological Survey for wildlife law enforcement.

- 1935: Federal Power Act is enacted and requires the Federal Energy Regulatory Commission to accept the Service's prescriptions for fish passage.

- 1935: Lacey Act amended to prohibit foreign commerce in illegally taken wildlife.

- 1936: Convention between the US and Mexico for the protection of migratory birds and game mammals is signed.

- 1935: The Waterfowl Flyways of North America. In 1935, relying on data from waterfowl banding, Frederick Lincoln developed the Flyways concept. The concept gained widespread credence and is still applied in an administrative context with the annual development of migratory bird hunting regulations.

- 1936: Bureau of Fisheries hires Rachel Carson (1907-1964) as a biologist.

- 1937: Congress passes Federal Aid in Wildlife Restoration Act (Pittman-Robertson Act). The Act makes federal funds available for state wildlife protection and propagation. The funds are derived from taxes on rifles, archery equipment and ammunition and are used for purchasing game habitat and conducting wildlife research.

• 1940: Fish and Wildlife Service is created by combining the Bureau of Fisheries and the Bureau of Biological Survey within the Department of Interior. Ira Gabrielson named first Director of Fish and Wildlife Service

• 1940: Western Hemisphere Convention signed by the US (Convention on Nature Protection and Wildlife Preservation in the Western Hemisphere). -- Under this 1940 treaty, the governments of the United States and 17 other American republics expressed their wish to "protect and preserve in their natural habitat representatives of all species and genera of their native flora and fauna, including migratory birds" and to protect regions and natural objects of scientific value. The nations agreed to take certain actions to achieve these objectives, including the adoption of "appropriate measures for the protection of migratory birds of economic or esthetic value or to prevent the threatened extinction of any given species."

• 1940: Bald Eagle Act enacted.

• 1942: Fish and Wildlife Service Headquarters Office moves to Chicago for the duration of World War II.

• 1942: First Refuge Field Manual issued addressing a variety of organizational, personnel and management topics.

• 1946: The Service's River Basin Studies Program was founded in response to amendments to the Fish and Wildlife Coordination Act and growing demands for more protection of fish and wildlife resources threatened by large federal water projects. Created a growing network of field offices that would become our Ecological Services field offices of today, bringing fish and wildlife technical assistance to the public and state agencies throughout the country.

• 1946: Albert Day becomes FWS Director.

• 1949: A Sand County Almanac published.

• 1949: Duck Stamp Act increases fee to $2 while allowing up to 25% of any refuge's area to be used for hunting.

• 1951: Administrative Flyway system for waterfowl management adopted.

• 1953: John Farley becomes FWS Director.

• 1955: The Continental Waterfowl Population Survey Program begins standardized cooperative surveys performed by the US Fish and Wildlife Service, the Canadian Wildlife Service, state and provincial biologists, and non-governmental cooperators. The survey program is believed to be the most extensive, comprehensive, long-term annual wildlife survey effort in the world. The results of these surveys determine the status of North America's waterfowl populations; play a significant role in setting annual waterfowl hunting regulations; and help to guide the decisions of waterfowl managers throughout North America.

• 1956: The Fish and Wildlife Act of 1956 established a comprehensive national fish and wildlife policy and broadened the authority for acquisition and development of refuges.

•1956: The Fish and Wildlife Service re-organized into the United States Fish and Wildlife Service consisting of the Bureau of Sport Fisheries and Wildlife and Bureau of Commercial Fisheries.

• 1957: Daniel Janzen becomes FWS Director.

• 1958: Amendments to the Fish and Wildlife Coordination Act require coordination between Federal and State agencies and consideration of fish and wildlife impacts, thereby laying the groundwork for the creation of the National Environmental Policy Act (NEPA) and portions of the Clean Water Act.

• 1960: Arctic National Wildlife Range established

• 1962: Recognizing new public demands for recreational activities after World War II, Congress passed the Refuge Recreation Act of 1962 which authorized the recreational use of refuges when such uses did not interfere with the area's primary purposes and when sufficient funds were available to conduct recreational activities.

• 1962: Rachel Carson publishes Silent Spring.

• 1962: Bald Eagle Protection Act amended to become the Bald and Golden Eagle Protection Act.

• 1964: John Gottschalk becomes FWS Director.

• 1964: Congress passes the Land and Water Conservation Fund and provides a dedicated funding stream for land acquisition.

• 1964: Wilderness Act creates National Wilderness Preservation System which includes national wildlife refuges.

• 1966: Congress passes the National Wildlife Refuge System Administration Act for the administration and management of all areas in the system including "wildlife refuges, areas for the protection and conservation of fish and wildlife that are threatened with extinction, wildlife ranges, game ranges, wildlife management areas, and waterfowl production areas."

• 1967: Bald eagles declared an endangered species

• 1969: The National Environmental Policy Act (NEPA) passed by Congress and becomes the principle tool for assessing the impacts of major federal development projects on fish and wildlife. NEPA planning is now the center piece of nearly all federal resource planning and mitigation.

• 1970: Spencer Smith becomes FWS Director.

• 1970: The Endangered Species Conservation Act of 1969 became effective prohibiting the importation into the United States of species "threatened with extinction worldwide," except as specifically allowed for zoological and scientific purposes, and propagation in captivity.

• 1970: Bureau of Commercial Fisheries is moved out of the US Fish and Wildlife Service and transferred to Department of Commerce, renamed

National Marine Fisheries Service as part of new National Oceanic and Atmospheric Administration.

- 1970: The peregrine falcon is listed as endangered, a victim of the pesticide DDT, which caused eggshell thinning and prevented breeding success

- 1970: First Earth Day celebrated on April 22.

- 1971: The Alaska Native Claims Settlement Act (ANCSA), an outgrowth of the Alaska Statehood Act, authorized the addition of immense acreages of highly productive, internationally significant wildlife lands to the Refuge System.

- 1971: Convention on Wetlands of International Importance Especially as Waterfowl Habitats; adopted in Ramsar, Iran, on February 3, 1971, and opened for signature at UNESCO headquarters on July 12, 1972. On December 21, 1975, the Convention entered into force after the required signatures of seven countries. The United States Senate consented to ratification of the Convention on October 9, 1986, and the President signed instruments of ratification on November 10, 1986. The Convention maintains a list of wetlands of international importance and works to encourage the wise use of all wetlands in order to preserve the ecological characteristics from which wetland values derive. The Convention is self-implementing, with the US Fish and Wildlife Service serving as the US administrative authority for the Convention, in consultation with the Department of State.

- 1972: The Environmental Protection Agency bans the use of DDT in the US because of its potential danger to both people and to wildlife, including the bald eagle, peregrine falcon, and brown pelican.

- 1972: US and Japan signed the Convention for the Protection of Migratory Birds and Birds in Danger of Extinction, and Their Environment. The Convention addresses the conservation of migratory birds in the US, its territories, and Japan.

• 1972: The Marine Mammal Protection Act was enacted, prohibiting the take (i.e., hunting, killing, capture, and /or harassment) of marine mammals, and enacting a moratorium on the import, export, and sale of marine mammal parts and products.

• 1973: Lynn Greenwalt becomes FWS Director.

• 1973: Congress passes the Endangered Species Act and puts Fish and Wildlife Service and National Marine Fisheries Service in charge of enforcing it. Over 25 refuges have been established for the specific protection of an endangered species, including the Attwater Prairie Chicken, Mississippi Sandhill Crane, and Crocodile Lake Refuges.

• 1975: The Convention on International Trade in Endangered Species of Wild Fauna and Flora (CITES) is ratified, regulating the importation, exportation, and re-exportation of species.

• 1976: Convention Between the US and the USSR Concerning the Conservation of Migratory Birds and Their Environment, signed in Moscow on November 19, 1976. The Convention provides for the protection of species of birds that migrate between the United States and the Soviet Union or that occur in either country and "have common flyways, breeding, wintering, feeding or moulting areas."

• 1977: The first plant species are listed as endangered—the San Clemente Island Indian paintbrush, San Clemente Island larkspur, San Clemente Island broom, and San Clemente Island bush-mallow.

• 1978: The US Supreme Court finds the Tennessee Valley Authority in violation of the ESA by building a dam that would threaten the continued survival of the snail darter.

• 1978: The US Supreme Court finds the Tennessee Valley Authority in violation of the ESA by building a dam that would threaten the continued survival of the snail darter.

• 1980: Congress passes the Alaska National Interest Lands Conservation Act, creating 9 new wildlife refuges including the 18 million acre Arctic National Wildlife Refuge, and expanding 7 other units. The law adds 54 million refuge acres in Alaska, tripling the size of the Refuge System.

• 1980: Fish and Wildlife Conservation Act enacted protecting non-game species.

• 1981: Robert Jantzen becomes FWS Director.

• 1984: National Fish and Wildlife Foundation Establishment Act creates the Foundation as a federally chartered charitable, non-profit corporation to aid Service conservation efforts.

• 1985: Animal Damage Control moved from Fish and Wildlife Service to the Animal and Plant Health Inspection Service in United States Department of Agriculture.

• 1986: Frank Dunkle becomes FWS Director.

• 1986: North American Waterfowl Management Plan signed. Recognizing the importance of waterfowl and wetlands to North Americans and the need for international cooperation to help in the recovery of a shared resource, the US and Canadian governments developed a strategy to restore waterfowl populations through habitat protection, restoration, and enhancement. The strategy was documented in the North American Waterfowl Management Plan signed in 1986 by the Canadian Minister of the Environment and the US Secretary of the Interior, the foundation partnership upon which hundreds of others would be built. With its update in 1994, Mexico became a signatory to the Plan.

• 1988: The African Elephant Conservation Act became law, providing additional protection for the species, whose numbers had declined by 50 percent in the last decade. The Lacey Act was amended to include, among other things, felony provisions for commercial guiding violations.

• 1989: John Turner becomes FWS Director.

• 1989: Congress passes the North American Wetlands Conservation Act. The North American Wetlands Conservation Act was passed, in part, to support activities under the North American Waterfowl Management Plan, an international agreement that provides a strategy for the long-term protection of wetlands and associated uplands habitats needed by waterfowl and other migratory birds in North America. The Act provides matching grants to organizations and individuals who have developed partnerships to carry out wetlands conservation projects in the United States, Canada, and Mexico for the benefit of wetlands-associated migratory birds and other wildlife.

• 1989: The National Fish and Wildlife Forensics Laboratory was dedicated in Ashland, Oregon, providing expertise to assist in investigations, ranging from species identification to technical assistance such as surveillance and photography.

• 1990: Northern Spotted owl listed as threatened species.

• 1993: Mollie Beattie becomes first female FWS Director.

• 1995: Bald eagle upgraded from endangered to a threatened species.

• 1997: National Wildlife Refuge System Improvement Act strengthens the mission of the Refuge System, clarifies priority public uses, and requires comprehensive conservation plans for every refuge.

• 1997: Jamie Clark becomes FWS Director.

• 1997: The National Conservation Training Center in Shepherdstown, West Virginia is officially dedicated.

• 1998: Reauthorization of the Rhinoceros-Tiger Conservation Act prohibited the import, export, or sale of any product, item or substance containing, or labeled as containing, any substance derived from tigers or rhinos.

• 1999: The peregrine falcon delisted following recovery.

• 2000: Congress passes the Neotropical Migratory Bird Conservation Act to protect and conserve neotropical migrants both in the US and in their winter homes in Latin America and the Caribbean.

• 2002: Steven Williams becomes FWS Director.

• 2004: The California Condor reproduces in the wild for the first time in 17 years.

• 2005: H. Dale Hall becomes FWS Director.

• 2006: White nose syndrome first discovered in a single cave in New York. The fungal disease has since spread to 19 states and four Canadian provinces, and killed more than 5.7 million bats.

• 200: Papahanaumokuakea Marine National Monument--the first marine national monument--was established by Presidential proclamation under the authority of the Antiquities Act of 1906. Papahanaumokuakea Marine National Monument, which extends 1200 miles from Nihoa to Kure Atoll in the Northwestern Hawaiian Islands, is the largest protected area in the United States.

• 2007: As a result of the banning of DDT and ESA protection, the bald eagle is delisted due to recovery.

• 2009: Sam Hamilton becomes FWS Director.

• 2009: Three additional marine national monuments were established in the Pacific. In total, these 4 marine monuments protect the biological and geological heritage on nearly 214,777,000 acres of small islands, atolls, coral reefs, submerged lands, and deep blue waters.

• 2009: As a result of the banning of DDT and ESA protection, more than 650,000 brown pelicans could be found across Florida and the Gulf and Pacific

Coasts. Therefore, it is removed from Federal protection as an endangered species.

• 2010: On April 20, the Deepwater Horizon drilling rig exploded and sank in the Gulf of Mexico, triggering the largest oil spill in history. Oil gushed from the sea floor until the well was capped on July 15. About 4.9 million barrels of oil are estimated to have been spilled during these 87 days. During the response and continuing in the damage assessment FWS employees worked to rescue oiled wildlife, patrol beaches, wetlands, and estuaries, relocate sea turtles, assist the States and local landowners, and evaluate the ecological impacts of the spill.

• 2011: Dan Ashe becomes FWS Director.

• 2013: On November 14, 2013, the United States destroyed its six-ton stock of confiscated elephant ivory, sending a clear message that the nation will not tolerate wildlife crime that threatens to wipe out the African elephant and a host of other species around the globe. The destruction of this ivory, which took place at the US Fish and Wildlife Service's National Wildlife Property Repository on the Rocky Mountain Arsenal National Wildlife Refuge near Denver, Colorado, was witnessed by representatives of African nations and other countries, dozens of leading conservationists, and international media representatives.

• 2014: On February 5, 2014, the US Fish and Wildlife Service proposed delisting the Oregon chub from the Endangered Species Act. If finalized, it would be the first ever fish removed from the ESA due to recovery, a monumental success for the Service and the many partners who worked together to make this happen, and for all Americans concerned about the health of our nation's wildlife.

Statutory Authority and Functions

A 1940 reorganization plan (54 Stat. 1232) in the Department of the Interior consolidated the Bureau of Fisheries and the Bureau of Biological Survey into one agency to be known as the Fish and Wildlife Service. The Bureau of Sport Fisheries and Wildlife was created as a part of the US Fish and Wildlife

Service in the Department of the Interior on November 6, 1956, by the Fish and Wildlife Act of 1956 (70 Stat. 1119). That act was amended on July 1, 1974, by Public Law 93-271 (88 Stat. 92) to, among other purposes, abolish the position of Commissioner of Fish and Wildlife and designate the Bureau as the US Fish and Wildlife Service.

Offices and Divisions

Division of Conservation Business Management

Conservation Business Management describes an integrated set of business processes, practices & tools that enable the Service to better define, invest in, and deliver measurable improvements to populations of targeted species – improving its ability to prioritize efforts and focus its limited resources on the conservation actions that will have the greatest impacts, and make the greatest difference to the species that it is charged to conserve

Organizational Performance Management

Organizational performance management at FWS was developed to streamline business processes and develop a performance based culture. Its comprehensive performance management solution integrates budgeting and planning processes with financial and performance management solutions. The integrated framework aligns and cascades performance information from DOI to FWS Programs.

Business Process Innovations

The Human Capital Management System (HCMS) is an automated, web-based tool that managers use to create and store position descriptions and job analysis components (such as knowledge required by the position and selective factors). The tool provides managers and supervisors an automated suite of relevant and reliable reference materials that pre-populate PDs and job analysis components.

Support Tools Training

The Division of Conservation Business Management provides basic video tutorials and PowerPoint presentation materials to assist FWS Employees in using the automated tools needed to support performance management. Additional information and user guides are also available to support

Conservation Management tools, Business Process Innovations tools (i.e. PD Express) and SES Performance Accomplishment Reporting.

Office of the Assistant Director for Business Management and Operations (ABMO)

The ABMO organization provides a foundation and the necessary tools for all natural resources programs to accomplish their day-to-day operations and to accomplish the Service's mission.

The Office is responsible for the development of policy and Service-wide guidance on a myriad of business management and operational activities. ABMO directs, formulates, and manages Service-wide financial management activities, contracting and acquisition management, engineering and construction management, Service-wide safety, occupational health, industrial hygiene programs, economic analyses, and other associated operational support functions.

Division of Engineering

The Division of Engineering (DEN) manages the Service's construction, dam safety, bridge safety, seismic safety and environmental compliance programs. Key areas of responsibility include: engineering program management, civil and facility design, construction management, dam safety, bridge safety, seismic safety, and environmental compliance. In addition, engineering staffs in the headquarters office and regional offices provide technical leadership in energy management, the sustainability of Service facilities, hazardous materials management and mitigation, environmental compliance, and compliance with other Federal regulations and codes

Division of Financial Management

The Division of Financial Management (DFM) develops and implements policies and procedures for Service-wide financial management, financial system policies and analysis, billings and collections, travel management, external financial reporting, charge card management, stewardship accounting and reporting, accounting operations, cost recovery, financial statement preparation, reporting and auditing, and the Service's investment management program.

Division of Economics

The Division of Economics (ECN) provides socio-economic reviews and analyses including: designation of critical habitat for threatened and endangered species, regulatory impact statements, natural resource damage assessments, record of compliance statements, and hydroelectric dam relicensing reviews. Depending on the requirements of the analysis, the Division has both in-house and contracting capabilities relevant to the Service's mission and goals, including regulatory analysis, hydropower relicensing, endangered species critical habitat designation, natural resource damage assessments, recreation associated with National Wildlife Refuge visitation and National Fish Hatchery production and distribution, invasive species and natural resource based economic development.

Division of Safety and Health

The Division of Safety and Health (DSH) oversees the Service's accident prevention program, accident investigations, and safety reporting and analysis. Its mission is to provide the authority, policy and has responsibility for execution of a safety and occupational health management program to cover all Fish and Wildlife Service activities.

Division of Contracting and General Services

The Division of Contracting and General Services (CGS) develops policy and manages programs for Federal acquisition and financial assistance, purchase cards, personal property, Government quarters, space leasing, and the motor vehicle fleet. Also manages office facilities at the Washington Headquarters.

Endangered Species

As the principal federal partner responsible for administering the Endangered Species Act (ESA), FWC takes the lead in recovering and conserving the Nation's imperiled species by fostering partnerships, employing scientific excellence, and developing a workforce of conservation leaders.

Working in partnership with others, FWS's two major goals are to:

1) Protect endangered and threatened species, and then pursue their recovery; and

2) Conserve candidate species and species-at-risk so that listing under the ESA is not necessary.

These goals are achieved through the following activities:

Candidate Conservation

Working in partnership with public and private landowners, the Candidate Conservation Program assesses species and develops and facilitates the use of voluntary conservation tools for collaborative conservation of candidate and other species-at-risk and their habitats, so that these species do not need the protection of the Endangered Species Act.

The Candidate Conservation Program uniquely bridges the non-regulatory and regulatory approaches to species conservation. Two key elements:

Conducting assessments to identify species most in need of the ESA's protection and the activities that threaten them; and

Working through partnerships to conserve these species by improving habitat and removing threats.

Species Assessments

FWS identifies candidates for listing and provides conservation recommendations that can remove or reduce threats so that listing becomes unnecessary. This process:

Emphasizes coordination with States and other partners to obtain the best available information on species status and recommendations for conservation; and

Provides the foundation for planning and implementing voluntary conservation efforts that are most likely to be effective in improving the status of the species.

Cooperative Conservation

Through a broad suite of public and private partners, FWS provides technical assistance and leverage funding for conservation of candidate and other at-risk species. The program:

Provides information to guide strategic approaches to ensure voluntary efforts occur where they are most needed and most likely to be effective in making listing unnecessary;

Facilitates development and implementation of Candidate Conservation Agreements and Candidate Conservation Agreements with Assurances; and

Leverages resources by facilitating funding for landowners to engage in voluntary conservation (e.g. through various FWS grants and agreements, Farm Bill programs, DOD programs).

Consultations

The ESA directs all Federal agencies to use their existing authorities to conserve threatened and endangered species and, in consultation with the Service, to ensure that their actions do not jeopardize listed species or destroy or adversely modify critical habitat. This applies to management of Federal lands as well as other Federal actions that may affect listed species, such as Federal approval of private activities through the issuance of Federal permits, licenses, or other actions.

The purposes of the Endangered Species Act are to provide a means for conserving the ecosystems upon which endangered and threatened species depend and a program for the conservation of such species. The ESA directs all Federal agencies to participate in conserving these species. Specifically, section 7 (a)(1) of the ESA charges Federal agencies to aid in the conservation of listed species, and section 7 (a)(2) requires the agencies, through consultation with the Service, to ensure that their activities are not likely to jeopardize the continued existence of listed species or adversely modify designated critical habitats.

Early coordination is one of the most effective methods of (1) streamlining section 7 consultation, (2) reducing the need to make project modifications during the consultation process, and (3) improving the ability of section 7 to fulfill its role as a recovery tool. Federal agencies, applicants, and the Service engage in early coordination to develop methods of integrating proposed activities with the conservation needs of listed resources before the proposed actions are fully designed.

Before initiating an action, the Federal agency or its non-Federal permit applicant should coordinate with the Service as to the species that may be within their action area. If a listed species is present, the Federal agency must determine whether the project may affect it. If so, consultation may be required. If the action agency determines (and the Service agrees) that the project is not likely to adversely affect a listed species or designated critical habitat, and the Service concurs in writing, then the consultation (informal to this point) is concluded.

If the Federal agency determines that a project is likely to adversely affect a listed species or designated critical habitat, the agency initiates formal consultation by providing information with regard to the nature of the anticipated effects. The ESA requires that consultation be completed within 90 days, and the regulations allow an additional 45 days for the Service to prepare a biological opinion. The analysis of whether or not the proposed action is likely to jeopardize the continued existence of the species or adversely modify designated critical habitat is contained in a biological opinion. If a jeopardy or adverse modification determination is made, the biological opinion must identify any reasonable and prudent alternatives that could allow the project to move forward.

The Service must anticipate any incidental take that may result from the proposed project and, provided that such take will not jeopardize the continued existence of the listed species, authorize that take in an incidental take statement. The latter contains clear terms and conditions designed to reduce the impact of the anticipated take to the species involved. The authorization of incidental take is contingent upon the Federal agency carrying out the terms and conditions. If the Service issues either a non-jeopardy opinion or a jeopardy opinion that contains reasonable and prudent alternatives, it may include an incidental take statement.

Grants

Grants for states and territories, offered through the Cooperative Endangered Species Conservation Fund, fund participation in a wide array of voluntary conservation projects for candidate, proposed and listed species. These funds may in turn be awarded to private landowners and groups for conservation projects.

Because more than half of all species currently listed as endangered or threatened spend at least part of their life cycle on privately owned lands, the US Fish and Wildlife Service (Service) recognizes that success in conserving species will ultimately depend on working cooperatively with landowners, communities, and Tribes to foster voluntary stewardship efforts on private lands. States play a key role in catalyzing these efforts.

A variety of tools are available under the Endangered Species Act (ESA) to help States and landowners plan and implement projects to conserve species. One of the tools, the Cooperative Endangered Species Conservation Fund (section 6 of the ESA) provides grants to States and Territories to participate in a wide array of voluntary conservation projects for candidate, proposed, and listed species. The program provides funding to states and territories for species and habitat conservation actions on non-federal lands. States and territories must contribute a minimum non-federal match of 25 percent of the estimated program costs of approved projects, or 10 percent when two or more States or Territories implement a joint project. A state or territory must currently have, or enter into, a cooperative agreement with the Secretary of the Interior to receive grants. Most states and territories have entered into these agreements for both plant and animal species.

Habitat Conservation Plans

To obtain a permit for conducting activities that might incidentally harm endangered or threatened wildlife, private landowners, corporations, State or local governments, Tribes or other non-Federal landowners need to develop a Habitat Conservation Plan (HCP), designed to offset any harmful effects the proposed activity might have on the species. The Service assists applicants throughout the HCP process, allowing development to proceed consistent with conserving listed species.

Congress answered this question in the introduction to the Endangered Species Act of 1973 (Act), recognizing that endangered and threatened species of wildlife and plants "are of esthetic, ecological, educational, historical, recreational, and scientific value to the Nation and its people."

After this finding, Congress said that the purposes of the Act are "...to provide a means whereby the ecosystems upon which endangered species and threatened species depend may be conserved [and] to provide a program for the conservation of such ... species..." Habitat Conservation Plans (HCPs) under section 10(a)(1)(B) of the Act provide for partnerships with non-Federal parties to conserve the ecosystems upon which listed species depend, ultimately contributing to their recovery.

HCPs are planning documents required as part of an application for an incidental take permit. They describe the anticipated effects of the proposed taking; how those impacts will be minimized, or mitigated; and how the HCP is to be funded. HCPs can apply to both listed and nonlisted species, including those that are candidates or have been proposed for listing. Conserving species before they are in danger of extinction or are likely to become so can also provide early benefits and prevent the need for listing.

Listing and Critical Habitat

Through the Listing Program, the Service determines whether to add a species to the Federal list of endangered and threatened wildlife and plants. Listing affords a species the full range of protections available under the ESA, including prohibitions on killing, harming or otherwise "taking" a species. In some instances, listing can be avoided by the development of Candidate Conservation Agreements which may remove threats facing the candidate species.

Before a plant or animal species can receive the protection provided by the Endangered Species Act (ESA), it must first be added to the federal lists of endangered and threatened wildlife and plants. The List of Endangered and Threatened Wildlife (50 CFR 17.11) and the List of Endangered and Threatened Plants (50 CFR 17.12) contain the names of all species of mammals, birds, reptiles, amphibians, fishes, insects, plants, and other creatures that have been determined by the US Fish and Wildlife Service (Service) or the National Marine Fisheries Service (for most marine life) to be in the greatest need of federal protection.

A species is added to the list when it is determined to be endangered or threatened because of any of the following factors:

the present or threatened destruction, modification, or curtailment of its habitat or range;

overutilization for commercial, recreational, scientific, or educational purposes;

disease or predation;

the inadequacy of existing regulatory mechanisms;

other natural or manmade factors affecting its survival

The ESA provides that any interested person may petition the Secretary of the Interior to add a species to, or to remove a species from, the list of endangered and threatened species. Through the candidate assessment process, Service biologists identify species as listing candidates.

What it means to be listed

Among the conservation benefits authorized for threatened and endangered plants and animals under the ESA are: protection from being jeopardized by federal activities; restrictions on take and trade; a requirement that the Service develop and implement recovery plans for listed species under US jurisdiction; authorization to seek land purchases or exchanges for important habitat; and federal aid to State and Commonwealth conservation departments with cooperative endangered species agreements. Listing also lends greater recognition to a species' precarious status, encouraging conservation effort by other agencies (foreign, federal, state, and local), independent organizations, and concerned individuals.

Section 7 of the ESA directs federal agencies to use their legal authorities to carry out conservation programs for listed species. It also requires these agencies to ensure that any actions they fund, authorize, or carry out are not likely to jeopardize the survival of any endangered or threatened species, or to adversely modify its designated critical habitat (if any).

When an agency finds that one of its activities may affect a listed species, it is required to consult with the Service to avoid jeopardy. If necessary, "reasonable and prudent alternatives," such as project modifications or rescheduling, are suggested to allow completion of the proposed activity while still conserving the species. Where a federal action may jeopardize the survival of a species that is proposed for listing, but has not yet been finalized and added to the list, the federal agency is required to "confer" with the Service (although the recommendations resulting from such a conference are not legally binding).

Additional protection is authorized by section 9 of the ESA, which makes it illegal to take, import, export, or engage in interstate or international commerce in listed animals except by permit for certain conservation purposes. The ESA also makes it illegal to possess, sell, or transport any listed species taken in violation of the law. For plants, trade restrictions are the same but the rules on "take" are different. It is unlawful to collect or maliciously damage any endangered plant on lands under federal jurisdiction. Removing or damaging listed plants on state and private lands in knowing violation of state law, or in the course of violating a state criminal trespass law, also is illegal under the ESA. In addition, some states have more restrictive laws specifically prohibiting the take of state or federally listed plants and animals.

Recovery

The goal of the Endangered Species Act is the recovery of listed species to levels where protection under the Act is no longer necessary. Towards that goal, we develop and implement recovery plans that provide detailed site-specific management actions for private, Federal, and State cooperation in conserving listed species and their ecosystems.

Working with partners, the Service uses a range of conservation tools to "recover" endangered and threatened species—to ensure that they are secure members of their ecosystems. These tools include restoring and acquiring habitat, removing introduced animal predators or invasive plant species, conducting surveys, monitoring individual populations, and breeding species in captivity and releasing them into their historic range.

Collaborative efforts are critical to recovery success. Service partners include Federal, State, and local agencies, Tribal governments, conservation organizations, the business community, landowners, and other concerned citizens.

As a result of these efforts, the ESA has been credited with saving species such as the California condor, blackfooted ferret, peregrine falcon, and our Nation's symbol, the bald eagle, from extinction.

To delist or downlist species, the Service follows a process similar to what is used in considering whether to list species. Populations and recovery achievements in eliminating or reducing threats are assessed, and peer-review is sought.

Working with Tribes

Actions taken under authority of the ESA may affect Indian lands, tribal trust resources, or the exercise of American Indian tribal rights. Accordingly, the Service carries out its responsibilities in a manner that harmonizes the Federal trust responsibility to tribes, tribal sovereignty, and our mission, and strives to ensure that Indian tribes do not bear a disproportionate burden for the conservation of listed species, so as to avoid or minimize the potential for conflict and confrontation.

American Indian lands in the lower 48 States comprise over 45 million acres of reserved lands and an additional 10 million in individual allotments. There are another 40 million acres of traditional Native lands in Alaska. Much of this acreage remains relatively wild and unspoiled.

Home to more than 560 Federally recognized tribes, these lands provide the living space, the sacred and cultural sites, and many of the natural resources that tribes need to keep their people and cultures alive. The importance of these lands to the tribes cannot be overstated. They provide spiritual and physical sustenance, and increasingly, the means for economic self-sufficiency. Tribal governments generally place a high priority on preserving these lands and their natural resources, including many vulnerable wildlife species, for future generations.

As a representative of the Federal government and a steward of our country's natural resources, the US Fish and Wildlife Service has a responsibility to manage these natural resources in a way that:

reflects our Federal trust responsibility toward Indian tribes

respects tribal rights

acknowledges the treaty obligations of the United States toward tribes

uses the government-to-government relationship in dealing with tribes

protects natural resources that the Federal government holds in trust for tribes.

The Service and Indian tribes have a common goal of conserving sensitive species (including candidate, proposed, and listed species) and the ecosystems upon which they depend. Indian lands are not federal public lands or part of the public domain, and are not subject to federal public land laws. They were retained by tribes or were set aside for tribal use pursuant to treaties, statutes, judicial decisions, executive orders or agreements. These lands are managed by Indian tribes in accordance with tribal goals and objectives, within the framework of applicable laws. Many Indian lands have remained untouched by conventional land use practices and therefore are an island of high quality ecosystems, attracting many sensitive species.

Partnerships in Conservation

Invasive Species Program

Invasive species are organisms that are introduced into a non-native ecosystem and which cause, or are likely to cause, harm to the economy, environment or human health. Invasive species are often part of the reason other species can be threatened.

An invasive species is one that is not native to an ecosystem and which causes, or is likely to cause, economic or environmental harm or harm to human health. It is important to note that when we talk about a species being invasive, we are talking about environmental boundaries, not political ones. In addition to the many invasive species from outside the US, there are many species from within the US that are invasive in other parts of the country.

The US Fish and Wildlife Service is the only agency of the US Government whose primary responsibility is the conservation of the nation's fish, wildlife, and plants. Because of its responsibilities, the Service is very concerned about the impacts that invasive species are having across the Nation. Invasive plants and animals have many impacts on fish and wildlife resources. Invasive species degrade, change or displace native habitats and compete with our native wildlife and are thus harmful to our fish, wildlife and plant resources

Migratory Bird Program

Migratory birds are some of nature's most magnificent resources. They have a significant role in the health of the environment, economy, and culture in the US and internationally. The mission of the Fish and Wildlife Service's Migratory Bird Program is to conserve migratory bird populations and their habitats for future generations, through careful monitoring, effective management, and by supporting national and international partnerships that conserve habitat for migratory birds and other wildlife.

As the lead Federal agency for managing and conserving migratory birds in the United States, many Service programs are actively involved in migratory bird conservation activities. Although these activities are generally developed within a specific Service Program, the success of these activities is also dependent upon close intra-Service coordination in addition to building and sustaining vital partnerships with other Federal and State agencies, tribes, and private entities.

The Migratory Bird Program utilizes a number of different lists to direct US Fish and Wildlife Service actions and priorities to manage and protect migratory birds.

The Migratory Bird Treaty Act makes it illegal for anyone to take, possess, import, export, transport, sell, purchase, barter, or offer for sale, purchase, or barter, any migratory bird, or the parts, nests, or eggs of such a bird except under the terms of a valid permit issued pursuant to Federal regulations. The migratory bird species protected by the Act are listed in 50 CFR 10.13. View more information and the list at Migratory Bird Treaty Act.

Focal Species - the US Fish and Wildlife Service initiated the Focal Species strategy to better measure its success in achieving its bird conservation priorities and mandates. The Focal Species strategy involves campaigns for selected species to provide explicit, strategic, and adaptive sets of conservation actions required to return the species to healthy and sustainable levels.

Birds of Conservation Concern - The 1988 amendment to the Fish and Wildlife Conservation Act mandates the US Fish and Wildlife Service to "identify species, subspecies, and populations of all migratory nongame birds that, without additional conservation actions, are likely to become candidates for listing under the Endangered Species Act (ESA) of 1973." *Birds of Conservation Concern 2008 (BCC 2008)* is the most recent effort to carry out this mandate.

Birds of Management Concern - are a subset of Migratory Bird Treaty Act - protected species which pose special management challenges because of a variety of factors (e.g., too few, too many, conflicts with human interests, societal demands). These species are of concern because of documented or apparent population declines, small or restricted populations, dependence on restricted or vulnerable habitats, or overabundant to the point of causing ecological and economic damage.

Environmental Contaminants Program

Pollution is one of the American public's greatest environmental concerns. Like the proverbial "canary in the coal mine," fish and wildlife often signal pollution problems that ultimately affect people and their quality of life. The US Fish and Wildlife Service (Service) is the main federal agency dedicated to protecting wildlife and their habitat from pollution's harmful effects, helping to create a healthy world for all living things.

The Environmental Contaminants Program includes contaminants specialists stationed around the country that are on the front lines in the fight against pollution. They specialize in detecting toxic chemicals; addressing their effects; preventing harm to fish, wildlife and their habitats; and removing toxic chemicals and restoring habitat when prevention isn't possible. They are experts on oil and chemical spills, pesticides, water quality, hazardous materials disposal and other aspects of pollution biology. The Contaminant Program's operations are integrated into all other Service activities and the Service's contaminants specialists often work in partnership with other agencies and organizations which have come to rely on their expertise.

". . . synthetic pesticides have been so thoroughly distributed throughout the animate and inanimate world that they occur virtually everywhere. They have been recovered from most of the major river systems and even from streams of groundwater flowing unseen through the earth. Residues of these chemicals linger in soil to which they may have been applied a dozen years before. . . They have been found in fish in remote mountain lakes, in earthworms burrowing in soil, in the eggs of birds--and in man himself."
- Rachel Carson, Silent Spring

Contaminants specialists review environmental documents, legislation, regulations, and permits and licenses with pollution potential to ensure that harmful effects on fish, wildlife, and plants are avoided or minimized. Some examples include:

- analysis of documents and permits related to control of nonpoint source pollution from agriculture and urban runoff, point source pollution from industrial and municipal waste treatment facilities, and discharges of dredge and fill material;
- review of proposed Federal projects related to mining, agricultural irrigation, range management, and oil and gas development to ensure that habitat quality concerns are adequately addressed;
- review of EPA pesticide registration proposals to ensure that potential impacts to fish and wildlife are considered; and,
- review of pesticide use on FWS lands to ensure these chemicals are properly applied and, in some cases, to recommend the use of acceptable alternatives.

Service environmental contaminant specialists conduct field studies to determine sources of pollution, to investigate pollution effects on fish and wildlife and their habitat, and to investigate fish and wildlife die-offs. Sites typically assessed include those impacted by pesticides, industrial wastes, oil and hazardous waste spills, and drain water from agricultural irrigation and mining, as well as Superfund sites and other sites contaminated at some time in the past.

Contaminants specialists have also developed tools such as the Contaminants Assessment Process (CAP), which was developed in cooperation with the US Geological Survey's Status and Trends of Biological Resources Program to assist in evaluating contaminant threats to national wildlife refuges, as well as other Service lands. In addition, field specialists conduct contaminant surveys prior to the Service buying new lands.

Data collected in contaminant assessments is often used to secure compensation for resources lost or degraded by hazardous waste releases or spills. These efforts are part of the Natural Resource Damage Assessment and Restoration Program (Restoration Program). The Service also takes part, through contaminants identification, assessment, planning and restoration, in the Department of Interior's National Irrigation Water Quality Program (NIWQP).

Contaminant specialist are often called in by the US Environmental Protection Agency (EPA), US Coast Guard, or various other Federal or State agencies responsible for cleaning up a contaminated area, to ensure that fish and wildlife and their habitat are adequately protected during, and upon completion of, the cleanup. Contaminants specialists also work closely with National Wildlife Refuge managers to design and implement actions to cleanup oil and hazardous material on refuge lands.

Training field office staff, analyzing contaminant samples, and managing information are all key to the Contaminants Program's success. A large part of the Program's technical support comes from the Analytical Control Facility (ACF), part of the National Conservation Training Center in Shepherdstown, West Virginia. Staff at ACF are responsible for such things as overseeing all Service chemical analysis and managing the Environmental Contaminants Data Management System. This system is designed to electronically store, analyze, and create reports on the vast amount of analytical information obtained from fish and wildlife tissue samples collected by FWS biologists.

National Conservation Training Center

The National Conservation Training Center trains and educates natural resource managers to accomplish the common goal of conserving fish, wildlife, plants, and their habitats. As the "home of the Fish and Wildlife Service," NCTC brings exceptional training and education opportunities to

Service employees and others. The Center supports the mission of the U.S Fish and Wildlife Service in five critical ways:

Home and Heritage: NCTC serves as the physical and virtual home of the US Fish and Wildlife Service, where the history and heritage of the Service are preserved and shared;

Training for the Mission: NCTC provides exemplary training and professional development tailored to support Service employees and conservation partners in accomplishing the agency's mission;

Youth in Conservation: NCTC helps the Service engage, educate, and employ the next generation of conservationists who reflect our diverse society, ensuring that our natural resource legacy is left in capable hands;

Partnerships: NCTC helps solve urgent conservation challenges, such as climate change, by bringing together diverse partners representing multiple points of view;

Sustainability: NCTC is a national leader in the conservation community for its state-of-the art facility and green practices.

Fisheries

In 1871, the US Department of State fostered the establishment of the Commission of Fish and Fisheries for the following reasons:

a growing concern over the observed decline in the Nation's fishery resources

a lack of information concerning the status of the Nation's fisheries

a need to define and protect US fishing rights

Spencer Fullerton Baird, a prominent research scientist, was appointed the first US Commissioner of Fish and Fisheries. Baird had previously been serving as the Assistant Secretary of the Smithsonian Institution since 1850. Before his appointment Baird had already recognized the urgent need to assemble the necessary information to help analyze the magnitude of declining fisheries and identify the factors which were contributing to the decrease in fish populations.

Consequently, it is not surprising that the first national funding for fisheries conservation occurred one year before the establishment of the US Commission of Fish and Fisheries.

Commissioner Baird's primary duty, as directed by the President and the Senate, was to "ascertain whether any and what diminution in the number of food fishes of the coast and inland lakes has occurred." He was also required to report to Congress the necessary remedial measures to be adopted and was authorized to take fish from lakes and coastal waters, regardless of any state law.

In 1872, the Senate and the House charged the Fisheries Commission with an additional task of "supplementing declining native stocks of coastal and lake food fish through fish propagation."

America's fish and aquatic resources are among the world's richest, and provide substantial social, economic, and ecological benefits to the Nation. The US Fish and Wildlife Service's Division of Fisheries and Habitat Conservation is committed to working with partners to promote healthy fish and wildlife, healthy habitats, healthy people, and a healthy economy.

The Fisheries Program applies scientific data to focus conservation activities on high-priority species and habitats. We are committed to protecting and maintaining stable populations and healthy habitats and restoring degraded habitats and depleted populations. The healthy habitat is vital to well managed aquatic resources, continuing ecological, recreational, commercial, and subsistence contributions to our nation's prosperity.

Law Enforcement

Law enforcement is essential to virtually every aspect of wildlife conservation. The Office of Law Enforcement contributes to Service efforts to manage ecosystems, save endangered species, conserve migratory birds, preserve wildlife habitat, restore fisheries, combat invasive species, and promote international wildlife conservation.

Service law enforcement today focuses on potentially devastating threats to wildlife resources -- illegal trade, unlawful commercial exploitation, habitat destruction, and environmental contaminants. The Office of Law Enforcement investigates wildlife crimes, regulates wildlife trade, helps Americans understand and obey wildlife protections laws, and works in partnership with international, state, and tribal counterparts to conserve wildlife resources. This work includes:

- Breaking up international and domestic smuggling rings that target imperiled animals
- Preventing the unlawful commercial exploitation of protected US species
- Protecting wildlife from environmental hazards and safeguarding critical habitat for endangered species
- Enforcing federal migratory game bird hunting regulations and working with states to protect other game species from illegal take and preserve legitimate hunting opportunities
- Inspecting wildlife shipments to ensure compliance with laws and treaties and detect illegal trade
- Working with international counterparts to combat illegal trafficking in protected species
- Training other federal, state, tribal, and foreign law enforcement officers
- Using forensic science to analyze evidence and solve wildlife crimes
- Distributing information and outreach materials to increase public understanding of wildlife conservation and promote compliance with wildlife protection laws

When fully staffed, the Office of Law Enforcement includes 261 special agents and some 140 wildlife inspectors. Most are "officers on the beat" who report through eight regional law enforcement offices. A headquarters Office of Law Enforcement provides national oversight, support, policy, and guidance for Service investigations and the wildlife inspection program; trains Service law enforcement personnel; fields a special investigations unit; and provides budget, management and administrative support for the Office of Law Enforcement.

The Clark R. Bavin National Fish and Wildlife Forensics Laboratory conducts scientific analyses that support federal, state, and international investigations of wildlife crime. The Office of Law Enforcement also maintains a National Wildlife Property Repository, which supplies abandoned and forfeited wildlife items to schools, universities, museums, and non-government organizations for public education, and operates the National Eagle Repository, which meets the needs of Native Americans for eagles and eagle feathers for religious use.

Wetlands

The Service is the principal Federal agency that provides information to the public on the extent and status of the Nation's wetlands. The agency has developed a series of topical maps to show wetlands and deep water habitats. This geospatial information is used by Federal, State, and local agencies, academic institutions, and private industry for management, research, policy development, education and planning activities.

Wetlands provide a multitude of ecological, economic and social benefits. They provide habitat for fish, wildlife and a variety of plants. Wetlands are nurseries for many saltwater and freshwater fishes and shellfish of commercial and recreational importance. Wetlands are also important landscape features because they hold and slowly release flood water and snow melt, recharge groundwater, recycle nutrients, and provide recreation and wildlife viewing opportunities for millions of people.

There are an estimated 110.1 million acres (44.6 million ha) of wetlands in the Conterminous US Wetlands composed 5.5 percent of the surface area of the U. S. An estimated 95 percent of all wetlands are freshwater and five percent are in the marine or estuarine (saltwater) systems. There are an estimated 104.3 million acres (42.2 million ha) of freshwater wetland and 5.8 million acres (2.4 million ha) of intertidal (saltwater) wetlands.

Wetlands are found in all 48 states and in every physiographic region of the country. Of the freshwater wetland population contained in the national sample, ponds are the most prevalent wetland type found in urban areas, whereas freshwater emergent wetlands are the least common type. On agricultural lands, there is a fairly even distribution of wetland types with forested, emergent and ponds represented. Land predominantly in silviculture has the highest percentage of forested and shrub wetland. Rural areas exhibiting growth have a mix of all freshwater wetland types, as this represents an interface with new development activities.

International Affairs

While the Endangered Species Program deals primarily with species found in the US and its territories, and the International Affairs Program deals primarily with foreign endangered species, these species occasionally overlap. Both programs work closely with the governments of Canada and Mexico to cooperatively conserve species at risk across North America.

The **Branch of Foreign Species** (BFS), like the domestic listing side of the Endangered Species Program, determines the status of foreign species and whether they should be added to the Federal list of threatened and endangered wildlife and plants and receive protections provided by the Endangered Species Act of 1973, as amended. The BFS also assesses foreign species already listed as threatened or endangered to determine whether they should be reclassified from threatened to endangered, reclassified from endangered to threatened, or removed from the list (delisted).

The Endangered Species Act (ESA) requires the Service to list species as endangered or threatened regardless of which country the species lives in. Benefits to the species include prohibitions on certain activities including import, export, take, commercial activity, interstate commerce, and foreign commerce. By regulating activities, the United States ensures that people under the jurisdiction of the United States do not contribute to the further decline of listed species. Although the ESA's prohibitions regarding listed species apply only to people subject to the jurisdiction of the United States, the ESA can generate conservation benefits such as increased awareness of listed species, research efforts to address conservation needs, or funding for in-situ conservation of the species in its range countries. The ESA also provides for limited financial assistance to develop and manage programs to conserve listed species in foreign countries, encourages conservation programs for such species, and allows for assistance for programs, such as personnel and training.

International Affairs works to conserve living resources around the world by working with people to conserve nature and regulating international wildlife trade.

Fish, wildlife, and plants don't recognize national boundaries. Wildlife and natural resources all over the world are under pressure from human activities such as poaching, illegal harvesting of bushmeat, resource extraction, habitat destruction and pollution. If we want to have any hope at all of saving these important animals and habitats from extinction, we have to work across national boundaries, saving wildlife without borders. In addition, international conservation efforts are of strategic importance to US national security and economic interests because a degraded environment destabilizes communities thus putting people's livelihoods at risk. This sets the stage for political instability and conflict.

The Division of International Conservation implements the **Wildlife Without Borders** program, launched in 1972, to help conserve the world's most treasured wildlife and habitats. The program builds the capacity of local people to identify, value, and conserve the wildlife and their habitats. It partners with other nations at all levels - from grassroots capacity building to applied conservation research, to wildlife management training and improving the coexistence of people and wildlife.

The program operated through a number of branches.

Global Branch. Focusing on species, ecosystems, and emerging and cross cutting issues worldwide, the Wildlife Without Borders Global Program seeks to ensure international cooperation to conserve habitats and endangered species. The Global Branch focuses on international treaties and conventions; partnerships; cross cutting and emerging issues; communications; and grant programs. The Global Branch partners with federal agencies, non-government organizations, private sector corporations, philanthropic institutions, multilateral agencies, and other entities to align priorities for international wildlife conservation and societal impact and to leverage collaborative efforts.

Latin America and Caribbean Branch. The principal goal of the Latin America and the Caribbean Branch is to strengthen the ability of local people and institutions to manage and conserve species, habitats, and ecological processes. The three core strategies implemented by the Latin America and Caribbean Branch are built upon a holistic and inter-disciplinary approach to conservation with a primary emphasis on the social context: building the capacity of key stakeholders through innovative training programs, fostering networks to facilitate learning and collaboration across sites, and enhancing conservation values and behaviors to achieve environmental sustainability.

Mexico Branch. The principal goal of the Mexico Branch is to strengthen Mexico's capacity to conserve its globally important biological resources. The Branch achieves this through the development of signature initiatives which develop local capacity for biodiversity conservation and management. The Mexico Branch also supports regional approaches, working with the governments of Mexico and Canada, through implementation of the Canada/Mexico/US Trilateral Committee for Wildlife and Ecosystem Conservation and Management MOU, and related legislation.

Near East, South Asia, and Africa Branch. The Near East, South Asia, and Africa Branch's principle goal is to strengthen the capacity of conservation and natural resource managers, institutions, and communities of the region to conserve biological diversity. This includes species ecosystem conservation. In order to accomplish this goal, the Branch cooperates with domestic and foreign governmental agencies, national and international non-governmental conservation organizations, and universities through legal mandates, international treaties, conventions, protocols, agreements, the Multinational Species Conservation Funds (African and Asian elephant, great apes, rhinoceros and tiger, and marine turtle) and other regional initiatives.

Policy and Partnerships Branch. The Branch of Policy and Partnerships coordinates grant functions and partnership activities to support conservation of wildlife around the globe. The Branch develops and implements grant management policy in accordance with regulatory requirements, while accommodating the logistical concerns of effective on-the-ground conservation work. The Branch also leads strategic planning activities to engage external and internal audiences in supporting and guiding the Service's international conservation work. The Branch seeks to strengthen partnerships with other federal agencies, foreign countries, non-governmental organizations, and other interested entities and individuals in order to enhance sustainability of conservation achievements and maximize conservation project funding through appropriations and matching resources.

Russia and East Asia Branch. The principal goal of the Russia and East Asia Branch is to promote the conservation of wildlife resources in Russia and East Asia. To accomplish this goal, the Branch cooperates with domestic and foreign governmental agencies, national and international non-governmental organizations, universities, and other interested parties. Since 1972, the US Fish & Wildlife Service and its counterpart agencies in the former Soviet Union have studied and conserved wildlife and their habitats. These collaborative efforts have grown to encompass topics such as shared species of migratory birds; fish and marine mammals; refuges and other protected lands; and the vast ecosystem represented by the Bering and Chukchi Seas. Since 1986, the Service has had ongoing cooperation with wildlife managers in China, exchanging ideas for addressing wildlife trade issues as well as wetlands, river, and floodplain management.

The **Division of Management Authority** (DMA) and the **Division of Scientific Authority** (DSA) work together to implement domestic laws and international treaties that promote the long-term conservation of plant and animal species by ensuring that international trade does not threaten their survival in the wild.

DMA implements domestic laws and international treaties to promote long-term conservation of global fish and wildlife resources. In response to ever-increasing global pressures of wildlife trade and habitat loss on species worldwide, the office dedicates its efforts to conserving species at risk from trade and implementing policies that have a broad impact on conservation overall.

DMA is one of three divisions within the International Affairs Program. International cooperation is essential to safeguarding the survival of many wild animals and plants in trade. The Convention on International Trade in Endangered Species of Wild Fauna and Flora (CITES) provides a framework for nations to work together to prevent further declines in wildlife populations. Most U.N. recognized nations are now party to CITES, the total number of signatories now stands at 180 countries. Each country has a Management Authority to oversee implementation of CITES. In the United States, this role is carried out by DMA.

DMA's Branch of Permits and Wildlife Trade and Conservation Branch work together to accomplish the following:

- implement an international permit program
- monitor trade
- coordinate with inspection and enforcement officials
- communicate on CITES issues with others
- work with State and Federal agencies
- provide technical assistance to other countries
- represent the United States at CITES meetings

DSA serves as the US Scientific Authority for the Convention on International Trade in Endangered Species of Wild Fauna and Flora (<u>CITES</u>). It provides scientific advice on the issuance of permits for international trade; the listing of native and foreign species under CITES; implementation of the Wild Bird Conservation Act (WBCA); and other policy matters, particularly as they may relate to international wildlife trade and exotic species.

Duck Stamps

Since 1934, the sales of Federal Duck Stamps has generated more than $800 million which has been used to help purchase or lease over 6 million of acres of waterfowl habitat in the US These lands are now protected in the US Fish & Wildlife Service's National Wildlife Refuge System. Waterfowl are not the only wildlife to benefit. Numerous other bird, mammal, fish, reptile, and amphibian species that rely on wetland habitats have prospered. Further, an estimated one-third of the Nation's endangered and threatened species find food or shelter in refuges established using Federal Duck Stamp funds.

People, too, have benefited from the Federal Duck Stamp. Hunters have places to enjoy their sport and other outdoor enthusiasts have places to hike, watch birds, photograph and explore. Moreover, these protected wetlands help purify water supplies, store flood water, reduce soil erosion and sedimentation, and provide spawning areas for fish important to sport and commercial fishermen.

Federal Duck Stamps are vital tools for wetland conservation. Ninety-eight cents of every dollar generated by the sale of Federal Duck Stamps goes directly to purchase or lease wetland habitat for protection in the National Wildlife Refuge System. The Federal Duck Stamp has been called one of the most successful conservation programs ever initiated and is a highly effective way to conserve America's natural resources.

Besides serving as a hunting license and a conservation tool, a current Federal Duck Stamp also serves as an entrance pass for national wildlife refuges where admission is charged. Duck Stamps and products that bear stamp images are also popular collector items.

The Junior Duck Stamp conservation education program teaches students across the nation "conservation through the arts." Revenue generated by the sales of Junior Duck Stamps funds environmental education programs in all 50 states, the District of Columbia and several territories.

Today, many states issue their own duck stamps. In some states, the stamps are purely a collector's item, but in others, the stamps have a similar role in hunting and conservation as Federal Duck Stamps.

10

US Geological Survey

The US Geological Survey (USGS), part of the Department of the Interior, is a science organization that provides impartial information on the health of our ecosystems and environment, the natural hazards that threaten us, the natural resources we rely on, the impacts of climate and land-use change, and the core science systems that help us provide timely, relevant, and useable information.

The USGS serves the nation by providing reliable scientific information to describe and understand the Earth; minimize loss of life and property from natural disasters; manage water, biological, energy, and mineral resources; and enhance and protect our quality of life.

Its expert staff of 10,000 scientists, technicians, and support personnel working at over 400 locations around the US, bring a range of earth and life science disciplines to bear on a wide range of problems. By integrating its diverse scientific expertise, the USGS is able to understand complex natural science phenomena and provide scientific products that lead to solutions.

As the Nation's largest water, earth, and biological science and civilian mapping agency, the US Geological Survey also collects, monitors, analyzes, and provides scientific understanding about natural resource conditions, issues, and problems. The diversity of its scientific expertise enables it to carry out large-scale, multi-disciplinary investigations and provide impartial scientific information to resource managers, planners, and other customers.

History

The United States Geological Survey was established on March 3, 1879, just a few hours before the mandatory close of the final session of the 45th Congress, when President Rutherford B. Hayes signed the bill appropriating money for sundry civil expenses of the Federal Government for the fiscal year beginning July 1, 1879.

The sundry civil expenses bill included a brief section establishing a new agency, the United States Geological Survey, placing it in the Department of the Interior, and charging it with a unique combination of responsibilities: "classification of the public lands, and examination of the geological structure, mineral resources, and products of the national domain." The legislation stemmed from a report of the National Academy of Sciences, which in June 1878 had been asked by Congress to provide a plan for surveying the Territories of the United States that would secure the best possible results at the least possible cost. Its roots, however, went far back into the Nation's history.

The first duty of the Geological Survey required by Congress was the classification of the public lands, originated in the Land Ordinance of 1785. These were the lands west of the Allegheny Mountains claimed by some of the colonies, which became a source of contention in writing the Articles of Confederation until 1781 when the States agreed to cede their western lands to Congress. The extent of the public lands was enormously increased by the Louisiana Purchase in 1803 and later territorial acquisitions.

At the beginning of Confederation, the decision was made not to hold the public lands as a capital asset, but to dispose of them for revenue and to encourage settlement. The Land Ordinance of 1785 provided the method of surveying and a plan for disposal of the lands, but also reserved "one-third part of all gold, silver, lead, and copper mines to be sold or otherwise disposed of, as Congress shall thereafter direct," thus implicitly requiring classification of the lands into mineral and non-mineral. Mapping of the public lands was begun under the direction of the Surveyor-General, but no special provision was made for classification of the public lands, and it thus became the responsibility of the surveyor.

By 1879, eight classes of public lands had been recognized, each of which had separate regulations for disposition, but, except in a few cases, no special provision had been made to secure an accurate classification in advance of disposition. Of the mineral lands listed in the 1785 Ordinance, lead lands had been leased for a time and later sold, and copper lands had been sold, but no regulations were made about the lands bearing precious metals until 1866 when they were declared free and open to exploration and purchase. Iron lands, not mentioned in the 1785 Ordinance, were ruled "not mineral lands," and coal lands, also not mentioned, were offered for sale in 1863. The surveyors were still responsible for classification of the public lands, but, in actual practice, did not make the classification themselves but relied on affidavits from the interested parties.

The earliest geological surveys were made in support of agriculture, which was the basic occupation in the United States in the early 1800's. Manufacturing was then of importance only in a few areas, and mining was a quite insignificant part of the economy. Farmland in the Eastern and Southern States, however, was beginning to lose its fertility, and farmers were abandoning their holdings and moving westward.

In 1834, just a year before the Geological Survey of Great Britain was established, Congress authorized the first Federal examination of the geological structure, mineral resources, and products of the public lands by permitting the Topographical Bureau of the US Army to use $5,000 of its appropriation for geological investigations and the construction of a geological map of the United States.

In 1839, the Federal Government for the first time called on a geologist to classify public lands as Congress made plans to authorize the sale of the mineral lands in the Upper Mississippi Valley. David Dale Owen organized a force that made a survey of 11,000 square miles in a little more than 2 months, which led the Commissioner of the General Land Office to propose that "an officer skilled in the sciences of geology and mineralogy" be appointed to explore all the public lands and thus enable the Commissioner to discriminate between agricultural and mineral lands before putting them on the market. That idea came to naught, but in 1847, when Congress authorized the sale of mineral lands in the Lake Superior Land District in Michigan and the Chippewa Land District in the Territory of Wisconsin, it specified that geological examinations be made prior to the sale.

In 1853, Congress appropriated $150,000 for surveys to ascertain the most practical and economical route for a railroad from the Mississippi River to the Pacific Ocean and authorized the Secretary of War to employ the Corps of Topographical Engineers to make the explorations and surveys.

During the 1850's, while the Topographical Engineers explored four routes for the transcontinental railroad, the industrialization of the Nation quickened. In 1859, for the first time, the value of the products of US industry exceeded the value of agricultural products. In that same year, gold was discovered in Colorado, silver was discovered at the Comstock Lode in western Nevada to begin the era of silver mining in the West, and the first oil well in the United States was successfully drilled in northwestern Pennsylvania. By that time, the relationship between geological surveys and mineral resources was sufficiently clear that when gold mining in California became difficult and costly, the State Legislature established a Geological Survey, on April 21, 1860, to make an accurate and complete geological survey of the State.

By 1867, the developing industries were making radical demands on the Nation's natural resources. Joseph S. Wilson, the Commissioner of the General Land Office, in his annual report written in the fall of 1866, assessed at some length the mineral resources of the public domain, and afterward stated that the proper development of the geological characteristics and mineral wealth of the country was a matter of the highest concern to the American people. On March 2, 1867, Congress for the first time authorized western explorations in which geology would be the principal objective: a study of the geology and natural resources along the fortieth parallel route of the transcontinental railroad, under the Corps of Engineers, and a geological survey of the natural resources of the new State of Nebraska, under the direction of the General Land Office. Looking back at that day's work in 1880, Clarence King, Director of the US Geological Survey, remarked that "Eighteen sixty-seven marks, in the history of national geological work, a turning point, when the science ceased to be dragged in the dust of rapid exploration and took a commanding position in the professional work of the country."

Establishment of the US Geological Survey

Inevitably, conflicts developed between civilian versus military control of mapping. Congress turned to the National Academy of Sciences and asked it to recommend a plan for surveying and mapping the Territories of the United

States that would secure the best possible results at the least possible cost. A committee of seven members appointed by the Academy recommended that the Coast and Geodetic Survey be transferred from the Department of the Treasury to the Department of the Interior, renamed the "Coast and Interior Survey," and be given responsibility for geodetic, topographic, and land-parceling surveys in addition to its existing work. The Academy committee also recommended that an independent organization, to be called the US Geological Survey, be established in the Interior Department to study the geological structure and economic resources of the public domain.

Congress also established a public lands commission, of which the Director of the US Geological Survey would be a member, to prepare a codification of laws relating to the survey and disposition of the public domain, a system and standard of classification of public lands, a system of land-parceling surveys adapted to the economic use of the several classes of lands, and recommendations for disposal of the public lands in the western portion of the United States to actual settlers.

On March 20, 1879, President Hayes sent to the Senate the nomination of Clarence King to be the first Director of the US Geological Survey. The Senate confirmed the nomination on April 3, and King took the oath of office on May 24.

The Fortieth Parallel Exploration under King's direction had led the way in converting western exploration to an exact science. His new position gave him a unique opportunity to influence the development of Federal geology.

In the year that the Geological Survey was established, the Federal Government still held title to more than 1.2 billion acres of land, nearly all of it west of the Mississippi River, of which only 200 million had been surveyed. The edge of settlement was at about 102° West; beyond the frontier were only isolated pockets or belts of settlement, and in vast areas beyond the frontier, the population was officially less than 1 per square mile.

King planned a series of land maps to provide information for agriculturists, miners, engineers, timbermen, and political economists. The mining geology program began in 1879 with comprehensive studies of the geology and technology of three great mining districts--Leadville in Colorado, and the Comstock and Eureka in Nevada--and the collection of mineral statistics in the Western States, while mineral statistics were collected in the Eastern States, and iron resources in all parts of the country.

In 1882, topographic mapping began to provide a base for geologic maps in Eastern as well as Western States. Topographic mapping became the largest part of the Geological Survey program. Paleontologic and stratigraphic studies to support the geologic mapping program were also begun throughout the country.

In 1894, a small appropriation was obtained for the purpose of "gauging the streams and determining the water supply of the United States." In 1895, the work was transferred to the Geologic Branch, and studies of underground water and water utilization were gradually added to the stream gaging. Appropriations were increased regularly, and in 1896 a new series of publications was inaugurated to make available the ever-increasing volume of information. The Irrigation Congress that met in Phoenix in December 1896 reversed the opinions of earlier congresses with regard to the Geological Survey's role in public-land management by recommending establishment of a Public Lands Commission, including the Director of the Geological Survey as a member, to be responsible for preparing a topographic map, determining the water supply, ascertaining the character and value of the timber, and making regulations for the occupation and utilization of the public lands.

By 1897, the Forest Management Act placed management of the forest reserves in the Department of the Interior and required that surveys of the "public lands that have been or may be designated forest reserves" be made under the supervision of the Director of the Geological Survey. Survey topographers within the next 3 years mapped more than 32,000 square miles in and adjacent to the reserves, even though most were in wilderness areas. At the same time, a program of topographic mapping on the larger scales needed for more urbanized areas was steadily growing in cooperation with the Eastern States.

In the late 1890's, geologic work was extended into new fields and went beyond the national domain. In 1897, a Survey geologist and a hydrographer were detailed to the Nicaraguan Canal Commission to study the proposed canal route between the Atlantic and Pacific Oceans. The Commission made extensive use of their findings, marking perhaps the first time on this continent that geological evidence provided support for a great engineering project. After the Spanish-American War in 1898, Survey geologists were sent to investigate the mineral resources of Cuba and the Philippine Islands.

In 1897, a Senate resolution called for a three-man commission, including the Director of the Geological Survey, "to determine the best method of ascertaining all the facts of general importance relating to mines and mining within the United States, whether by a mining bureau, a Secretary of Mines and Mining, a Commissioner of Mines, or a commission."

In December 1898, a Senate resolution called for a Division of Mines and Mining in the Geological Survey to gather statistics on mineral resources and mineral production and to make investigations related to mines and mining.

The reorganization of the Geologic Branch on July 1, 1900, was an experiment designed to separate scientific and administrative control. Seven divisions were established, covering specified subject areas, each in charge of a specialist who would prepare plans of work, establish priorities, recommend geologists to undertake particular projects, and review manuscripts. Party chiefs would plan the conduct of the work.

The accession of Theodore Roosevelt to the Presidency in September 1901, after the assassination of President William McKinley, very quickly had an effect on the Survey program. By inclination and training, Roosevelt was in full sympathy with the movement for scientific management of the Nation's resources, and in his first State of the Union message, in December 1901, outlined a national forest and water policy. The long effort to promote reclamation of the arid lands culminated in passage of the Newlands Act in June 1902 and the establishment of the Reclamation Service. At the same time, the appropriation for the Geological Survey's water-resources investigations was increased and the total appropriation for the Geological Survey for the first time was more than $1 million. At the direction of President Roosevelt, the Reclamation Service became an adjunct of the Geological Survey.

In 1904, the US Geological Survey celebrated the 25th anniversary of its establishment. It had grown from an organization of 38 employees at the end of its first year to one with 491 employees (and another 187 in the adjunct Reclamation Service) in 1904. Its first appropriation had been $106,000; the appropriation for the fiscal year that ended on June 30, 1904, was $1.4 million.

To mark the anniversary, a bulletin describing the Survey and its operations during the 25 years was published. Among the achievements noted were preparation of topographic maps of 929,850 square miles of the United States (26 percent of the country including Alaska) published as 1,327 atlas sheets; geologic mapping of 171,000 square miles and publication of 106 geologic folios; experimental and theoretical investigations of the physical characteristics of rocks in various processes of formation, of volcanic and geyser action, and of rock composition and structure; paleontologic and stratigraphic studies; streamflow measurements and their analysis, which, among other things, had stimulated the development of water power, especially in the Southern States; and studies of irrigable lands and detailed examination and classification of 110,000 square miles of the forest reserves.

During the Survey's first 25 years, the United States had become an urban industrial world power. The population had increased from 48.9 million in 1879 to 81.8 million in 1904. The number of manufacturing establishments and the value of manufactured products had more than doubled during this period, and the value of the mineral products had increased from $365 million in 1879 to more than $1 billion in 1904. At the same time, settlement of the West had proceeded so rapidly that by 1890 the frontier had disappeared.

In 1905, the Survey obtained additional funds to increase its field investigations of iron and coal, the staples of industry, and a new program of mapping western coal deposits was started. As the emphasis in the Survey's program in economic geology shifted to nonmetallic resources, specifically fuel resources, a new Section of the Geology of Fuels was set up in the Geologic Branch.

In May 1910, Congress established a new agency, the Bureau of Mines, designating the Technologic Branch of the Geological Survey as its nucleus, and n 1912, the Land Classification Board was separated from the Geologic Branch and made an independent branch.

During World War 1 Europe was in urgent need of American agricultural products and then in still more urgent need of American steel, copper, and explosives. Within 2 years, some minerals became difficult to obtain, and the Survey reoriented its work to aid the search for both metals and fuels. When the United States entered the war in April 1917, the Geological Survey was almost wholly on a war basis.

The strategic-minerals concept was born at this time when it became clear that domestic supplies of a dozen minerals were inadequate in quantity or quality or both, another half dozen adequate for peace but insufficient for war, and petroleum production barely sufficient to meet the Nation's normal demand and much too small for the abnormal demands of war. In August 1917, Congress passed the Lever Act empowering the President to make regulations and issue orders to stimulate and conserve the production and control the distribution of fuels necessary to the war effort. A similar bill for the control of other mineral commodities was passed shortly before the war ended but never put into effect.

During the war years, the Survey sought intensively for deposits of war minerals at home and, in time, extended the search to Central and South America and the West Indies. The results were highly successful; adequate supplies of all essential materials were found before the war's end. The Geological Survey also became the main source of information on mineral production, both domestic and foreign, and its data were used to solve a variety of industrial and transportation problems.

Oil shortages in 1919 and 1920 gave credibility to predictions of the exhaustion of domestic supplies within a decade. The postwar shortages also convinced Congress that it was necessary to open up the public mineral lands to development. In February 1920, the Mineral Leasing Act was passed. Under the terms of that act, mineral lands were to be leased by competitive bidding, and royalties and other income were to be divided between the Federal Government and the States.

Waterpower as an alternative source of energy was given new status by passage of the Federal Water Power Act in June 1920, establishing the Federal Power Commission to issue licenses for development of waterpower on Federal lands. Under the Water Power Act, the Survey took responsibility for the necessary streamflow records and for examination of proposed projects on the public lands outside the National Forests. In 1921, Congress authorized a superpower survey to investigate if economy in fuel, labor, and material could be gained by a comprehensive system for generation and distribution of electric power in the region between Boston and Washington. The study was made under the direction of the Geological Survey by independent engineers who proposed a power grid that anticipated the present northeast power network.

Another postwar problem that demanded action was the lack of maps, which had become evident even before war was declared when the Army had found itself without maps upon which to base its defense of the border areas. Industrial development, land reclamation, power generation projects, and highway construction were also creating a demand for topographic data. Nearly 60 percent of the country was still totally unmapped, and much that had been mapped was in need of resurvey.

Professional organizations urged the President and Congress to make provision for completing the topographic map of the United States in the shortest possible time compatible with requisite accuracy. The Survey proposed a plan whereby the mapping could be effectively and economically completed by 1932, but no funds were made available to inaugurate the plan. Meanwhile, several West Indian republics sought the assistance of the Geological Survey in both topographic and geologic mapping, and Survey scientists and engineers were given leave to supervise their mapping programs.

Research was begun on the source materials of petroleum, the physical properties of reservoir rocks, microfaunas as aids to the identification and correlations of beds, and salt-dome cap rocks. Survey physicists and chemists joined the effort by developing improved recovery techniques and by laboratory and field tests of geophysical methods of exploration. In addition, geologic mapping for classification purposes and mapping of potential oil areas was continued, especially in Wyoming, where there was some oil company interest, and in Montana, where only the Survey had done any detailed work. In 1923, the Survey extended its intensive study of possible oil-bearing areas to Naval Petroleum Reserve No. 4 on the Arctic Coast of Alaska. The Survey's long-range stratigraphic correlation studies also became a contribution valued by industry in its exploration for petroleum.

By the mid-1920's, new discoveries in the midcontinent region, the Gulf Coast, and California resulted in an oil surplus, and overproduction and competition leading to reckless waste became a major public concern. This postwar expansion of the oil industry from famine to glut was in part the result of the striking developments in the geological sciences in the industry, as well as Government surveys and the academic world.

The Survey also became involved in energy policy. After the great coal strike in 1922, a Coal Commission was established to study the problems of the industry and to aid Congress on legislation that would ensure the Nation of an adequate supply of coal. The Geological Survey's resource data provided the basis for much of the Commission's report.

In February 1925, Congress passed the Temple bill which called for completion of a topographic map of the United States within 20 years and authorized both an appropriation of $950,000 for the first year and cooperative arrangements with States and other civic subdivisions to expedite the mapping.

In June 1934, the Taylor Act was passed, providing for organization of the public grasslands into grazing districts under the control of the Secretary of the Interior. The work of agricultural and grazing classification, which the Survey had begun in 1909, was transferred to the new Grazing Service as the third spinoff from the Survey.

By the1930s, Germany, Italy, and Japan were already perceived to be aggressor nations and the Survey called attention to the need for strategic-mineral investigations. The need for a national mapping program had been outlined as early as 1934. Strategic-mineral investigations were begun in 1938 with funds from the Public Works Administration. Congress passed the Strategic Materials Act in June 1939 and appropriated funds for strategic-mineral studies in August, only days before Hitler's armies marched into Poland to begin World War II. Topographic mapping of strategic areas in accordance with military priorities was begun in 1940. In 1940 also, the State Department allotted funds to the Geological Survey to begin investigations in cooperation with other American republics to identify mineral deposits of potential importance in hemisphere trade.

The Japanese attack on Pearl Harbor on December 7, 1941, abruptly ushered the United States from defense to war and united Americans in a determination to defeat the Axis powers. For the next several years, the Geological Survey bent its entire energies to the war effort. The Geologic, Topographic, Water Resources, and Conservation Branches each made its own special contribution.

Postwar and Cold War

World War II was a watershed in the history of the US Geological Survey. Wartime developments in science and technology provided new tools for the solution of prewar problems that had been put aside and new ones created by the exigencies of the war. The contribution of science to the security and prosperity of the Nation was more widely recognized than ever before, and greater demands were made for both traditional and innovative research in solving postwar problems. The growth of the Geological Survey, begun under the spur of war needs, continued after 1945, and thus within only a few years, the Survey had become a very different organization than the prewar Survey.

Half the Nation, including a large part of the public lands, was still without topographic maps, and many of the available maps were inadequate to meet the needs of the postwar world. Geologic mapping of the country was even less complete. Less than 10 percent of the country had been mapped geologically on scales suitable for an appraisal of natural resources and land potential to meet modern needs, and the rate of mapping possible with funds available was only one-sixth of that needed to complete the job by 1980. Base-metal reserves had been greatly depleted during the war, the limit of the Nation's capacity to produce efficiently from known oil fields had been reached, and appraisal of coal reserves and the search for new supplies was considered urgent.

The Geological Survey prepared a plan to provide adequate topographic maps for the entire Nation within 20 years, needing only funds to implement it, planned major studies on copper, lead, zinc, iron, and the ferroalloy metals, and the continuation or expansion of regional studies to aid the search for new petroleum supplies.

By 1950, the Geological Survey began undertaking investigations in new areas to meet the demand for current information. Geologic mapping was needed in fast-growing industrial areas to provide geologic data for the many types of engineering construction. The demand for construction of large dams to impound water for irrigation, power development, flood control, and industrial use focused attention on the need for information on the effect of waterloss by evaporation and the limitation of the useful life of reservoirs by deposition of sediment as well as on stream flow and sediment load. The heavy drain on ground-water resources during the war had resulted in critical conditions in many areas; saltwater encroachment was a subject of special concern in some coastal areas. Efforts to upgrade the Nation's highways required hydrologic data and flood studies to aid highway drainage design.

In late June 1950, the Korean War broke out and again the Geological Survey focused on locating strategic minerals. The military geology program was expanded, as was the search for radioactive raw materials. The new program of urban geology was accelerated to aid in civil defense. In response to a request from the Army's Corps of Engineers, the topographic mapping program was expanded in an effort to complete mapping of about 600,000 square miles of strategic importance in 6 years. A unit newly established to investigate the quantity and quality of water required to produce various manufactured products began with an investigation of the needs of the steel industry. The Geological Survey was also given new responsibilities under the Defense Production Act of 1950, which provided for stockpiling of critical materials, including, for the Defense Minerals Administration, the evaluation of applications for loans and the preparation and enforcement of contracts for the loans.

Although only 33 percent of the topographic mapping of the Nation met modern standards, the use of aerial photographs and photogrammetric methods for production of most topographic maps, the continuing development of more accurate instruments and methods, and the use of helicopters to transport topographic engineers to mountaintops and other remote spots to obtain survey control measurements resulted in a significant increase in the amount of mapping accomplished each year. Data on streamflow were being obtained at some 6,400 gaging stations, about 500 ground water investigations were in progress, and the chemical quality of more than 85,000 samples of water was being determined in Survey laboratories.

The Survey had responsibility for supervising more than 100,000 lessee operations on mining or oil-and-gas properties on public, acquired, or Indian lands and, since 1953, of oil-and-gas lease operations on the Outer Continental Shelf.

Science and technology by this time were helping the Nation to meet many of its increasing demands for raw materials through improved methods of exploration, the ability to exploit lower-grade sources, and the substitution of common for less common materials, but new dimensions were added to the problem. Overspecialized exploitation of mineral resources in some areas caused economic problems; competition for resources, where development of one precluded use of others, created resource-management problems; the increasing industrial development and urbanization were creating wastes that caused health hazards and heightened vulnerability to damage by natural geologic processes.

On May 25, 1961, President John F. Kennedy proposed as a goal "landing a man on the moon and returning him safely to earth" before the end of the decade, and in 1963, the Geological Survey, in cooperation with the National Aeronautics and Space Administration, began to train astronauts in geology and to investigate and evaluate methods and equipment for geological and geophysical exploration of the Moon. Congress had by that time already expanded the Survey's Earth-bound investigations, to Antarctica and the Trust Territory of the Pacific Islands in 1958, and to "outside the national domain" in 1962.

In 1962, the Geological Survey began a program of marine studies to identify and evaluate potential mineral resources on or beneath the sea floor and to aid in solving the problems caused by rapid population growth, urbanization, and industrial expansion in coastal areas.

On September 3, 1964, Congress passed the Wilderness Act, by which 9.1 million acres of national forest lands were made part of the National Wilderness Preservation System to be safeguarded permanently against commercial use and construction of permanent roads and buildings. New mining claims and mineral leases would be allowed only until December 31, 1983. The Geological Survey and the Bureau of Mines were authorized to assess the mineral resources of each area proposed or established as wilderness if no prior mineral survey had been made, and a new program of geologic mapping and mineral-resource assessment was begun. At the same time, new studies and investigations in space, under the sea, and on land were expanded.

In 1970, the Geological Survey published the "National Atlas of the United States of America," a reference tool comprising more than 700 physical, historical, economic, sociocultural, and administrative maps compiled through the combined efforts of more than 80 Federal agencies and a score of specialists and consultants over a period of several years. In cooperation with the Department of Housing and Urban Development, the Survey began a pilot study in the San Francisco Bay region of the application of geology, geophysics, hydrology, and topography in improving regional urban planning and decisionmaking. The Survey also played a major role in representing the United States at meetings of the United Nations Committee on the Peaceful Uses of the Seabeds and Ocean Floors Beyond the Limits of National Jurisdiction

Planetary studies were extended to Mars and other planets. A program to map the geology of Mars systematically, managed by the Geological Survey but involving both Survey and university geologists, was formalized with the National Aeronautics and Space Administration in 1971. A shaded-relief map of Mars was published in 1973, and by the time two Viking spacecraft landed on the surface of Mars in the summer of 1976, at sites selected by scientists at the Survey's Flagstaff, Arizona, office, the Survey had prepared more than 100 maps of Mars, Mercury, Venus, and the Moon in support of space exploration.

In 1977, Congress directed the Survey to establish a national water-use information program. It became part of the Federal-State cooperative program and by the late 1980's, 49 States and Puerto Rico were participating in it.

The National Mapping Division continued the quiet revolution in mapping. The development and application of advanced cartographic techniques and systems to geographic information systems was continued, a National Digital Cartographic Data Base was established, and standards of digital cartographic data were developed for the US mapping community. Primary map coverage for the United States was 97 percent complete in early 1989.

The disposal and release of hazardous chemical and radioactive wastes and ground-water contamination problems were also under investigation to provide data to help alleviate their effects on the Nation's water resources, some of them to assist the Department of Energy in developing procedures and guidelines for identifying suitable waste disposal sites.

Now several years into its second century, the Geological Survey continues to fulfill its original mission of classification of the public lands and examination of the geological structure, mineral resources, and products of the national domain. It continues to conduct research both on the cutting edge of science and with reference to economic and other issues of national concern, to develop and apply innovative means of solving problems in resource management.

Programs

Core Science Systems Strategy

Core Science Systems is a new mission of the Survey that resulted from the 2007 Science Strategy, "Facing Tomorrow's Challenges: US Geological Survey Science in the Decade 2007–2017." This report described the Core Science Systems vision and outlined a strategy to facilitate integrated characterization and understanding of the complex Earth system. The vision and suggested actions are bold and far-reaching, describing a conceptual model and framework to enhance the ability of the USGS to bring its core strengths to bear on pressing societal problems through data integration and scientific synthesis across the breadth of science.

The context of this report is inspired by a direction set forth in the 2007 Science Strategy. Specifically, ecosystem-based approaches provide the underpinnings for essentially all science themes that define the USGS. Every point on Earth falls within a specific ecosystem where data, other information assets, and the expertise of USGS and its many partners can be employed to quantitatively understand how that ecosystem functions and how it responds to natural and anthropogenic disturbances. Every benefit society obtains from the planet—food, water, raw materials to build infrastructure, homes and automobiles, fuel to heat homes and cities, and many others, are derived from or affect ecosystems.

The vision for Core Science Systems builds on core strengths of the USGS in characterizing and understanding complex Earth and biological systems through research, modeling, mapping, and the production of high quality data on the Nation's natural resource infrastructure. Together, these research activities provide a foundation for ecosystem-based approaches through geologic mapping, topographic mapping, and biodiversity mapping. The vision describes a framework founded on these core mapping strengths that makes it easier for USGS scientists to discover critical information, share and publish results, and identify potential collaborations that transcend all USGS missions. The framework is designed to improve the efficiency of scientific work within USGS by establishing a means to preserve and recall data for future applications, organizing existing scientific knowledge and data to facilitate new use of older information, and establishing a future workflow that naturally integrates new data, applications, and other science products to make interdisciplinary research easier and more efficient. Given the increasing need for integrated data and interdisciplinary approaches to solve modern problems, leadership by the Core Science Systems mission will facilitate problem solving by all USGS missions in ways not formerly possible.

The report lays out a strategy to achieve this vision through three goals with accompanying objectives and actions. The first goal builds on and enhances the strengths of the Core Science Systems mission in characterizing and understanding the Earth system from the geologic framework to the topographic characteristics of the land surface and biodiversity across the Nation. The second goal enhances and develops new strengths in computer and information science to make it easier for USGS scientists to discover data and models, share and publish results, and discover connections between scientific information and knowledge. The third goal brings additional focus to research and development methods to address complex issues affecting society that require integration of knowledge and new methods for synthesizing scientific information. Collectively, the report lays out a strategy to create a seamless connection between all USGS activities to accelerate and make USGS science more efficient by fully integrating disciplinary expertise within a new and evolving science paradigm for a changing world in the 21st century.

Climate and Land Use Change Science Strategy

The Survey is uniquely positioned to serve the nation's needs in understanding and responding to global change, including changes in climate, water availability, sea level, land use and land cover, ecosystems, and global biogeochemical cycles. Global change is among the most challenging and formidable issues confronting our nation and society. Scientists agree that global environmental changes during this century will have far-reaching societal implications (Intergovernmental Panel on Climate Change, 2007; US Global Change Research Program, 2009). In the face of these challenges, the nation can benefit greatly by using natural science information in decision making.

Since the passage of the US Global Change Research Act of 1990, the USGS has made substantial scientific contributions to understanding the interactive living and nonliving components of the Earth system. USGS natural science activities have led to fundamental advances in observing and understanding climate and land-cover change and the effects these changes have on ecosystems, natural-resource availability, and societal sustainability. Most of these major advances were pursued in partnership with other organizations within and outside the Department of the Interior. The inherent value of partnerships with other US Global Change Research Program agencies and natural-resource managers is emphasized in all aspects of the planning and implementation of this Science Strategy for the coming decade.

Over the next 10 years, the USGS will make substantial contributions to understanding how Earth systems interact, respond to, and cause global change. The USGS will work with science partners, decision makers, and resource managers at local to international levels (including Native American tribes) to improve understanding of past and present change; develop relevant forecasts; and identify those lands, resources, and communities most vulnerable to global change processes. Science will play an essential role in helping communities and land and resource managers understand local to global implications, anticipate effects, prepare for changes, and reduce the risks associated with decision making in a changing environment. USGS partners and stakeholders will benefit from the data, predictive models, and decision-support products and services resulting from the implementation of this strategy.

This Science Strategy recognizes core USGS strengths that are applied to key societal problems. It establishes seven goals for USGS global change science and strategic actions that may be implemented in the short term (1–5 years) and the longer term (5–10 years) to improve our understanding of the following areas of inquiry:

1. Rates, causes, and impacts of past global changes;
2. The global carbon cycle;
3. Biogeochemical cycles and their coupled interactions;
4. Land-use and land-cover change rates, causes, and consequences;
5. Droughts, floods, and water availability under changing land-use and climatic conditions;
6. Coastal response to sea-level rise, climatic change, and human development; and
7. Biological responses to global change.

In addition to the seven thematic goals the Survey address the central role of monitoring in accordance with the USGS Science Strategy recommendation that global change research should rely on existing "...decades of observational data and long-term records to interpret consequences of climate variability and change to the Nation's biological populations, ecosystems, and land and water resources" (US Geological Survey, 2007, p. 19). It also briefly describe specific needs and opportunities for coordinating USGS global change science among USGS Mission Areas and address the need for a comprehensive and sustained communications strategy.

Energy and Minerals Science Strategy

The economy, national security, and standard of living of the United States depend heavily on adequate and reliable supplies of energy and mineral resources. Based on population and consumption trends, the nation's use of energy and minerals can be expected to grow, driving the demand for ever broader scientific understanding of resource formation, location, and availability. In addition, the increasing importance of environmental stewardship, human health, and sustainable growth places further emphasis on energy and mineral resources research and understanding. Collectively, these trends in resource demand and the interconnectedness among resources will lead to new challenges and, in turn, require cutting- edge science for the next generation of societal decisions.

The long and continuing history of US Geological Survey contributions to energy and mineral resources science provide a solid foundation of core capabilities upon which new research directions can grow. This science strategy provides a framework for the coming decade that capitalizes on the growth of core capabilities and leverages their application toward new or emerging challenges in energy and mineral resources research, as reflected in five interrelated goals.

Goal 1.—Understand fundamental Earth processes that form energy and mineral resources

Goal 2.—Understand the environmental behavior of energy and mineral resources and their waste products

Goal 3.—Provide inventories and assessments of energy and mineral resources

Goal 4.—Understand the effects of energy and mineral development on natural resources and society Goal 5.—Understand the reliability and availability of energy and mineral supplies

Within each goal, multiple actions are identified. The level of specificity and complexity of these actions varies, consistent with the reality that even a modest refocus can yield large payoffs in the near term whereas more ambitious plans may take years to reach fruition. As such, implementation of these actions is largely dependent on available resources and the sequencing of prerequisite steps. This science strategy places an emphasis on interdisciplinary collaboration and leveraging of expertise across the US Geological Survey and with external partners.

Energy and mineral resources are essential to society. The Survey, as the nation's principal natural science bureau, advances the science of energy and mineral resources and provides statistical information and analysis on the global flow of minerals and mineral materials. The Organic Act of 1879 defines the role of the USGS as "... the classification of the public lands and examination of the geological structure, mineral resources, and products of the national domain." Understanding the science, quality, quantity, and spatial distribution of energy and mineral resources has been a core function of the USGS since its inception.

The USGS is recognized by industry, nongovernmental organizations, and international, Federal, State, tribal, and local governments for its reliable, high-quality energy and minerals science, information, fundamental research, and expertise. This science strategy, intended to reach multiple audiences, describes the USGS role and suggests actions that can be taken in the next 10 years to provide the Nation with high-impact energy and minerals science and information on recognized and emerging issues. The goals represent broad directions; the actions represent specific research thrusts to advance these goals. Collectively, the understanding gained from these actions provides information for decision making with respect to such issues as economic vitality, environmental health, national security, and responsible resource management and protection on US Department of the Interior (DOI) and other lands. The United States uses substantial amounts of energy and mineral resources each year.

Industries that consume processed mineral materials add about $2,230 billion, or approximately 15 percent, to the US gross domestic product, and the nation's mines and quarries produced raw materials with a total estimated value of $74 billion, with production varying by state. Domestic energy resource production activities also take place throughout the nation (such as oil and gas production). The US also consumes about 7 billion barrels of oil, 24 trillion cubic feet of natural gas, and 1 billion short tons of coal a year. To meet these needs, energy and mineral production (extraction) occurs in every State, with substantial amounts also imported from other countries. The United States faces challenges in meeting its current and future energy and minerals needs.

These challenges range in scale from global competition for resources to local decisionmaking about the appropriate use of individual land parcels. Decisions on every scale may affect the availability of energy and minerals and have far-reaching economic, geopolitical, and social consequences. For example, the increasing demand for both traditional and emerging energy and mineral resources is driving exploration and production into geological settings for which there may be little data available, such as in the Arctic, deeper in the Earth's crust, and beneath deeper regions of the oceans. Activities in these locations may pose considerable technical and engineering challenges or be colocated with sensitive environments or other natural resources of importance. At the same time, consideration of alternative sources of energy and minerals is increasing, which may involve mining of deposits of lower concentration, recovering resources from waste and recycling streams, and sourcing from countries with different political systems or environmental stewardship practices. The USGS serves the national interest by providing impartial information across this range of scales and about alternatives, thereby enabling decision makers and society at large to make informed decisions and better understand the potential outcomes of those decisions.

An additional challenge facing the nation is the need to balance the reliability and availability of energy and mineral supplies with other considerations including the availability of other natural resources; the viability of energy and mineral development amidst changes in climate, natural hazards, and demand; and the need to prevent or mitigate environmental degradation (Gundersen and others, 2011). This challenge is especially noteworthy given the long-term nature of resource development and associated infrastructure and the comparable or longer recovery times stemming from any adverse effects. The concept of sustainability, defined as "development that meets the needs of the present without compromising the ability of future generations to meet their own needs" (United Nations World Commission on Environment and Development, 1987, p. 54), underpins many land use and environmental policies that address this challenge. From the perspective of nonrenewable energy and mineral resources, sustainability focuses on stewardship of lands, protection of the environment, and identification of alternative sources. To provide society with the knowledge needed to address these challenges, there is growing recognition that it is incumbent on "earth scientists to redirect their scientific research, to assemble data that are usable in policy analysis and decision making, and ultimately transmit their findings more clearly to policymakers and the public" (National Research Council, 1996, p. 5).

The USGS leads research and monitoring studies to address these challenges and provide a scientific foundation for decision making with respect to sustainable resource use, protection, and adaptive management. In this strategy, we identified a set of overarching questions that drive the science needed to address energy and mineral resources use issues during the coming decade. All parts of this science strategy are designed to reflect one or more of these challenges:

- How or where might energy and mineral commodities be obtained to meet present and future needs?
- What economic, environmental, geopolitical, and health consequences must also be considered in both the short term and the long term?
- How can decisions more effectively incorporate scientific complexity and uncertainty?
- What science is needed to anticipate and respond to future events?

Using these questions as a guide, five interdependent goals were constructed that collectively provide the needed scientific research, information, and analysis:

Goal 1.—Understand fundamental Earth processes that form energy and mineral resources

Goal 2.—Understand the environmental behavior of energy and mineral resources and their waste products

Goal 3.—Provide inventories and assessments of energy and mineral resources

Goal 4.—Understand the effects of energy and mineral development on natural resources and society

Goal 5.—Understand the reliability and availability of energy and mineral supplies

The overarching concept for these goals is a resource lifecycle for energy and minerals, which traces the flow of these resources from generation and occurrence through interaction with society and the environment to ultimate disposition and disposal. Each goal addresses one or more stages of the resource lifecycle. Through targeted research, the first two goals expand basic knowledge of the formation of energy and mineral deposits and their interaction with the atmosphere, biosphere, and hydrosphere. The next two goals build on this research foundation and develop additional science and information products. The final goal extends beyond identified concerns to focus and deliver science on emerging issues and unanticipated events affecting energy and mineral supplies.

Together, these goals form a dynamic science strategy for advancing USGS science to a new level of understanding and effectiveness in the next 10 years. Each goal presents several specific "actions," intended to fill the highest priority needs and address key gaps in data and understanding. Actions range from those that incrementally build on existing USGS capabilities and core strengths to new, ambitious efforts. In most cases, successful achievement of these actions cannot be accomplished solely within the energy and minerals mission area but rather depends on collaboration and leveraging of expertise and capabilities across the USGS and among stakeholders and partners.

Environmental Health Science Strategy

America has an abundance of natural resources. We have bountiful clean water, fertile soil, and unrivaled national parks, wildlife refuges, and public lands. These resources enrich our lives and preserve our health and wellbeing. These resources have been maintained because of our history of respect for their value and an enduring commitment to their vigilant protection.

Awareness of the social, economic, and personal value of the health of our environment is increasing. The emergence of environmentally driven diseases caused by exposure to contaminants and pathogens is a growing concern worldwide. New health threats and patterns of established threats are affected by both natural and anthropogenic changes to the environment. Human activities are key drivers of emerging (new and re-emerging) health threats. Societal demands for land and natural resources, quality of life, and economic prosperity lead to environmental change.

Natural earth processes, climate trends, and related climatic events will compound the environmental impact of human activities. These environmental drivers will influence exposure to disease agents, including viral, bacterial, prion, and fungal pathogens, parasites, synthetic chemicals and substances, natural earth materials, toxins, and other biogenic compounds.

Organisms can be exposed to environmental contamination through multiple routes of exposure (consumption, inhalation, contact) and in many forms (drinking water, food, air, soil, sediment, dusts, and other aerosols), which are affected by contaminant occurrence and distribution in the environment. Similarly, pathogens spread in the environment and via other living organisms, and are transmitted to other organisms or people via host-to-host transmission, vector-borne transmission, or environmental exposure.

Changes in the use, handling, and disposal of chemical wastes affects the environment, the health of fish and wildlife, and human health by affecting the quality of the air (and dust) we breathe, the water we drink, the soil we till, and the food we eat. Other human-induced alterations such as changes in land use and increasing urbanization alter fish and wildlife habitats and ultimately species diversity. The increasing spatial interconnections between human communities and natural and disturbed ecosystems enhance the risk of transmission of zoonotic diseases from wildlife to people. Weathering, runoff of natural and disturbed landscapes, windblown particulates, and dissolution of harmful minerals in rocks and aquifers, as well as the environmental disruption from natural hazards increase the potential for exposure to contaminants and pathogens. New approaches to meet the increasing demands for food, water, energy, and other resources can introduce more contamination to the environment and increase exposure to contaminants and pathogens. Furthermore, unprecedented increases in international travel and trade, as well as climate change, further complicate efforts to protect the health of the environment, fish and wildlife, domesticated animals, and people.

A WHO study determined that an estimated 24 percent of the global burden of disease and 23 percent of all global deaths can be attributed to environmental factors (Prüss-Ütün and Corvalán, 2006). The threat of contaminants to the health of the environment and public health is widely acknowledged. The National Institute of Environmental Health Sciences (NIEHS) stated "Experience tells us that virtually all human diseases can be caused, modified, or altered by environmental agents," where they describe environmental agents as pollutants and chemicals, commercial products we use that enter our environment, and naturally occurring toxins (National Institute of Environmental Health Sciences, 2006).

Only a small fraction of the 80,000 chemicals in use in the United States today have been tested for safety according to the Annual Report of the President's Cancer Panel. They said "A growing body of research documents myriad established and suspected environmental factors linked to genetic, immune, and endocrine dysfunction that can lead to cancer and other diseases. ... the consequences of cumulative lifetime exposures to known carcinogens and the interaction of specific environmental contaminants remain largely unstudied" (President's Cancer Panel, 2010).

Continued increases in the types and number of contaminants and limited understanding of the mechanisms by which contaminants can cause adverse health effects are challenges to continued efforts to safeguard environmental health. Environmental release of engineered nanomaterial is an example of a new type of contaminant; new approaches and methods are needed to measure their presence in the environment and to assess their potential ecological and human health effects (National Science and Technology Council, 2008).

Scientists are reevaluating current approaches for assessing risk and the potential health outcomes associated with exposure to environmental contaminants (Birnbaum, 2012). New challenges include defining the potential health effects of chronic exposures to extremely low (sub part-per-billion) concentrations, potential increased vulnerability of some populations such as the elderly or early life stages, the fact that exposures in early life stages can cause impacts much later in life or in subsequent generations, and exposure to mixtures of environmental contaminants that have unknown combined effects. The effect of endocrine-disrupting chemicals (EDCs) on exposed organisms is an example of the need for improved understanding of the mechanisms by which contaminants affect organisms (Vandenberg and others, 2012).

EDCs increasingly are being recognized as serious environmental health threats, and in their first Scientific Statement, the Endocrine Society implicated EDCs as a significant concern to public health (Diamanti-Kandarakis and others, 2009). Like contaminants, pathogens threaten the health and security of the Nation and its resources.

Of particular concern are pathogens that can lead to global pandemics, and they are featured prominently in the National Security Strategy (The White House, 2010), the National Response Framework (Department of Homeland Security, 2008), and the National Health Security Strategy (Department of Health and Human Services, 2009). Most pathogens that infect humans are of animal origin (zoonotic) (Woolhouse and Gowtage-Sequeria, 2005); the Institute of Medicine (IOM) stated "The significance of zoonoses in the emergence of human infections cannot be overstated" (Lederberg and others, 1992).

Virtually all of the major pandemics to date have been caused by zoonotic diseases, including the Black Death, Spanish influenza, and HIV/AIDS (Morens and others, 2008). Between 1940 and 2004, more than 60 percent of emerging infectious diseases were zoonotic; more than 70 percent of these originated in wildlife (Jones and others, 2008). Many emerging diseases, such as Ebola, HIV/AIDS, Lyme disease, Severe Acute Respiratory Syndrome (SARS), and highly pathogenic avian influenza (HPAI) had their genetic origins in wildlife (Friend, 2006). Many zoonotic disease outbreaks are evident in wild animal populations before they affect people or domesticated animals. Therefore, wildlife health and disease monitoring serve as early warning indicators of environmental and ecosystem health and are essential to any information system designed to protect human health.

Increasing coordination among wildlife, domesticated animal, and human health agencies will improve our ability to understand the potential for cross-species transmission (Jerolmack, 2012). Diseases can no longer simply be regarded as natural regulators of wild populations; they often pose a serious threat to fish and wildlife conservation, an increasing challenge for natural resource management, and may threaten the health of humans and domesticated animals. Numerous endangered species are threatened by disease. For example, chytridiomycosis, caused by an emerging fungal pathogen, has resulted in global extinction of amphibian species, and continues to jeopardize the persistence of a number of species.

In addition, the impacts of disease on populations of common species may result in major losses to ecosystem services on which we depend. White-nose syndrome in bats, for instance, has resulted in dramatic declines of insectivorous species that control important pests. The loss of these natural insect predators may result in damage to crops and forestry products, increased use of insecticides, and negatively impact the economy. The scientific community increasingly is acknowledging the complex interaction within organisms of exposure to both contaminants and pathogens, and considering implications for the health of an organism, of populations, and of sensitive subpopulations.

Environmental drivers influence the environment, human and ecological exposure to disease agents, and ultimately the complex responses from exposure to contaminants and pathogens that result in disease. The "One Health" paradigm, advocated by the WHO (World Health Organization, 2011) and the AVMA (American Veterinary Medical Association, 2008) among others, is based on recognition by the scientific community that the health of humans, the health of animals, and the quality of the environment are inextricably linked. Thus, successful health protection will require increased interdisciplinary research and increased communication and collaborations among the broader scientific community. This strategy is built upon that paradigm.

The Survey defines environmental health science broadly as the interdisciplinary study of relations among the quality of the physical environment, the health of the living environment, and human health. The interactions among these three spheres are driven by human activities, ecological processes, and natural earth processes; the interactions affect exposure to contaminants and pathogens and the severity of environmentally driven diseases in animals and people. This definition provides USGS with a framework for synthesizing natural science information from across the Bureau and providing it to environmental, natural resource, agricultural, and public health managers.

USGS specializes in science at the environment-health interface, by characterizing the processes that affect the interaction among the physical environment, the living environment, and people, and the resulting factors that affect ecological and human exposure to disease agents.

The "One Health" paradigm advocated by the World Health Organization (WHO; World Health Organization, 2011), and the American Veterinary Medical Association (AVMA; American Veterinary Medical Association, 2008), among others, is based on a general recognition that the health of humans, animals, and the environment are inextricably linked. Thus, successful efforts to protect that health will require increased interdisciplinary research and increased communication and collaboration among the

The vision, mission, and five cornerstone goals of the USGS Environmental Health Science Strategy were developed with substantial input from a wide range of stakeholders.

Vision—The USGS is a premier source of the environmental health science needed to safeguard the health of the environment, fish and wildlife, domesticated animals, and people.

Mission—The mission of USGS in environmental health science is to contribute scientific information to environmental, natural resource, agricultural, and public health managers, who use that information to support sound decision making. USGS will provide science to achieve the following societal goals:

Goal 1: Identify, prioritize, and detect contaminants and pathogens of emerging environmental concern. Goal 2: Reduce the impact of contaminants on the environment, fish and wildlife, domesticated animals, and people.

Goal 3: Reduce the impact of pathogens on the environment, fish and wildlife, domesticated animals, and people.

Goal 4: Discover the complex interactions between, and combined effects of, exposure to contaminants and pathogens.

Goal 5: Prepare for and respond to the environmental impacts and related health threats of natural and anthropogenic disasters.

Goals 1 through 4 are intended to provide science to address environmental health threats in a logical order, from informing prevention and preparedness, to supporting systematic management response to environmental health issues. Goal 4 addresses the interaction among contaminants and pathogens, an issue of emerging concern in environmental health science. Goal 5 acknowledges the fact that natural and anthropogenic disasters (for example, earthquakes, volcanic eruptions, floods, droughts, fires, industrial accidents, oil spills, acts of terrorism, and pandemics) can cause immediate and prolonged adverse environmental health threats. This strategy proposes that USGS take the following strategic science actions to achieve each of the five goals of this strategy:

- Goal 1: Identify, prioritize, and detect contaminants and pathogens of emerging environmental concern.
- Strategic Science Action 1.—Prioritize contaminants and pathogens of emerging concern to guide research, detection, and management activities.
- Strategic Science Action 2.—Conduct research, surveillance, and monitoring to provide early warning of emerging health threats. • Strategic Science Action 3.—Develop approaches and tools that identify vulnerable environmental settings, ecosystems, and species.
- Goal 2: Reduce the impact of contaminants on the environment, fish and wildlife, domesticated animals, and people.
- Strategic Science Action 1.—Systematically characterize the sources, occurrence, transport and fate of environmental contaminants to guide efforts to manage and mitigate contamination. Strategic Science Action 2.—Evaluate the threat of environmental contamination to the health of the environment, fish and wildlife, domesticated animals, and people, and inform the associated management and protection efforts.
- Strategic Science Action 3.—Characterize potential human exposure to support establishment of health standards and contamination-reduction efforts.

- Goal 3: Reduce the impact of pathogens on the environment, fish and wildlife, domesticated animals, and people.
- Strategic Science Action 1.—Determine the biotic and abiotic factors that control the ecology of infectious diseases in natural populations of aquatic and terrestrial species and potential transmission to other animals and humans.
- Strategic Science Action 2.—Establish how natural and anthropogenic environmental changes affect the distribution and severity of infectious diseases in natural populations of aquatic and terrestrial species and potential transmission to other animals and humans.
- Strategic Science Action 3.—Develop surveillance systems to identify changing patterns of disease activity in priority geographic areas.
- Goal 4: Discover the complex interactions between, and combined effects of, exposure to contaminants and pathogens.
- Strategic Science Action 1.—Identify how exposure to one class of disease agents (contaminants or pathogens) can make an organism more susceptible to adverse effects from exposure to the other class of disease agents.
- Strategic Science Action 2.—Implement interdisciplinary studies that characterize the effects of combined exposure to pathogens and contaminants.
- Goal 5: Prepare for and respond to the environmental impacts and related health threats of natural and anthropogenic disasters.
- Strategic Science Action 1.—Establish a formal interdisciplinary science capability to rapidly assess the environmental health risks associated with disasters.
- Strategic Science Action 2.—Enhance methods to anticipate, prepare for, and identify environmental and related health impacts of future disasters. This strategy is one of seven USGS science strategies developed concurrently: • Climate and Land Use Change • Core Science Systems • Ecosystems • Energy and Mineral Resources • Environmental Health • Natural Hazards • Water

This strategy describes how USGS will address the highest priority environmental health issues facing the nation. The ultimate intended outcome of this science strategy is prevention and reduction of adverse impacts to the quality of the environment, the health of our living resources, and human health. Communication with, and receiving input from, partners and stakeholders regarding their science needs is essential for successful implementation of this strategy. It is incumbent on USGS to reach out to all stakeholders to ensure that USGS efforts are focused on the highest priority environmental health issues, and that products are provided in the most timely and usable form to all those who can use them. USGS must reach out to the scientific community, internally and externally, to ensure that our efforts are integrated.

Ecosystems Science Strategy

Ecosystem science is critical to making informed decisions about natural resources that can sustain our Nation's economic and environmental well-being. Resource managers and policymakers are faced with countless decisions each year at local, regional, and national levels on issues as diverse as renewable and nonrenewable energy development, agriculture, forestry, water supply, and resource allocations at the urbanrural interface.

The urgency for sound decisionmaking is increasing dramatically as the world is being transformed at an unprecedented pace and in uncertain directions. Environmental changes are associated with natural hazards, greenhouse gas emissions, and increasing demands for water, land, food, energy, mineral, and living resources. At risk is the Nation's environmental capital, the goods and services provided by resilient ecosystems that are vital to the health and wellbeing of human societies. Ecosystem science—the study of systems of organisms interacting with their environment and the consequences of natural and human-induced change on these systems—is necessary to inform decision makers as they develop policies to adapt to these changes.

This Ecosystems Science Strategy is built on a framework that includes basic and applied science. It highlights the critical roles that US Geological Survey (USGS) scientists and partners can play in building scientific understanding and providing timely information to decision makers. The strategy underscores the connection between scientific discoveries and the application of new knowledge, and it integrates ecosystem science and decisionmaking, producing new scientific outcomes to assist resource managers and providing public benefits. We envision the USGS as a leader in integrating scientific information into decisionmaking processes that affect the Nation's natural resources and human well-being.

The USGS is uniquely positioned to play a pivotal role in ecosystem science. With its wide range of expertise, the Bureau can bring holistic, cross-scale, interdisciplinary capabilities to the design and conduct of monitoring, research, and modeling and to new technologies for data collection, management, and visualization. Collectively, these capabilities can be used to reveal ecological patterns and processes, explain how and why ecosystems change, and forecast change over different spatial and temporal scales. USGS science can provide managers with options and decision-support tools to use resources sustainably. The USGS has long-standing, collaborative relationships with the Department of the Interior (DOI) and other partners in the natural sciences, in both conducting science and applying the results. The USGS engages these partners in cooperative investigations that otherwise would lack the necessary support or be too expensive for a single bureau to conduct.

The heart of this strategy is a framework for USGS ecosystems science that focuses on five long-term goals, which are seen as interconnected components that reinforce our vision of the USGS providing science that is at the forefront of decision making.

Natural Hazards Science Strategy

The mission of the US Geological Survey in natural hazards is to develop and apply hazard science to help protect the safety, security, and economic well-being of the Nation. The costs and consequences of natural hazards can be enormous, and each year more people and infrastructure are at risk. USGS scientific research—founded on detailed observations and improved understanding of the responsible physical processes—can help to understand and reduce natural hazard risks and to make and effectively communicate reliable statements about hazard characteristics, such as frequency, magnitude, extent, onset, consequences, and where possible, the time of future events.

To accomplish its broad hazard mission, the USGS maintains an expert workforce of scientists and technicians in the earth sciences, hydrology, biology, geography, social and behavioral sciences, and other fields, and engages cooperatively with numerous agencies, research institutions, and organizations in the public and private sectors, across the Nation and around the world. The scientific expertise required to accomplish the USGS mission in natural hazards includes a wide range of disciplines that this report refers to, in aggregate, as hazard science.

In October 2010, the Natural Hazards Science Strategy Planning Team (H–SSPT) was charged with developing a long-term (10-year) Science Strategy for the USGS mission in natural hazards. This report fulfills that charge, with a document hereinafter referred to as the Strategy, to provide scientific observations, analyses, and research that are critical for the Nation to become more resilient to natural hazards. Science provides the information that decision makers need to determine whether risk management activities are worthwhile.

Moreover, as the agency with the perspective of geologic time, the USGS is uniquely positioned to extend the collective experience of society to prepare for events outside current memory. The USGS has critical statutory and nonstatutory roles regarding floods, earthquakes, tsunamis, landslides, coastal erosion, volcanic eruptions, wildfires, and magnetic storms—the hazards considered in this plan. There are numerous other hazards of societal importance that are considered either only peripherally or not at all in this Strategy because they are either in another of the USGS strategic science plans (such as drought) or not in the overall mission of the USGS (such as tornados).

The USGS conducts hazard research to inform a broad range of planning and response activities at individual, local, State, national, and international levels. A sustainable society requires a responsive government to reduce the loss of life and disruption caused by natural hazards. People who are potentially affected by natural hazards need robust assessments to prepare for hazardous events, and they need information about updated hazards for situational awareness during times of crisis. To meet these needs, scientists, in turn, require fundamental understanding of natural processes and observations of natural events. Thus, the H–SSPT developed four overarching and interrelated goals regarding observations, understanding, assessments, and situational awareness.

To accomplish each goal, this Strategy identifies core responsibilities and strategic actions. Core responsibilities are activities that the USGS must continue in order to uphold its mission. In many cases, these are mandated activities that help to protect lives and assets, or strengths developed as a consequence of long-standing national need. Strategic actions are high-value, priority efforts that go beyond the core responsibilities and will reduce uncertainties about hazards, improve communication, and thus enhance the ability to provide accurate, effective assessments and situational awareness.

The Survey provides a prioritization philosophy, to be applied through the collaborative efforts of the USGS Executive Leadership Team, Program Coordinators, and Science Centers, to accomplish prioritization effectively. For each goal, this Strategy identifies key strategic actions that were synthesized from hundreds of suggestions provided by USGS hazards stakeholders.

Given the spectrum of hazards under consideration in this report, along with the broad administrative controls for funding USGS hazards science, this report does not prioritize the strategic actions. The first and highest priority is to maintain the basic and applied research, observations, and communication efforts such as assessments and warnings that form the core responsibilities. These are areas of USGS activity that must be safeguarded in times of decreased funding.

Given sufficient funding to support the core responsibilities, the strategic actions indicate areas of advancement that will have greatest impact on improved understanding and on the efficacy of assessments and situational awareness. The H-SSPT recommends that strategic actions be prioritized based on the degree to which the strategic action does the following:

- Helps meet USGS core responsibilities (particularly statutory responsibilities).
- In a larger context, helps the Federal Government to meet its responsibilities in the hazards arena.

- Is important for risk reduction, protecting human health, the economy, or national security.
- Addresses a large gap in hazards science understanding and reduces uncertainty.
- Enhances areas where the USGS has a unique role and expertise.
- Holds a high potential for investment return in the form of improved assessments and awareness.

Goal 1: Enhanced Observations The USGS acquires comprehensive observations important to natural hazards to improve fundamental understanding, assessments, and situational awareness.

Core Responsibilities that Must be Sustained
- Operate monitoring networks for earthquakes, streamflow, volcanic activity and geomagnetic storms, and produce datasets of observations and near-real-time products.
- Conduct surveys, such as geological mapping and acquisition of geophysical data, to enable a better understanding of hazardous processes including sources and impacts.
- Collect the ephemeral data during hazardous events that will support future research to reduce loss.
- Develop long-term chronologies, with associated magnitudes, of hazardous events from both historical and paleohazard studies.
- Distribute this information to the wide range of users through a variety of data portals.

Strategic Actions for the Future
- Enhance the existing monitoring networks to provide reliable operation, ensure full interoperability with other agencies that rely on uninterrupted data flow from the USGS, and improve early warning.
- Improve the use of monitoring information through better near-real-time delivery, new tools for use of data, and the merger of existing, critical datasets.
- Take advantage of rapidly changing technology, recognizing that the ability to monitor effectively depends on the technology used and the ability to adapt to changes.
- Improve overall data quality standards governing quality assurance, metadata, additions, curation, and timeliness.

- Expand observations of geologic setting, including geological mapping and geophysical data acquisition, as these observations are essential to understanding the frequency, physical mechanisms, and impacts of events.
- Improve data collection during and after hazardous events to protect public safety and gather critical, ephemeral information.
- Use geological and historical methods to expand hazard chronology and magnitude distribution studies needed to define probabilities of occurrence.

Goal 2: Fundamental Understanding of Hazards and Impacts. The USGS advances and applies fundamental understanding of natural hazards to improve assessments and situational awareness.

Core Responsibilities that Must be Sustained

- Increase understanding of the underlying physical processes that produce the hazard and determine where and under what conditions hazards occur.
- Uphold the tradition of innovation in instrumentation, measurement and experimental techniques.
- Foster USGS scientific expertise to provide expert advice as needed in crisis and noncrisis situations.
- Publish results with peer review and distribute to appropriate audiences through relevant mechanisms.
- Support innovation and creativity in the conduct of our science.

Strategic Actions for the Future

- Promote targeted research on physical hazard initiation processes, because limited understanding about these processes limits the ability to make accurate predictions.
- Promote research on extreme events, which are the rare, potentially catastrophic events with the greatest societal consequences.
- Promote research about natural hazard vulnerability, risk estimation, and communication.
- Encourage interchange of ideas in research about the role of fluids in physical processes, because this broad topic of investigation is essential to understanding a multitude of hazards phenomena.

- Promote research in the triggering and interaction of multiple hazard processes, which frequently happen in nature and have distinct probabilities of occurrence and potential impacts.

Goal 3: Improved Assessment Products and Services. The USGS develops assessments of natural hazards, vulnerability and risk to inform decisions that can mitigate adverse consequences.

Core Responsibilities that Must be Sustained

- Create hazard assessments used to inform decision making, based on fundamental understanding of natural hazards.
- Evaluate the assessments using observations made at national and regional scales and over long time periods to capture significant and infrequent events.
- Develop new assessment tools to improve the scientific foundation of assessments as new understanding evolves.
- Inform the public about natural hazards to promote risk-wise behavior by publishing assessments and providing assessment tools using USGS scientific information.

Strategic Actions for the Future

- Improve the formulation of assessments, in particular, by ensuring there is a process to update assessments with the most current understanding, methodology, and observations.
- Create and distribute effective multimedia assessments developed through partnerships with users, social and behavioral researchers, and educators.
- Develop multihazard assessments to compare the relative risk of multiple hazards or assess the combined risk of multiple hazards.
- Balance investments in hazard, vulnerability and risk assessment to ensure that the USGS improves the accuracy, resolution, and timeliness of hazard assessments while engaging with other entities who make use of the hazard information.
- Develop event and disaster scenarios and other strategic assessments to incorporate research results into decision-making processes.
- Evaluate the accuracy, use, validity and effectiveness of assessments, working with social and behavioral scientists and assessment users, in order to improve future assessments and demonstrate the value of USGS assessments.

Goal 4: Effective Situational Awareness

The USGS provides situational awareness to improve emergency response, inform the public, and minimize societal disruption.

Core Responsibilities that Must be Sustained

- Collect the data and conduct analyses to inform warnings by the USGS or others of impending crises.
- Issue warnings and advisories of impending potential hazardous events and their termination.
- Provide timely information to other agencies, emergency managers, the media, and the public about hazardous events as they occur.
- Invest appropriate resources in hazard education during crisis as well as noncrisis times.

Strategic Actions for the Future

- Develop and provide training for the next generation of tools for rapid event detection and response, which will require targeted partnerships to define the products and delivery mechanisms that most effectively put USGS information into the hands of decision makers.
- Improve data systems critical to situational awareness responsibilities, a need that includes making monitoring networks that are more robust, expanding monitoring coverage as needed, and delivering information in usable formats.
- Implement 24x7 operations for critical USGS monitoring efforts in order to maximize USGS ability to inform partner agencies, respond to hazards, and deliver expertise when it is needed.
- Improve provision of scientific expertise for decisions and assessments during rapidly changing situations. This necessitates training of scientific staff in media response.
- Improve internal hazards coordination, which is conducted across the Bureau and over many regions and includes data, research, and geospatial support activities.
- Evaluate warning and response products to improve their accuracy, timeliness, and communication, and demonstrate the value of the USGS hazard investment in observations and fundamental understanding.
- Involve the whole community in the evaluation of the response products so as to increase the reach of the products.

A Vision of the Future

If these core responsibilities are upheld, and these strategic actions are taken, the USGS will move closer to the H-SSPT vision of the future, where the Nation will be more resilient because of USGS hazards science. That vision includes a USGS that does the following:

- Operates a robust, comprehensive network of instruments that monitor hazardous conditions.
- Leads the Nation in hazards science because of its diverse, expert staff.
- Creates easily understood assessments that are routinely used to reduce risk.
- Employs newly developed software tools that bring together data and understanding to better manage natural disasters and shares these tools with emergency managers.

Water Science Strategy

The Water Science Strategy expands on the US Geological Survey (USGS) Science Strategy, "Facing Tomorrow's Challenges—US Geological Survey Science in the Decade 2007–2017" (US Geological Survey, 2007), which developed seven integrated science Mission Areas. This water strategy builds on the strengths of water science in the USGS and links to other science disciplines and Mission Areas of the Bureau and our many partners outside of the USGS. In addition, it recognizes that "in the coming decades of the 21st century the United States faces serious and complex water problems.

Constraints on availability of water—quantity and quality—will impact what we do and where we do it as a society. To face these problems the Nation will need more, new, and improved water science, information and tools to manage and adapt to these constraints" (National Research Council, 2009).

The Water Mission Area is one of seven science areas that will lead to integrated science across the various USGS disciplines to address societal earth science needs. A Water Science Strategy Planning Team (SSPT) was charged with developing a long-term (10-year) strategic science plan for the USGS Water Mission Area and the programs that support it. This Science Strategy looks at the issues facing society and develops a strategy that observes, understands, predicts, and delivers water science by taking into account the water science and core capabilities of the USGS; the document also looks forward over the next 5 to 10 years toward building new capabilities, tools, and delivery systems to meet the Nation's water-resource needs. This Science Strategy serves as a guiding document for USGS leadership in science planning and execution and will be used as a basis for budget initiatives and national and regional guidance.

Through observing components of the water cycle, we can better quantify the water resource in terms of abundance and quality. Understanding the water cycle leads to development of better tools for assessing all aspects of the water resource, from water availability, to flooding, to degradation of surface waters and groundwater. Predicting modifications of the water cycle from factors such as human effects on watersheds and climate variability is important for decision making to ensure the sustainability and resilience of communities and ecosystems. Finally, USGS science related to observing, understanding, and predicting components of the water cycle must be delivered to managers, policymakers, and the public in understandable and relevant ways to be an effective force in managing the water resource.

The goals, objectives, and strategic actions presented in this report are a result of many meetings and forums with stakeholders and input from USGS scientists and staff, along with discussions with collaborators and partners of water science outside the Bureau. This information was considered in forming the Priority Actions discussed in the section by that name of this report. "Priority Actions" attempts to take the crosscutting objectives and strategic actions in the section entitled "Water Science
Goals and Objectives" and integrate them into science for the future to meet water needs of the 21st century. The Water SSPT recognized that water needs include sustaining ecosystems along with human uses. Competing uses of water including human consumption, industry, agriculture, and ecosystems are exacerbated by the challenges we face with population growth, energy demands, climate variability, and other factors. The science needed to address these issues requires a diverse workforce with expertise in hydrology, geology, physics, chemistry, and biology.

Priority actions focus on the following:

- Improve integrated science planning for water.
- Expand and enhance water-resource monitoring networks.
- Characterize the water cycle through development of state-of-the-art 3-D/4-D hydrogeologic framework models at multiple scales.
- Clarify the linkage between human water use (engineered hydrology) and the water cycle (natural hydrology).
- Advance ecological flow science.
- Provide flood-inundation science and information.
- Develop rapid deployment teams for water-related emergencies.
- Conduct integrated watershed assessment, research, and modeling.
- Deliver water data and analyses to the Nation.

The goals deal with the following:

1. Providing society the information it needs regarding the amount and quality of water in all components of the water cycle at high temporal and spatial resolution, nationwide;

2. Advancing our understanding of processes that determine water availability;

3. Predicting changes in the quantity and quality of water resources in response to changing climate, population, land use, and management scenarios;

4. Anticipating and responding to water-related emergencies and conflicts; and 5. Delivering timely hydrologic data, analyses, and decision support tools seamlessly across the Nation to support water-resource decisions.

The USGS will provide unbiased knowledge of the Nation's water resources to support human well-being, healthy ecosystems, economic prosperity, and anticipate and help resolve impending water-resource conflicts and emergencies. The USGS Water Mission Area, through integrated activities with other USGS Mission Areas and partners, will serve society through water-resource monitoring, assessment, modeling, and research to provide tools that managers and policymakers can use for the following:

- Preserving the quality and quantity of the Nation's water resource, which is critical to the survival of our society, the support of our economy, and the health of our environment;
- Balancing water quantity and quality in relation to potential conflicting uses among human consumption, industrial use and electric power

production, agricultural use, mineral and energy extraction, and ecosystem needs;

- Understanding, predicting, and mitigating water-related hazards such as floods, droughts, and contamination events, as well as understanding the effects of climate variability on the water resource, to foster more sustainable and resilient communities and ecosystems; and
- Quantifying the vulnerability of human populations and ecosystems to water shortages, surpluses, and degradation of water quality.

To manage water resources and to meet human and environmental needs, it is necessary to understand the effects of water quantity, timing, and quality on these systems. The USGS is in a position to provide data, understanding, and prediction tools regarding the responses of human water-resource management systems and ecosystems to hydrologic variability and change.

Societal Issues and Water Science

Water is essential to life on our planet and is the most widely used natural resource. Our own species cannot go more than 36 hours without water before our lives are endangered. Water is essential to every biological function of life. Water provides energy, food, habitat, hygiene, recreation, transportation, waste assimilation, and more.

Water availability encompasses aspects of water supplies (quantity and quality) and water needs. Water supplies are governed by a complex system of natural and human-induced processes, ranging in scope from local to global. Many of the processes affecting water supplies have changed in the past, and will continue to change in the future, on various time scales. Water needs are diverse, and they are increasingly in conflict. Water is a critical commodity for human consumption, agriculture, energy, and industry. Water is a fundamental requirement for ecosystem health, biodiversity, and resilience, and it has important recreational and aesthetic values. In many areas of the world, one or more of these aspects of water availability is under stress. Yet, the diversity of values associated with water availability makes it difficult to assess, predict, and manage water resources effectively. Improvements are needed in the characterization and understanding of water quantity and water quality if we are to maintain our society and quality of life.

Water supplies are not evenly distributed across the landscape. At all scales ranging from small subwatersheds to the Nation as a whole, water storage, movement, and quality are heterogeneous. Similarly, water needs are highly variable spatially and temporally. It is increasingly the case that water needs and water supplies are not well matched. For example, electric power plants, community water systems, and cities occupy relatively small areas in comparison to the catchment areas that ultimately supply the water they need. In many localities, water needs are being met by depleting resources that took an extended period of time to accumulate (for example, groundwater in aquifers recharged over hundreds of years). Even in some large areas of the United States, such as the Colorado River Basin, consumptive water use and losses now equal or exceed water supply. Therefore, it is essential to understand the spatial and temporal interactions between water supplies and needs at all scales.

Competition over water has involved conflicts over differing human uses and human uses versus ecosystem values throughout time. It is an unavoidable outcome of growing populations and increasing demands. Important issues regarding water availability include understanding and quantifying the vulnerability of human populations and ecosystems to water shortages and surpluses. Water-quality concerns include toxic chemicals, pathogens, excess nutrients and sediments, salinity, and oxygen depletion. As society has developed, questions about the quantity and quality of water have evolved from simple to complex issues in need of investigation and answers. As the population in the United States has increased, pressures on water supplies have increased. Of interest, water withdrawals in the United States increased steadily until 1980 and then declined and leveled off, indicating that some critical choices were made about water use in the last 30 years.

Water can also present itself as a hazard to society in the form of droughts, floods, and debris flows. Scarcity or overabundance of water causes some of society's most dangerous, costly, and damaging situations to human life and property. Droughts and floods rank first and second, respectively, as the most costly natural hazards we face (Bryant, 2005). It is of vital importance for our nation to understand, predict, and mitigate these hazardous situations, and the science of hydrology is critical to undertaking this endeavor.

These situations prompt questions related to the magnitude and frequency of extreme events, the landscapes and property that are at risk, and the ability of water to assimilate the wastes and chemicals accidentally or intentionally introduced into it.

To fully understand the importance of the nation's water resources, society must assess a multitude of water-resource issues, ask the pertinent questions, and find the critical answers that will address our concerns. Broadly, the first set of societal questions relate to the need to observe the water resource.

- Where does our water come from?
- How much water do we have?
- How much water do we use?
- Is our water supply safe for people, industries, and ecosystems?
- What are the trends in our supplies of and demand for water?
- Do we have adequate information to make water resource decisions?

Next, society moves to questions about our level of understanding and ability to predict the resource.

- How much water does our society need for the future, and is that amount sustainable?
- How can we protect our water supply, both quantity and quality, for the future?
- What can the past tell us about the future of water availability? Can human effects be clearly distinguished from natural variability? Can critical thresholds or "tipping points" be recognized or predicted?
- What new tools will be needed to improve assessment, understanding, and prediction of water availability in the future?
- Do we understand the processes near hydrologic boundaries or interfaces (for example, groundwater/ surface water, sediment/water, freshwater/seawater, and shallow/deep flow systems)?
- What are potential benefits and limitations of increased reliance on "unconventional" water resources (for example, deep saline groundwater; brackish coastal waters; enhanced water storage, recovery, and reuse)?
- How can contamination of groundwater and surface water be prevented or mitigated?
- How can water-related hazards be prevented or mitigated?

- What principles should guide optimization of water availability for multiple uses (that is, drinking water, ecosystems, agriculture/energy/industry), and how should water management adapt to changing conditions?

The Water Science Strategy is based on four guiding principles: observe, understand, predict, and deliver. Integrated observations of the entire water cycle are the cornerstone for water-availability science in terms of quantity and quality. Understanding the water cycle is a hallmark of the unbiased science that the USGS is known for. The science produced is applied to societal relevance by predicting changes to water availability in response to events such as sea-level rise and climate and land-use change, and informing society during water conflicts and emergencies such as floods, droughts, and water quality degradation.

To sustain the resource and contribute to safety in society, water data and science must be delivered to the public and other scientists. These guiding principles are reflected throughout this strategy and the development of its goals, objectives, and strategic actions. The USGS is the premier water-monitoring and science Bureau within the Federal Government.

The USGS works within the Water Mission Area through a variety of programs that serve to observe, understand, and predict components of the water cycle, which are the guiding principles of this report. The guiding principles are critical to societal issues involving water resources.

Core capabilities include the following:
- Observe.—The USGS operates and maintains national hydrologic monitoring networks consisting of more than 8,000 streamgages, 1,900 continuous waterquality monitoring stations, and 250 precipitation monitoring stations, and monitors 20,000 groundwater observation wells. USGS programs that support these networks include the Water Cooperative Program, National Streamflow Information Program, National Stream Quality Accounting Network, as well as others. Nationwide assessments and discontinuous monitoring of water storage, movement, and quality are conducted periodically by various USGS programs. The USGS also maintains the Nation's only

comprehensive program for estimating water use. The USGS operates a system of state-of-the-art water-quality laboratories for aqueous chemistry, isotope hydrology, microbiology, and sediment. The USGS laboratory capabilities include the National Water Quality Laboratory, producing more than 30,000 analyses per year. USGS laboratories have pioneered efforts to establish protocols for the collection and analysis of constituents that occur at very low concentrations. The USGS Hydrologic Instrumentation Facility provides hydrologic instrumentation, hardware, and software to support water-resource science. Support also is provided through development, testing, evaluation, repair, calibration, and quality control of hydrologic instrumentation. The USGS is the steward of Landsat—the world's longest continuously acquired collection of space-based moderate-resolution land remote-sensing data. Nearly four decades of imagery provide a unique resource for water-resource understanding and research. Landsat images are also invaluable for rapid response to water-related emergencies. In addition, the use of extensometers coupled with satellite radar (InSAR) imagery is a technique used by the USGS to characterize and model aquifer system compaction and land subsidence. Furthermore, the USGS has an institutional commitment to make the data collected by the Bureau available to the public, including Internet access through the Web pages of the National Water Information System.

- Understand.—The USGS carries out numerous scientific investigations designed to improve understanding of processes affecting water availability that can lead to more informed decisions by water managers dealing with national, regional, and local water-resource issues. Many such investigations are carried out through the USGS network of Water Science Centers and through a variety of programs such as the Water Cooperative Program, the Groundwater Resources Program, the National Water-Quality Assessment Program, and the Toxic Substances Hydrology Program. The USGS also maintains a strong research presence in water-resource science through its National Research Program. The USGS conducts intensive research and develops new tools and concepts for use by the scientific community at large. USGS research adds value to monitoring and assessment activities, provides unbiased interpretations of specific water-resources issues, and advances general knowledge of hydrologic principles. An important feature of USGS research is the synergy of local studies, national surveys and syntheses, laboratory experiments, and method-development activities that are dispersed among its varied programs. USGS scientists also contribute expertise and maintain proficiency by interacting externally with academia, industry, and other government agencies.

- Predict.—The USGS provides data, information, and tools that are useful to predicting long- and short-term changes within the water cycle. Historical data from hydrologic networks, combined with other tools such as paleohydrology, can provide information on trends such as the effect of climate change on timing of seasonal streamflow in rivers— an important consideration for flood control and water supply. The USGS produces, maintains, and freely distributes numerous computer programs that are used for research and predictions in hydrology and geochemistry. Examples include SPARROW, a model that computes delivery of water-quality constituents in rivers and streams, based on watershed characteristics; MODFLOW, considered the international standard for simulating and predicting groundwater conditions and groundwater/surface-water interactions; PHREEQC, one of the most popular codes used for modeling chemical reactions and movement in groundwater; and GSFLOW, a rapidly developing integrated tool for understanding and predicting transient stream responses to precipitation and complex watershed processes, and many other codes.
- Deliver.—The USGS is known for long-term storage and delivery of real-time and historical hydrologic data. The USGS National Water Information System (NWIS) database includes millions of data entries for surface water, groundwater, and water quality that are easily accessible through the World Wide Web. USGS real-time water data are served more than 20 million times per month. The USGS also delivers numerous scientific reports and journal articles on our Nation's water resources every year; these publications are the product of a stringent peer review system and are almost without exception publicly available through multiple outlets, including the Internet.

The USGS is distinguished for its proficiency in the following:

- Measurements of streamflow.
- Flow statistics.

- Flood monitoring and post-flood data recovery.
- Flood-frequency analysis.
- Measurement and understanding of groundwater at local and regional scales.
- Understanding geologic framework controls on groundwater.
- Development of computer models of water, sediment, and chemical transport.
- Understanding aquifer-system compaction and land subsidence.
- Age-dating of water and sediments.
- Chemical and isotopic tracer techniques in hydrologic and biogeochemical investigations.
- Water-quality sampling and analysis.
- Relating water quality to causative factors. • Development of water-quality statistical models.
- Field methods, data collection, and preservation of hydrologic information.
- Water-use estimation.
- Development of water-information databases.
- Training the next generation of water scientists and technicians.

Along with this proficiency, however, is acknowledgment of the uncertainty in water science. Scientists struggle with uncertainty in terms of how to adequately assess it; how to understand uncertainty; how to control it; and how to effectively communicate the uncertainty of the science with science information products. Understanding uncertainty in water science is essential for resource managers and others who use water data and information in decision making. Uncertainty is an inherent factor in hydrologic data collection, estimation techniques, and simulation modeling. Errors associated with measurement techniques arise from the inability to accurately measure specific aspects of the hydrologic system, such as streamflow, the water level in a well, or soil properties that control evapotranspiration and runoff.

Uncertainty arises from the inadequacy of data collection networks to fully characterize natural spatial and temporal variability associated with hydrology, geology, climate, and land use. Uncertainty also is present in simulation models because it is impossible to thoroughly reproduce a natural hydrologic system in a model. An additional USGS objective is to reduce uncertainty in the highest priority water data and information. Improvements in the spatial and temporal coverage of data collection networks, the techniques for measuring flows, and improved estimation techniques with data layers that account for more of the factors that influence variability will lead to reduced uncertainty in the information provided to the public.

Additionally, the USGS will make a strategic effort in the future to estimate or quantify uncertainty associated with its information products. USGS strengths that benefit the Water Mission Area and underscore the above four guiding principles include national quality-assurance standards and policies; the long-term retention of hydrologic data, reports, and other products; and the unbiased science that underlies every mission activity of the Bureau.

Two other major strengths of the USGS are a business model that supports a high level of partnering with other agencies, academia, and the private sector; and a diverse workforce of scientists and physical-science technicians from multiple disciplines that allows the Bureau to bring an integrated scientific approach to water-resource problems. USGS water science starts within Water Science Centers, located in every State and in Puerto Rico. These Water Science Centers build important relationships with State and local agencies that are vital to the management of water resources in the United States. These Water Science Centers are supported by a regional and national structure that includes offices dedicated to the development of models, methods, tools, databases, and quality-assurance measures to support the Water Science Centers and maintain consistency in USGS work. Many of the national priorities of the USGS Water Mission Area are carried out through the network of Water Science Centers. Another hallmark of the USGS is the nationwide consistency that it brings to water data collection, analysis, and interpretation. This consistency allows the valid comparison of data across many locations and at multiple scales. Water science is furthered by the USGS National Research Program, which advances the science of hydrology to keep the USGS on the cutting edge. Finally, collaboration and joint project investigations with other USGS Mission Areas lend strength to USGS integrated science.

Critical to understanding and optimizing water availability is knowledge about how geology, climate, and humans interact with the water cycle at all-time scales. An important component of such research is analysis of former conditions (historical and pre-historical) for insights about modern processes and trends. A few examples of where the USGS has worked effectively to help answer interdisciplinary questions include research into how climate affects water movement and storage, how geology affects movement of water and persistence of contaminants, how streamflow affects aquatic and riparian ecosystems, and how energy and mineral-resource development affect water resources, among many other questions. An additional key strength of the USGS is its development of partnerships in the conduct of its water science.

Through the Cooperative Water Program, the USGS partners with more than 1,800 State, Tribal, county, local, regional, and watershed agencies in accomplishing its mission. Key Federal partners include Bureau of Reclamation, US Fish and Wildlife Service, National Park Service, Bureau of Land Management, Bureau of Indian Affairs, US Department of Defense (including US Army Corps of Engineers), US Environmental Protection Agency (USEPA), National Oceanic and Atmospheric Administration (NOAA) and National Weather Service, US Department of Agriculture (USDA), National Atmospheric and Space Administration (NASA), National Geospatial Intelligence Agency, National Science Foundation, and US Department of Energy. USGS scientists also work with numerous academic institutions, providing training and collaboration for faculty and students. Without these partnerships, the Water mission of the USGS could not be fulfilled. The USGS is always seeking opportunities to strengthen and expand its network of partners.

To this end, the USGS will increase its role in the future in interagency collaborative work through institutions such as the Advisory Committee on Water Information (ACWI), the Integrated Water Resources Science and Services (IWRSS) consortium, and the National Integrated Drought Information System (NIDIS). The USGS Water Mission Area brings hydrologic understanding to questions that logically intersect with the missions of these partner agencies. A good example of how partnership could be strengthened around mutual interests in the future is an opportunity to work with the USDA to integrate studies of agriculture and water availability. USDA expertise, models, and data for crop systems, soils, and drainage could be coordinated with USGS expertise in groundwater and surface-water movement and quality to yield important insights for best management practices relating to water use and water quality. Similarly, collaborative work with NOAA could result in integrated studies of climate, precipitation, and watershed processes, with each agency providing strength in its areas of expertise.

Collaboration with NASA could further improve understanding of earth and hydrologic processes through remote sensing and spatial imagery. Collaborative work with USEPA could improve understanding of linkages between contaminant distributions, hydrogeologic processes, and human and ecosystem effects. Partnership opportunities extend well beyond Federal agencies to academia and nongovernmental organizations (NGOs). USGS does, and should in the future, look to these prospects for mutual advancement of hydrologic science. The USGS through the National Cooperative Geologic Mapping Program (NCGMP) STATEMAP component partners with State geological surveys to provide geologic maps and frameworks important for identification and characterization of the Nation's aquifers. NCGMP had determined that most geologic maps in the United States are related to groundwater issues (Orndorff and others, 2008). In the recent past the USGS has advanced the area of environmental flow science through a liaison position with the Nature Conservancy. The USGS has worked to advance access to hydrologic information through joint opportunities with the Consortium of Universities for the

Advancement of Hydrologic Science (CUAHSI). The USGS is also a partner in the Western States Federal Agency Support Team (WestFAST). WestFAST is a collaboration between 11 Federal agencies with water management responsibilities in the West. WestFAST was established to support the Western States Water Council (WSWC), and the Western Governors Association in coordinating Federal efforts regarding water resources. The USGS views WestFAST as a prime model of partnerships in action and should be replicated in other venues. The USGS also benefits from being informed, involved, and educated by other agencies and organizations on the science, monitoring, tools, and strategies they are developing. The USGS sees these and similar collaborative efforts as vital to successful water-resources science endeavors and important for the future of the Nation's water availability.

Activities

Natural Hazards

Every year in the United States, natural hazard events threaten lives and livelihoods, resulting in deaths and billions of dollars in damage. The USGS works with many partners to monitor, assess, and conduct targeted research on a wide range of natural hazards so that policymakers and the public have the understanding they need to enhance preparedness, response and resilience.

In 2010, the USGS realigned its organizational structure around the missions identified in the USGS Science Strategy. The Natural Hazards Mission Area includes six science programs: Coastal & Marine_Geology, Earthquake Hazards, Geomagnetism, Global Seismographic Network, Landslide Hazards, and Volcano Hazards. Through these programs, the USGS provides alerts and warnings of geologic hazards and supports the warning responsibilities of the National Oceanic and Atmospheric Administration (NOAA) for geomagnetic storms and tsunamis. The Coastal and Marine Geology Program supports all the missions of the USGS, characterizing and assessing coastal and marine processes, conditions, change and vulnerability.

The Natural Hazards Mission Area is responsible for coordinating USGS response following disasters and overseeing the bureau's emergency management activities. The mission area coordinates long-term planning across the full USGS hazards science portfolio, including activities funded through many other programs across the bureau, including floods, hurricanes and severe storms, and wildfires.

The future direction of the USGS hazards mission is guided by the recently released USGS Natural Hazards Science Strategy, which was developed by a team of USGS scientists with considerable input from partners and the public. This document is part of a broader USGS science strategy planning process across all our missions.

Coastal and Marine Geology Program (CMGP)

CMGP conducts research on the changes to the coastal and marine environment that impact lands, lives and livelihoods, and vulnerable ecosystems; providing science to inform decisions that ensure safe and resilient coastal communities and sustainable use and protection of marine resources. Supporting the Natural Hazards mission, CMGP conducts research on marine geohazards including earthquakes, tsunami, and submarine landslides and on coastal change hazards from erosion, hurricanes and other extreme storms, and sea-level rise.

Earthquakes

The Earthquake Hazards Program is part of the National Earthquake Hazards Reduction Program (NEHRP), a four-agency partnership led by the National Institute of Standards and Technology (NIST). Earthquakes pose significant risk to 75 million Americans in 39 States. The USGS provides research and information products for earthquake loss reduction, including hazard and risk assessments, comprehensive real-time earthquake monitoring, and public outreach.

Geomagnetism

The mission of the Geomagnetism Program is to monitor the Earth's magnetic field. Using ground-based observatories, the Program provides continuous records of magnetic field variations covering long timescales; disseminates magnetic data to various governmental, academic, and private institutions; and conducts research into the nature of geomagnetic variations for purposes of scientific understanding and hazard mitigation.

Global Seismographic network

The Global Seismographic Network (GSN) is a permanent digital network of state-of-the-art seismological and geophysical sensors connected by a telecommunications network. The GSN provides near-uniform, worldwide monitoring of the Earth, with over 150 modern seismic stations distributed globally. The GSN was formed in partnership among the USGS, the National Science Foundation (NSF) and the Incorporated Research Institutions for Seismology (IRIS).

Landslide Hazards

The Global Seismographic Network (GSN) is a permanent digital network of state-of-the-art seismological and geophysical sensors connected by a telecommunications network. The GSN provides near-uniform, worldwide monitoring of the Earth, with over 150 modern seismic stations distributed globally. The GSN was formed in partnership among the USGS, the National

Science Foundation (NSF) and the Incorporated Research Institutions for Seismology (IRIS).

Volcano Hazards

The Volcano Hazards Program advances the scientific understanding of volcanic processes in order to lessen the harmful impacts of volcanic activity. The USGS monitors active and potentially active volcanoes, assesses their hazards, responds to volcanic crises, and conducts research on how volcanoes work. The USGS also issues warnings of potential volcanic hazards to responsible emergency-management authorities and to the populace affected.

Science Applications for Risk Reductions (SAFRR) Project

The SAFRR project focuses on building partnerships to improve the use of natural hazards information from the USGS, to identify needs and gaps, and to develop new products that increase the use of USGS science by emergency managers and community decision makers in order to promote greater resilience to natural hazards. SAFRR evolved from the Multi-Hazards Demonstration Project in Southern California, which has developed interdisciplinary, science-based products that deliver information that starts with the hazard and carries through to impacts on the community.

USGS Emergency Management

The USGS Natural Hazards Mission Area has been given responsibility for overseeing the bureau's emergency management activities. This function includes the USGS Hazard Response Executive Committee, which provides executive direction, oversight, and support to USGS managers in responding to major hazard events. During incidents of national significance, the USGS provides support to certain National Response Framework emergency support functions.

Astrogeology

The Astrogeology Science Center serves the nation, the international science community, and the general public in the pursuit of new knowledge about our Solar System. The program has participated in analyzing data from numerous missions to planetary bodies, assisting in finding potential landing sites for exploration vehicles, mapping our neighboring planets, moons, and

asteroids, and conducting research to better understand the geologic processes operating on these bodies.

Floods and Droughts

The USGS is the Nation's primary provider of information on water. The bulk of the USGS activities related to floods and droughts are carried out through programs within the Water Mission Area. Web portals make it possible to view current water conditions and where floods and droughts are occurring.

Wildfire hazards

The USGS carries out a wide range of wildfire-related science activities that span multiple USGS mission areas, including landscape ecology studies, geospatial support for fire response, burned area hydrology, and post-fire debris flow warnings.